BROKEN ALLIANCE

The Turbulent Times Between Blacks and Jews in America

Jonathan Kaufman

A TOUCHSTONE BOOK
Published by Simon & Schuster
New York   London   Toronto   Sydney   Tokyo   Singapore

For my parents and Aunt Jean

≭

TOUCHSTONE
Rockefeller Center
1230 Avenue of the Americas
New York, NY 10020

Copyright © 1988, 1995 by Jonathan Kaufman
All rights reserved,
including the right of reproduction
in whole or in part in any form.

TOUCHSTONE and colophon are registered trademarks of
Simon & Schuster Inc.

Manufactured in the United States of America

10 9 8 7 6 5 4 3 2 1

Library of Congress Cataloging-in-Publication Data
Kaufman, Jonathan.
    Broken alliance: the turbulent times between Blacks and Jews
in America / by Jonathan Kaufman.
      p.   cm.
    Bibliography; p.
    Includes index.
    1. Afro-Americans—Relations with Jews. 2. United States—Race
relations.   I. Title.
E185.615.K33 1988
305.8'00973—dc19   88-1948
                                                     CIP

ISBN 0-684-18699-3
ISBN 0-684-80096-9 (Pbk)

Contents

Preface

In the fall of 1993, soon after returning to the United States after a three-year assignment in Berlin and Eastern Europe, I received a call from a reporter at *Time* magazine asking me what I thought about the latest attacks against Jews by a top official of the Nation of Islam, Khalid Abdul Muhammad. In a now notorious speech to students at a New Jersey college, Muhammad called Jews "blood suckers" who had financed the slave trade and now controlled the United States government and the Federal Reserve Bank. "You see, everybody always talks about Hitler exterminating 6 million Jews," Muhammad said. "But don't nobody ever ask what did they do to Hitler? They went in there, in Germany, the way they do everywhere they go, and they supplanted, they usurped. . . . They had undermined the very fabric of the society."

I collected my thoughts and began to talk about the history of black-Jewish relations, the sources of tension—when the reporter interrupted.

"No, No," she said, "What do you think about what he said about you and your book." She then read me two pages of his speech. I later received a transcript.

I wanna use white Jew references. Is that okay? ("Yes, sir!" the audience responded) Okay. Jonathan Kaufman in *Broken Alliance* admits that the Jews who first came to America in the seventeenth, eighteenth, and early nineteenth centuries were heirs to a conservative political tradition that tended to embrace the status quo. Slavery, of course, was a major part of that status quo. . . . According to Kaufman, in his book *Broken Alliance*, the switch to seeming liberalism . . . was facilitated . . . by the pursuit of enlightened self-interest, meaning that whatever they did, they did it for themselves first. And they used us so that we could clear a path for them. . . . Brothers and sisters, African-American assertions of independence did not sit well with Jews who had grown accustomed to overlordship of the civil rights movement.

On and on, Muhammad went, taking facts out of context, twisting quotations, cramming more and more misinformation into what he called "The Secret History of Blacks and Jews":

As it says here from *Broken Alliance*, from the Jewish writer himself, who talks with them, who eats bagels with them, lox with them, who goes to the synagogue with them, who plays golf with them, who sits with them out of and beyond our earshot—that they had a self-interest, that they were doing these things to use us as cannon fodder. Then they started moving against us and taking the opposite position every time an issue came up that was in our best interests.

That Muhammad, an anti-Semite, would twist and misrepresent my writings was upsetting. But it was not really surprising. Enlightened self-interest was one reason Jews joined the civil rights movement in such large numbers, but so was idealism, a shared experience of being oppressed and persecuted, a fierce sense of justice, and a desire to make America a better and more equal place. Jewish contributors were at the forefront of the founding of the National Association for the Advancement of Colored People in 1909 and two Jewish brothers, the Spingarns, served as the NAACP's first leaders. In the late

1940s and 1950s, Jewish organizations helped finance some of the earliest research on the ill effects of discrimination and prejudice—research that was influential in the Supreme Court's decision in *Brown* v. *Board of Education* to end segregation in schools. The cooperation of blacks and Jews in the early 1960s set the standard for the great coalition that became the civil rights movement. At the height of that movement, three-quarters of the money raised by the Reverend Martin Luther King, Jr., and other civil rights leaders was donated by Jews, from business executives to ordinary families. During Freedom Summer of 1964, two-thirds of the whites who went to the South to help blacks to register to vote were Jews, including Michael Schwerner and Andrew Goodman, murdered, along with black civil rights worker James Earl Chaney, by white racists that summer.

As tensions between blacks and whites grew in the 1960s, so did the tension between blacks and Jews—often with greater vehemence. By 1966, Jews were asked to leave some civil rights organizations. During the bitter 1968 teachers' strike in New York, Jews found themselves opposing growing black demands for community control of schools and became targets of black anger. In neighborhoods across the country, from New York to Chicago to Los Angeles, blacks and Jews found themselves at loggerheads as blacks tried to move into once-Jewish neighborhoods and Jews began to move out. In the 1970s, the challenge to affirmative action brewed not among conservative whites but among some Jewish intellectuals and organizations. They provided much of the intellectual underpinning to the attack on affirmative action mounted in the 1970s and 1980s.

Yet in the 1980s, despite growing tensions over affirmative action, blacks and Jews were still able to work together to elect a wave of black officials, and Jews were critical in the elections of the first black mayors of Chicago, Philadelphia, and New York. In city after city, Jews voted for black candidates in far greater proportion than any other white group, often providing the margin of victory.

It soon became clear, however, that Muhammad's speech was part of a concerted campaign by Louis Farrakhan, the

Nation of Islam, and other black radicals to spread a false history of black-Jewish relations, especially to a younger generation of blacks on college campuses. Muhammad became a regular speaker to black student groups on college campuses, including Howard University. As controversy over Muhammad increased, Farrakhan came under pressure to denounce him. At a nationally televised press conference, Farrakhan denounced Muhammad's speech and then endorsed most of what Muhammad had said. "I stand by the truths that he spoke," Farrakhan said. Farrakhan used the spotlight to spread his message further, appearing on the late night "Arsenio Hall" show and television news programs.

The most troubling news I heard came a few weeks after Muhammad's speech when a young black law student called me to say she had been reading Muhammad's speech and other inflammatory writings about black and Jews. "I had never really thought about it before," said the woman, who was thoughtful and curious. "It made sense to me."

It made sense to me. What is in danger of developing is a generation of blacks and Jews who do not know each other and grow up with bitter stereotypes etched in their minds. The student who called me may not grow up hating Jews. But she may carry around with her a lifelong suspicion of Jews—"They were the ones who financed the slave trade."

Similarly, young Jews may not hate blacks, but they will view them warily—"They are the ones who are anti-Semitic."

I had just spent three years in Eastern Europe, where anti-Semitism flourishes even where there are no Jews, where Bosnia is in flames over hatreds that reach back centuries. It was clear to me how long stereotypes linger, and how much damage they can do.

This new edition of *Broken Alliance* with a new epilogue explains the complex history of blacks and Jews—the forces, and people, that brought blacks and Jews together and then tore them apart so bitterly. The epilogue takes the story to the present day: the aftermath of the 1988 election, the Crown Heights riot in New York in 1991 in which blacks attacked Jews in street battles, and the latest spread of Farrakhan's message beyond a small group of Black Muslims to black colleges and black professionals. It looks at the factors now driving blacks and Jews apart and at the implications for blacks and Jews as well as for America.

America is at a turning point, not just between blacks and Jews but in race relations as a whole. The black-Jewish alliance, at its height, offered a shining example of what Americans could achieve by forging a true interracial coalition. Black-Jewish relations, at their recent nadir, now offer a chilling picture of what American race relations could become. It is important to understand the history of black-Jewish relations before angry voices shout down any hope of reconciliation. Only by understanding the history of blacks and Jews—what went right and what went wrong—can both groups, and America, begin to look to the future.

BROKEN ALLIANCE

Introduction

One morning in 1984, Black Muslim minister Louis Farrakhan, who had angered many Jews by saying that Hitler was a "great man . . . wickedly great" and denounced Judaism as a "dirty religion," spoke at *The Boston Globe*, where I work. For several years, at the *Globe* and at *The Wall Street Journal*, I had written about black issues: poverty in black families, problems facing black executives in business, and violent attacks against blacks in Boston. I had just finished a series on job discrimination and racism in Boston. Soon I would be working on a major story on Jews in politics. I was anxious to hear Farrakhan in person.

His speech, from a news point of view, was unremarkable. Farrakhan said more or less what he had been saying in public all year. What happened after Farrakhan left overwhelmed me. Within minutes, shouting matches erupted between blacks and Jews in the newsroom, many of them reporters and editors who had worked together for years. How, black reporters asked, could Jews claim to be political allies but be so opposed to quotas and critical of affirmative action? How, Jewish reporters responded, could blacks be so blind to the impact of the Holocaust and brush off the terror Jews felt at any anti-Semitic

1

slur, of feeling vulnerable in a world that could always turn hostile? The arguments were as much over personal responses as they were over politics. I stood in the newsroom arguing with a black college intern that banks and newspapers were not, in fact, owned by Jews. A black friend of mine stood in the parking lot for forty-five minutes saying that no one, no black, no white, no Jew could understand what it had been like to work for a white-owned newspaper for fifteen years. Allies in so many causes, friends at so many levels, it was clear how little blacks and Jews knew about each other.

It was there, in the aftermath of that visit by Farrakhan, that the idea for this book began.

As a young Jew—I was born in 1956: two years after the *Brown* v. *Board of Education* decision outlawed segregation in public schools, the year of the Montgomery bus boycott and the 1956 Arab-Israeli War—I grew up taking black-Jewish cooperation for granted. I knew how the two groups had marched together in Mississippi and had sung songs together along the road from Selma to Montgomery. I knew that Jews had contributed money to black organizations like the NAACP, the National Urban League, and CORE, the Congress of Racial Equality. The first two presidents of the NAACP had been Jewish brothers, the Spingarns. Jack Greenberg, head of the NAACP Legal Defense Fund and the architect of many landmark cases establishing civil rights, was a Jew. So were two victims of the civil rights struggle in Mississippi: Michael Schwerner and Andrew Goodman.

"The Negro identifies himself almost wholly with the Jew. The more devout Negro considers that he is a Jew, in bondage to a hard taskmaster and waiting for a Moses to lead him out of Egypt," James Baldwin had written. That made sense to me. I knew that, as Jews, my family and I would always be outsiders. Blacks were outsiders, too. Returning to my parents' home in 1986 for Passover, I watched as friends of my parents—longtime liberals whose oldest son, now nearing thirty, had as a toddler passed out leaflets for John F. Kennedy—led everyone at the table in a chorus of "We Shall Overcome."

I knew how proud my father, an advertising executive, had

been back in the 1960s when he was asked to write some ads for the NAACP. And I knew how hurt he seemed one day when he came home and said he had been fired from the account because he was white. It was clear long before 1984 that the alliance that fought for civil rights in the South in the 1950s was becoming shredded and wary. The growth of Black Power, coupled with the growth of city crime, much of it by blacks, unnerved our lives and my neighborhood on the Upper West Side of Manhattan. When Martin Luther King was killed in 1968, it seemed to break the final link many whites felt with a black movement that was becoming angrier and more frightening, filling the TV screens with images of people carrying guns and demanding reparations. The disputes over Israel in the 1970s and 1980s, the debates over affirmative action—all were evidence of blacks and Jews drifting further and further apart. In the 1984 presidential election, blacks and Jews were two of only a handful of groups—the others were Hispanics, Asians, and the unemployed—who deserted the Reagan landslide to vote for Democrat Walter Mondale, but that electoral coalition masked deep fissures in black-Jewish relations. The campaign of Jesse Jackson, the controversy over his "hymie" and "hymietown" remarks, highlighted pain and anger that had been brewing a long time.

Still, the passions unleashed by Farrakhan at the *Globe* surprised me. I wanted to find out what had happened. What was it that first brought blacks and Jews together, and why have they now split so bitterly apart?

This book is a result of that journey.

I decided to tell what I found out through a set of six serial biographies—the stories of five individuals and one family whose lives reflected the ebbs and flows, the triumphs and losses of black-Jewish relations over the past thirty years.

Three of the biographical chapters focus on blacks. Three focus on Jews. I chose to alternate the chapters between black and Jewish tellers to provide a sense of shifting perspectives. The biographical chapters are framed by an opening chapter that looks at the history of black-Jewish relations before the 1950s and a closing chapter that looks ahead to the future.

There are several things this book is not. It is not a comprehensive history of blacks in America or of Jews in America. It is not an encyclopedia of every encounter between blacks and Jews since 1954. Rather, it is a tapestry that evokes, I hope, a coalition that came together, worked great change, and then began to fall apart. One goal of all these chapters has been to allow people to speak for themselves and describe events as they saw them. But I was also interested in how their actions and feelings reflected the changing dynamic of relations between blacks and whites and, more broadly, changes in American politics, culture, and self-image. A great deal has changed in America between the 1950s and now, and it would be wrong to describe black-Jewish relations in a vacuum.

Thus, each chapter also includes moments from the history of the civil rights movement and profiles of others who played a key role. Interwoven with the narrative are snatches of what I call "newsreel footage"—glimpses of news events, excerpts from speeches, snatches from novels and poems and songs— that capture and evoke the spirit of the times. This newsreel footage acts as a kind of background music, recalling what these times were like and occasionally providing a counterpoint to the narrative.

I chose this method of serial biography for several reasons. While the story of black-Jewish relations is, in many ways, a political story, it is also an intensely personal story. Unlike many political coalitions that skimmed the surface or united people for an election or a cause, this one got under people's skin. I wanted to understand why this alliance seemed to touch people so deeply, create such hope, and produce such anger and bitterness as it collapsed. Focusing on real people also meant dealing with real issues and real motivations. Over and over again, the people I profiled upended my expectations, discussing issues in terms far different from the way I had expected or the way news reports had described them. There is very little, figuratively speaking, that is black or white in the chapters that follow. Much of it is gray.

Finally, telling the story of black-Jewish relations through the eyes of real people made the issues and the conflicts more real. These were not "blacks" and "Jews," abstract groups that dealt with these issues. They were Paul Parks and Jack Greenberg; Rhody McCoy and Bernie and Roz Ebstein; Martin Peretz and Donna Brazile.

I first met Paul Parks while doing a story about the fortieth anniversary of the end of World War II. He was a large, avuncular man, with a seemingly endless capacity to tell stories and reminisce about his past. I decided to return to him when I began this book. Parks, the more I got to know him, seemed to embody much of the early spirit and pragmatism that suffused the civil rights movement. He was an engineer who became an organizer and a negotiator. Like many blacks who joined the civil rights movement in the early 1960s, Parks was middle class and a churchgoer, part of what one civil rights activist called the "striving class." He had grown up before World War II in the Midwest, in Indianapolis, where blacks were a small minority. Parks grew up with a Jewish storeowner in his all-black neighborhood, a storeowner who extended Parks's mother credit that enabled them to get through the Depression. In college many of his closest friends were Jews. In the 1950s he worked with the NAACP in Boston to stop discrimination in housing. As the 1960s dawned, he began shuttling down South to march with King and work for him. There, too, he found that most of his allies were Jews. For Parks, as for many blacks in the South and Midwest in the early 1960s, Jews were the good white people. In his mind, the alliance between blacks and Jews was natural and strong. As I explored how the civil rights movement took shape and won its victories across the South and in the courts, I wanted to find out more from Parks about the roots of his alliances with Jews. I wanted to find out more about that early spirit of cooperation and what made it possible.

Jack Greenberg once bailed Paul Parks out of jail, as he— at one time or another—bailed out thousands of civil rights protesters. Greenberg was a Jewish lawyer from New York who, as a newly minted law school graduate, joined the NAACP Legal Defense and Educational Fund in 1949. Thurgood Marshall was running the Legal Defense Fund back then and it was, quite simply, the best civil rights law firm in the country. It brought the landmark *Brown* v. *Board of Education* case in 1954 that ended the segregation of public schools and set the stage for the civil rights protests that would convulse and enrich the country over the next decade. Greenberg rose to become one of the most powerful and influential lawyers in the civil rights movement, succeeding Marshall as head of the fund in 1961 and running it through the 1960s and 1970s, long after most whites had left or been kicked out of the civil rights movement and the question of civil rights had itself been pushed to the back shelves of American concerns—replaced by women's rights, the economy, Vietnam, and foreign policy.

Yet what drew me to Greenberg was an incident that took place at Harvard Law School in 1982. A black lawyer and colleague of Greenberg's was asked to teach a month-long course on civil rights law. Pleading a heavy caseload, the lawyer asked Harvard if he and Greenberg could teach it together. Harvard officials agreed but a group of black students objected. Harvard Law School, they charged, did not have enough full-time black faculty, and they decided to force their challenge when Greenberg came to Cambridge. Black students ended up boycotting the course, offering the painful spectacle of a young generation of black professionals refusing to take a class with one of the greatest civil rights lawyers of all time because he was white. Greenberg's life bridged the great distance traveled in race relations, between blacks and whites, and blacks and Jews: from the years of the civil rights movement when the two groups joined hands to fight, to the alienation that characterized their relationship after the 1960s. Why had Jews like Greenberg been so drawn to civil rights, I wanted to know. What was their motivation in joining? Why had Greenberg stayed while so many others left? And how did he feel about what had happened at Harvard?

My conversations with Parks and Greenberg focused on the period of black-Jewish cooperation from the mid-1950s to the mid-1960s. Beginning in the mid 1960s, the rise of Black Power, the movement of the civil rights struggle from the South to the North, and the changing economic status of blacks and whites caused relations between blacks and Jews to change. The period of cooperation was succeeded by a period of confrontation. To understand the emotions and issues of this period, I turned to Rhody McCoy and Roz and Bernie Ebstein.

For a time in the late 1960s, Rhody McCoy occupied a prominent place in the demonology of many Jewish New Yorkers. As head of the experimental Ocean Hill–Brownsville school district in Brooklyn, McCoy stood at the fulcrum of the bitter New York teachers' strike of 1968 that pitted working, middle-class Jewish teachers against poor, working-class black parents, exploding into a storm of charges of Jewish racism and black anti-Semitism. This was the strike that left as its legacy a black schoolteacher reading over the radio a poem written by a fifteen-year-old student that began:

Hey, Jew boy, with that yarmulke on your head
You pale-faced Jew boy—I wish you were dead.

My intent in speaking to McCoy was not to indict him for anti-Semitism, but to hear the story of the strike from his point of view. The New York City school strike was a seismic event for New York. For two years, Ocean Hill–Brownsville was the focal point of demands for Black Power and black control. Much of the bitterness between blacks and Jews that had been simmering for several years billowed to the surface, and the strike previewed many of the issues that would divide blacks and Jews over the next fifteen years. It foreshadowed the collapse of the liberal coalition. The story from Rhody McCoy—a man who had followed Malcolm X beginning in the 1960s and who saw the fight over Ocean Hill–Brownsville as a way to wrest power away from the white power structure of New York and give it to black children and their parents —made clear the aspirations and anger of blacks that made the conflict inevitable. It also confirmed a trend that grew as the 1960s ended: Blacks and Jews were looking at the same events and coming away with completely different interpretations.

The story of how a neighborhood in Chicago changed from

largely Jewish to largely black, and the effect the change had on a Jewish family that lived there, is at the heart of the next chapter. Roz and Bernie Ebstein prayed with their feet, marching with Martin Luther King when he came to Chicago in 1966. They returned to their small house in Merionette Manor on Chicago's Far South Side determined to live and raise their children in an integrated neighborhood. Soon, however, the neighborhood began to change. Their Jewish friends started moving out. More and more blacks moved in. The schools deteriorated. Their sons were mugged. Their temple closed down and the Jewish Community Center closed its doors. The Ebsteins' position was not unique. In the wake of the urban shifts of the 1960s, Jewish neighborhoods in city after city in the North became black. The shift was often accompanied by a rise in crime and a decline in the neighborhood, often the result of city governments cutting back police protection and other city services. Jewish attitudes toward blacks—whom Jews once knew as housekeepers, shoppers who needed credit, allies in the South marching against bigotry—were now shaped by searing acts of violence and intimidation. For a time in the 1960s, there seemed to be no Jew who did not have a grandmother, a cousin, an elderly aunt, a family friend living in a once Jewish, now black ghetto, hemmed in by crime and fear. By talking with the Ebsteins, their friends, and some of their neighbors, I wanted to trace what those years did to them and to their children, and what it did to their liberalism.

The confrontation between blacks and Jews in the late 1960s, symbolized by the clash at Ocean Hill–Brownsville and the changing of a Chicago neighborhood, expanded in the 1970s into a wide-ranging era of competition and conflict—over Israel, affirmative action, the rise of black political power, and the presidential candidacy of the Reverend Jesse Jackson. Tensions once whispered about or confined to working-class or poor neighborhoods began to dominate everywhere. To examine the growing importance of Israel to American Jews, their changing political attitudes, and the growing political power and assertion of rights by blacks, I looked at this period through the eyes of Martin Peretz and Donna Brazile.

Few people felt neutral about Martin Peretz. In the space of less than twenty years, Peretz moved from the center of civil rights and New Left politics to the fringes of the neoconservatives. Unlike neoconservatives, among them Norman Podhoretz and Irving Kristol, Peretz had genuine roots in the civil rights movement. He picketed in front of Woolworth's when the Greensboro students sat in at lunch counters in 1960, and became one of the most generous angels of the civil rights movement, contributing and raising tens of thousands of dollars. In many ways, Peretz reflected the shifting allegiances of many Jews as the 1970s gave way to the 1980s: the growing importance of Israel, the skepticism toward the liberalism of the Great Society, the hostility toward black leaders like Jackson and Farrakhan. But his conversion was far more public because it played out in the pages of *The New Republic*, a magazine Peretz bought in 1974 and, as editor-in-chief, shaped into a magazine that reflected his own skepticism and many of his own views. Like a man he resembled in many ways stylistically, Mayor Edward Koch of New York, Peretz made clear who were his enemies and who were his friends. He encouraged an acerbic, almost slashing style that belittled crooked black politicians and supporters of the PLO, attacked old liberal ideas and truths, defended Israel, and attacked Jesse Jackson. He represented the emergence of a new kind of "muscular Judaism" that made many people, including many Jews, uncomfortable.

To his critics, Peretz embodied the betrayal of the white liberal—particularly the white Jewish liberal whom economic success and concern for Israel had turned into an uncaring conservative. Yet in many of his private activities, and in the woman he married, Anne Peretz, Peretz showed a far more complex understanding of blacks and of black problems than one gleaned from his magazine. His anger toward many black leaders and his criticism of many black political positions appeared rooted in frustration and disillusionment rather than in hate. And although it was unpalatable to many liberal Jews, Peretz's impassioned commitment to Israel reflected a fundamental change in the way American Jews viewed Israel, and, through the prism of their concern for Israel, now viewed the world. To understand Peretz is to understand some of what happened to American Jews between 1954 and 1984.

Donna Brazile was three years old during the great March on Washington in 1963, the march that ended with King's famous "I have a dream" speech. The civil rights movement was something she read about in history books, or heard about from her parents and grandmother. Then, in 1983, Brazile landed a job coordinating a twentieth-anniversary march to commemorate the March on Washington. It would be a chance to work with some of the most famous names of the past two decades: Bayard Rustin, Andrew Young, Jesse Jackson, Coretta Scott King. But it soon became apparent that a great deal had changed in twenty years. Brazile found herself enmeshed not in the nostalgia of 1963 but in the politics and disputes of the 1980s. Blacks wanted representatives from Arab-American groups to appear on the speaker's platform. Jewish groups vehemently objected. Other blacks felt that the "call" or declaration accompanying the march should discuss the Middle East; Jews objected and threatened to withdraw if the declaration criticized Israel. As she desperately set up conference calls from a tiny office in Washington in an effort to patch things together, Brazile found blacks angry at Jews, Jews angry at blacks.

Brazile went on to work in the seminal event of black-Jewish relations in the 1980s: the 1984 campaign of Jesse Jackson. Talking with her, I believed, offered a chance to hear the views of a young, articulate black woman on the dilemma of black-Jewish relations. It also was a chance to find out how blacks and Jews in their twenties and thirties—too young to have marched with Martin Luther King—felt about the black-Jewish alliance. Did the black-Jewish alliance have a future? Or was it time each group went its separate way?

From the start, I was aware of the pitfalls that I, as a Jew, would face in writing about black-Jewish relations. Those concerns dwindled as I dived into the book and the two years of research and writing. I was pleasantly surprised by the candid, sometimes brutal, responses I received from both blacks and Jews. No one, I believe, pulled any punches. Still, I wanted the book to be balanced and to be perceived as balanced. On several occasions I have asked black colleagues and friends—editors, lawyers, academics—to read over chapters in manuscript and give me their reaction. I made it clear that I did not mind being criticized in the final draft for what I meant to say. I did not want to be criticized for things I didn't mean to say—for missing the significance of events or projecting my own beliefs onto others. A full list of those who helped me appears in the acknowledgments. I went through the same process with people concerned with Jewish affairs. Like good editors, they made suggestions, disputed points, sharpened my thinking. We disagreed on many things but I never regretted submitting myself to their scrutiny.

The subjects of two of the chapters—the Ebsteins and Peretz—expressed concern about their privacy and how their views would be portrayed. In exchange for cooperating, they asked to see the chapters concerning them before publication. We agreed that they would review their respective chapters and could make changes on matters of fact—understanding that the final interpretation and writing rested with me. The changes both suggested were minor.

It is inevitable in a book like this that one writes about "blacks" and "Jews" as if each were a homogeneous group. They are not. The cooperation between blacks and Jews was, more often than not, cooperation between some elite blacks and some elite Jews. But what those elites did resonated strongly in each community, and when they fell out that resonated strongly, too. By focusing on individuals, I no doubt emphasize certain tendencies and feelings in each group. That does not mean there were not equally strongly held countertendencies. There were blacks who disagreed with Paul Parks in the early 1960s and with Rhody McCoy several years later. There were Jews who disagreed with Jack Greenberg and Martin Peretz. Some of these disagreements are noted in the chapters. In focusing on the people I did, I have tried to cut as wide a swath as possible through black and Jewish opinion.

At times during the past two years I have wondered: Why should anyone care about blacks and Jews, about their onetime alliance and their subsequent falling-out? The disputes between blacks and Jews are most often compared to family squabbles—of great importance to the people involved but of limited interest to the people who surround them. Who cares when a family fights except those who live inside the house?

As I talked to people around the country, I came to the conclusion that—beyond the benefits of civil rights and integration—the story of the black-Jewish alliance said something very important about the idea of alliances and coalitions in this country. There was something very American about the way blacks and Jews worked together. America, certainly since the waves of immigration that began after the Civil War and accelerated toward the end of the nineteenth century, has never thought of itself as a homogeneous country, with a single culture and view of the world. We are not Japan or Korea, with a single ethnic strain that allows everyone to work together harmoniously. The greatness of the country has often come through the synergy of its parts—the mixing of various groups, each bringing different gifts and perspectives. Blacks and Jews as separate groups clearly had things to offer the American stew. But in cooperating, something dynamic happened, and they were able to change the country in profound and fundamental ways. Without the help of white allies, could blacks have pushed the civil rights revolution? Probably not. Without the courage of blacks and the history of wrongs against them, could Jews have knocked down the barriers that fenced in their own success, the "old-boy" network that kept out Jews as well as blacks? Probably not. Without the synergy of the two, would the country have become as vibrant and diverse as it is, being able to draw in later years on the talents of Vietnamese and Cambodian refugees, immigrants from Haiti, Jamaica, Guatemala, Mexico, and the Philippines? I don't think so.

In the decades since the 1960s, however, the country has become more and more balkanized, with each group—blacks and Jews included—pulling further into itself. Politics has become a matter of addition and subtraction. Each group emerges with its own list of issues, its own set of litmus tests. Politicians who can stitch together the most interest groups win. Gone among blacks and Jews is the dynamic energy of interaction, cooperation, and disagreement among people who must work together.

This balkanization of the country is happening at a time when the United States is becoming more, not less, diverse. By the year 2000, demographers say, the number of Hispanics will outnumber the population of blacks. We are moving slowly but inexorably to a country that will be made up of a majority of minorities, with no single group numerous enough to make up more than 50 percent of the population. This is already happening at a brisk rate in cities like New York, Chicago, Boston, and San Francisco, and in Texas and California. Splinter politics may one day mean the splintering of the country.

In practical political terms, blacks and Jews have shown their importance by the havoc their differences have wreaked in recent years in the Democratic Party. The debate over Jesse Jackson's "hymietown" remarks and his ties to Louis Farrakhan consumed huge amounts of energy during 1984. The Democrats had a big enough obstacle in trying to defeat a popular President, Ronald Reagan, even without such a damaging internal debate. Jackson's presidential candidacy in 1988 ensures that similar questions will come up again. Jews remain one of the largest groups of contributors to the Democratic Party; blacks are a growing voting bloc—24 percent of Democratic voters are black. That the two groups may find themselves in a stalemate, or in opposition to each other, is a problem that now lurks behind future national elections.

For liberals, the collapse of black-Jewish cooperation was one powerful symbol of the shattering of the New Deal coalition. It has enervated progressive causes and encouraged conservatives in search of black and Jewish allies. Concern over civil rights was the door through which many Jews entered liberalism. Anger with blacks is the door through which some have left it. For blacks especially, the loss of Jewish allies cannot bode well. As the country has moved more to the right in recent years, blacks have found themselves increasingly isolated. There are few who believe blacks can create major political and economic change on their own.

Blacks and Jews matter because alliances and coalitions are important. To some, the dissolution of the black-Jewish alliance is further proof that class interests inevitably triumph over politics and idealism or that racism always wins out over cooperation. I believe there are other lessons. There is a great deal of talking in the chapters that follow about blacks and Jews, civil rights, affirmative action, Israel, and the campaign of Jesse Jackson. But throughout the stories that follow runs a remembrance of a time when great changes seemed possible and people embraced alliances and coalitions—and puzzlement and sadness that politics and personal relationships have today become polarized and fragmented.

Perhaps by listening to these stories, we can begin to understand why.

1

Crossing Jordan to the Promised Land

The disappearance of the three civil rights workers dominated the news for weeks. Michael Schwerner, James Chaney, and Andrew Goodman drove into Mississippi on the last day of spring, 1964—part of the vanguard of black and white civil rights workers flooding the South in a massive voter-registration drive dubbed Freedom Summer. Goodman, a tall, slim, dark-haired twenty-year-old Jewish college student from an upper-middle-class family in New York, had decided to spend a summer down South after hearing the head of the Mississippi NAACP speak at his school. Schwerner, twenty-four, and his wife, Rita, both also Jewish, had come South in January after being stirred by television coverage of police clubbing blacks who were trying to register to vote in Birmingham. James Chaney, a twenty-one-year-old black civil rights worker from Meridian, Mississippi, had left high school at sixteen. In recent months he had become deeply involved with the civil rights movement and had befriended the white Schwerners and worked with them to register voters in Mississippi.

The three young men and Rita Schwerner met in Oxford, Ohio, at a series of training meetings designed to prepare the young civil rights workers for the grueling summer ahead. The

United States Senate had just passed the 1964 Civil Rights Act, abolishing Jim Crow laws. The legislation capped eight years of bus boycotts, sit-ins, and nonviolent demonstrations. Ross Barnett, the fire-breathing ex-governor of Mississippi, warned: "This action is repulsive to the American people. Turmoil, strife, and bloodshed lie ahead." Leaders of Freedom Summer warned the volunteers, especially the young white volunteers like Goodman who would be spending their summer vacations on the project, that they could be in grave danger. "This is for real," said Robert Moses, head of the Freedom Summer project. "Like for life and death." Added another civil rights organizer, "I may be killed. You may be killed. Recognize that, and it may save your life."

On June 20, 1964, Mickey Schwerner, Andy Goodman, and Jim Chaney drove to Mississippi together. The day after they arrived, the three young men set out to investigate the recent burning of a black church and the beating of church members in the tiny town of Longdale, where Schwerner had been organizing a voter-registration movement. The Ku Klux Klan was active, willing to burn down churches in order to scare the volunteers away and intimidate local blacks from cooperating. Around 11:00 A.M., Schwerner, Chaney, and Goodman, dressed in blue jeans, T-shirts, and sneakers, climbed into the front seat of a blue Ford station wagon and headed to Longdale. "If we're not back by four-thirty," Schwerner told one of his co-workers, "start phoning. But we'll be back by four."

Then, nothing.

The disappearance of the three civil rights workers sent a shiver of fear through the hundreds of students and civil rights workers descending on Mississippi for Freedom Summer. The three vanished on a Sunday. Local police in nearby Philadelphia, Mississippi, said they had stopped Chaney for speeding, held Schwerner and Goodman for "investigation," but released all three after six hours. By Tuesday, President Johnson had sent Allen Dulles, former head of the CIA, to Mississippi to report on their disappearance. Two hundred federal agents and local police were assigned to the investigation. Black civil rights workers had been kidnapped and killed, even shot in the open, for years. But this was the first time white civil rights workers had disappeared. Rita Schwerner demanded, and got, a meeting with Johnson in the White House and asked him to send 5,000 men to Mississippi to look for her husband. Robert Goodman left his engineering job in New York to fly to Washington, D.C., and appeal for federal help in finding his son. Johnson ordered 400 sailors from a Mississippi naval air station to join the search.

Finally, on August 4, three bodies were found buried in an earthen dam, caked with the red dirt of the Mississippi Delta. They had deteriorated beyond recognition. Police identified the bodies by fingerprints and dental plates. They were Schwerner, Chaney, and Goodman.

In later years, the murders of the three young men became the touchstone of black-Jewish cooperation in the civil rights movement. A writer dubbed their story "brotherhood beneath an earthen dam." Black and Jewish leaders invoked their names as evidence of the strong, indelible ties each group had once felt for the other. "Twenty years ago, tears welled up in our eyes as the bodies of Schwerner, Goodman, and Chaney were dragged from the depths of a river in Mississippi," Jesse Jackson told the Democratic convention in 1984, in an attempt to heal the breach between blacks and Jews caused by his campaign. "Twenty years later, our communities, black and Jewish, are in anguish, anger, and in pain. Feelings have been hurt on both sides." At Goodman's funeral, a friend of the Goodman family predicted: "The reverence in which Andrew Goodman, James Chaney, and Michael Schwerner are held will never cease to grow. Their deeds and their sacrifice will become an integral part of the culture of our nation: its literature, its songs, its monuments—and even part of its legend. People who do not yet know their names call them the 'civil rights workers.' The phrase is already part of the American language, like 'abolitionist' and 'underground railroad.' "

Here, it seemed, was a natural place to begin the search for the roots of the black-Jewish alliance.

Evidence was hard to come by. Newspaper reports at the time emphasized that a black and two white civil rights workers had been murdered. That Schwerner and Goodman were Jewish was rarely mentioned. Schwerner had considered himself an atheist and Goodman's parents, while Jewish, did not belong to a synagogue. Andy Goodman's funeral was held at the Ethical Culture Society, a New York group that attracted many Jewish liberals and intellectuals but shunned the trappings and traditions of organized religion. "It never even occurred to any of us or to Andy that he went down [to Mississippi] as a Jew," his mother, Carolyn Goodman, told me when I talked to her more than twenty years after her son's death. "They went down because it was the most important thing to do at the moment."

Among black historians, Chaney's funeral was remembered not for any talk of grand alliances but for the brutal eulogy of David Dennis, an organizer for CORE, the Congress of Racial Equality, who captured the frustration and anger that would soon boil over into the riots and confrontations of the mid-1960s. As he stood over James Chaney's casket, Dennis said, "I feel that he has got his freedom and we are still fighting for it. But what I want to talk about right now is the living dead that we have right among our midst, not only here in the state of Mississippi but throughout the nation. Those are the people who don't care. [And] those who do care but don't have the guts to stand up for it. And those people who are busy up in Washington and other places using my freedom and my life to play politics with. . . . I'm sick and tired of going to the funerals of black men who have been murdered by white men. . . . I've got vengeance in my heart tonight, and I ask you to feel angry with me. I'm sick and tired, and I ask you to be sick and tired with me. . . . We've got to stand up. The best way we can remember James Chaney is to demand our rights. Don't just look at me and go back and tell folks you've been to a nice service. Your work is just beginning. If you go back home and sit down and take what these white men in Mississippi are doing to us . . . if you take it and don't do something about it . . . then God damn your souls!"

Yet it was more than coincidence that the three civil rights workers murdered near Meridian in 1964 were black or Jewish. Well over half the white students heading South that summer were Jewish, and Jews wrote most of the checks that bank-rolled the fights of Martin Luther King and his Southern Christian Leadership Conference (SCLC); of SNCC, the Student Nonviolent Coordinating Committee; and of the Freedom Rides of James Farmer and CORE. Ever since the early years of the NAACP more than fifty years before, with a Jewish president and, a few years later, a black national organizer, leading Jews on the board of directors, and a vocal black membership, blacks and Jews had been linked in the fight to end discrimination.

Instead of finding symbols of cooperation in Mississippi in 1964, I found myself asking a different question: What was it that had first brought blacks and Jews together in the fight for civil rights? How had they ended up on the same side?

A routine by Lenny Bruce

Dig: I'm Jewish. Count Basie's Jewish. Ray Charles is Jewish. Eddie Cantor's goyish. B'nai B'rith is goyish, Hadassah, Jewish.

If you live in New York or any other big city you are Jewish. It doesn't matter even if you're Catholic; if you live in New York, you're Jewish. If you live in Butte, Montana, you're going to be goyish even if you're Jewish.

Kool-Aid is goyish. Evaporated milk is goyish even if the Jews invented it. Chocolate is Jewish and fudge is goyish. Fruit salad is Jewish. Lime Jell-O is goyish. Lime soda is very goyish.

Negroes are all Jews . . .

Unlike the Quakers, or even the blue-blooded Protestant Brahmins of Boston, American Jews did not have a history of becoming involved in liberal causes, even during the Civil

War. The Jews who first came to America in the seventeenth, eighteenth, and early nineteenth centuries were heirs to a conservative political tradition that tended to embrace the status quo and sought not to rock the boat. The tumult of Europe had rarely been good for the Jews. They had been chased from Jerusalem in A.D. 70 when the Romans destroyed the Second Temple, enslaving whatever Jewish inhabitants they could catch. From that time on, Jews had lived on the margins of society, pushed into ghettos and restricted to crafts or professions that Christians would not touch, such as money-lending. Country after country persecuted the Jews, then expelled them—England in 1290, France in 1306 and 1394, Sicily and Spain in 1492, the Kingdom of Naples in 1541. In Russia, the Czar restricted Jews to a narrow pale of settlement, then left them at the mercy of the pogroms, the riots of mobs that sacked and looted Jewish homes.

Where Jews survived, they often did so at the whim of the political ruler, relying on the king or emperor to protect their special status in the face of hostility by local people or the Church. Rapid political change often meant new perils. Mass, uncontrolled political movements could always turn into an attack against the Jews. Jews did not seek alliances with the oppressed. They were oppressed enough themselves, and it was often peasants and lower-class mobs that hated Jews the most. Hannah Arendt, the German-Jewish philosopher, wrote of this "paradox" of the political history of the Jews: "Of all European peoples, the Jews had been the only one without a state of their own and had been, precisely for this reason, so eager and so suitable for alliances with governments and states as such, no matter what these governments or states might represent. . . . they had somehow drawn the conclusion that authority, and especially high authority, was favorable to them and that lower officials, and especially the common people, were dangerous." An old Jewish saying put it more bluntly: "Any group bigger than a minyan [the ten men required for prayer] looks like a pogrom."

Conditioned to the perils of Europe, the Jews who came to

America starting in 1654 treaded cautiously. They burned for a land where they would be treated equally and escape bigotry, but they shied away from the reform movements that swept the United States in the mid-nineteenth century—for these reformers were heavily influenced by Protestant churches and Christian zeal. Hand in hand with demands for better schools and social works often came demands for a more "Christian" society with, for example, tighter blue laws that would close shops on Sunday. On Sunday, December 21, 1845, Sol A. Benjamin ran afoul of these laws when he had the temerity to sell a pair of gloves to W. C. Gatewood in Charleston, South Carolina. Benjamin was hauled before the Charleston Court of Errors and, despite what a newspaper called arguments of "great ability," was convicted and fined. The court agreed with the city prosecutor that "Christianity was part and parcel of the common law—that the common law was the law in South Carolina" and such law "was equally binding on Jews as well as Christians."

On the most crucial civil rights question of the nineteenth century—slavery—Jews were divided. The lack of broad Jewish involvement in the anti-slavery movement puzzled and angered the abolitionists. "The object of so much mean prejudice and unrighteous oppression as the Jews have been for ages," declared a report of the American and Foreign Anti-Slavery Society in 1853, "surely they, it would seem, more than any other denomination, ought to be the enemies of caste and friends of Universal Freedom." Perhaps they ought to have been, but they weren't. There were no opinion polls conducted in the mid-nineteenth century, but historians agree that Jews differed little from other Americans in their attitudes toward slaves: Jews in the North tended to oppose slavery; Jews in slave-owning states favored it. There were Jewish abolitionists: For example, three immigrant Jews fought side by side with John Brown in the battles over "Bloody Kansas," and a Jewish man named Michael Greenbaum led a mob in Chicago to free a slave captured under the Fugitive Slave Law. But there were also Jewish slave-owners. A Jewish South Carolina

businessman, Abraham Seixas, took to verse to advertise the
sale of Negro slaves in 1794:

Abraham Seixas
All so gracious
Once again does offer

His services pure
For to secure
Money in the coffer

He has for sale
Some negroes, male,
Will suit full well grooms

He has likewise
Some of their wives
Can man clean dirty rooms

Judah Benjamin, born of Jewish parents in the British West
Indies, though he had little connection with organized Judaism in his adult life, became secretary of state of the Confederacy, prompting Daniel Webster to call him an Egyptian in
Israeli clothing. In January 1861, Rabbi Morris Jacob Raphall
of Congregation B'nai Jeshurun in New York brought the full
force of Jewish learning to a defense of slavery, preaching a
lengthy sermon that defended its biblical roots and noting that
"Abraham, Isaac, Jacob, Job—the men with whom the Almighty conversed, with whose names he emphatically con-
nects his own most holy name . . . all these men were slave-
holders." Raphall was no fringe figure. He was one of the most
prominent rabbis of his day; the year before he had been chosen to be the first Jew to open a session of the House of Representatives with a prayer. Opponents of slavery shuddered at
the impact of Raphall's widely reprinted sermon for, as one
minister observed, "the impression on the minds of some is
that he must know the Hebrew of the Bible so profoundly that
it is absolutely impossible for him to be mistaken on the
subject of slavery; and that what he affirms respecting it is as
true almost as the word of God itself."

It was a paradox that America's Jews—who would come to

be seen in the twentieth century as defenders of the poor and the weak, eager to vote for social programs and back civil rights protests—largely sat out the epic battles of reform and emancipation that coursed through America in the nineteenth century. Notwithstanding the "prophetic tradition" of the Old Testament prophets who inveighed against injustice, inequality, and poverty, the Jews who came to America before the Civil War harbored a deep-seated—and historically justified—uneasiness of mass protest movements. They were unwilling to defy the law of the land or cast their lot with poor, oppressed people who might easily one day turn their anger on the Jews.

Yet by the summer of 1964, Jews had emerged at the forefront of the civil rights movement and the liberal wing of the Democratic Party. Not everyone was prepared to march down South or send money to the NAACP. But Jews, by and large, showed more sympathy with the growing black protest than any other white group. Jewish organizations lobbied relentlessly for civil rights, and in election after election Jews voted overwhelmingly for liberal over conservative candidates.

What happened?

Individual people made individual decisions. But it is also possible, from the vantage point of 1964, to see several strains in the history of Jews in America that shaped the outlook of Jews toward civil rights and set the stage for the liberal outlook that dominated Jewish political life from the end of the Second World War onward. Three factors set the stage for Jewish involvement in civil rights: the flood of Jewish immigrants from Eastern Europe that began in the later part of the nineteenth century, the rise of anti-Semitism in the United States, and the discovery of the Holocaust in Europe.

Most of the Jews who came to America before 1880 were German Jews with business on their minds and success in their future. Many came from striving lower-middle-class families in Germany and built on their connections and expertise as peddlers to make their way. The second wave of Jewish immigration that began in 1880 changed all that. The Jews who came to America between 1880 and 1920—more than 2 million—overwhelmed the 250,000 Jews already here. The new arrivals were overwhelmingly poor and working class. They came from Russia and Eastern Europe. In style, jobs, and politics they were light-years removed from the German or "uptown" Jews. Indeed, it was the German-Jewish community that first used the slur "kike" to describe the poor immigrants who crammed the Lower East Side of New York and moved on to the West Side of Chicago and to cities across the country. The newly arrived Jews found jobs in New York's "needle trades," the various clothing shops and garment factories often owned by wealthier German Jews. Whereas established Jews clung to the more conservative outlook they had brought with them from Europe, these new immigrants brought with them a new ideology, largely unknown in America: socialism.

The Jewish fascination with socialism had its roots in the broken promises of equality and freedom in Europe. Beginning with the French Revolution, a wave of civil reform had swept across Europe in the late 1700s and early 1800s, bringing greater equality, including equality for Jews. The revocation of these freedoms in Germany in the early 1800s had been one reason German Jews had decided to make the journey across the Atlantic. In 1855, Czar Alexander of Russia began a similar series of reforms. Twenty years later, these reforms, too, came to a grinding halt. Cynically, the czar turned the revolutionary fervor of Russia's peasants against the Jews, encouraging the pogroms that terrorized Jewish communities. In fear, frustration, and disappointment, Jews, especially Jewish intellectuals, turned to revolutionary and socialist movements. These ideologies seeped down to Jewish workers, and when they landed in America in the 1880s and 1890s, they brought socialism with them. The bosses were the enemies, even when the bosses were Jews. "Solidarity! Solidarity of the workers!"

The Eastern European Jews who immigrated to America duplicated to a dizzying degree the left-wing groups, bunds, socialist leagues, and communist leagues they had joined in Poland and Russia. There was a branch of the Socialist Labor Party, a Jewish workers' educational club, a socialist bund that promoted Yiddish but opposed Zionism, a territorialist group that backed Zionism but not necessarily in Palestine, and a labor Zionist group that backed a Jewish homeland in Palestine but insisted it be socialist. Their leaders read socialist newspapers, studied socialist doctrine, and were often members of the Socialist Party. They worried, with religious fervor, over the positions of workers in a capitalist society. In many ways, socialism became the new religion, union leaders the new rabbis, alliances with capitalists the new forbidden fruit. A socialist immigrant, formerly a religious Jew, wrote to a Yiddish newspaper confessing that he had fallen in love with the boss's daughter. Was this permissible? Could he spend his life with the daughter of an exploiter of the workers?

Socialism injected a new element into the American Jewish community. If Jews in America before 1880 had cut a low political profile on the issues of slavery and social reform, the new arrivals hurled themselves into politics, union organizing, and public life. In New York, Jewish immigrants formed the most militant labor unions. They marched with picket signs printed in Hebrew and Yiddish and forced passage of progressive labor laws. Jewish names dominated the labor movement: David Dubinsky, Abraham Cahan, Sidney Hillman, Morris Hillquit. Even among those Jews who did not consider themselves socialist, the commitment to improving the lot of workers was strong: two Jews, Samuel Gompers and Leo Strasser, led the American Federation of Labor. Whatever their personal feelings about blacks—and surely many Jews shared an uneasiness about blacks, whose lives and skin color were so different from their own—in the political universe of these men, blacks were not part of the problem; they were part of the solution. The catechism of socialism impelled an alliance with blacks. The brotherhood of the workers would overthrow the bosses and banish racism, anti-Semitism, war, and exploitation. Even more, socialism in America gave Jews an opportunity few could dream of in Poland or Russia—the chance to help people less fortunate than themselves. Blacks worked even lower-paid and less-skilled jobs in the sweatshops in New York than Jews did. There was something heady in the chance to help people whose sufferings dwarfed Jewish sufferings and who seemed happy to get the help. "You colored workers were exploited and mistreated in the shop worse than any other group," David Dubinsky, head of the Jewish-dominated International Ladies' Garment Workers' Union, told a rally of Harlem workers in 1934. When Dubinsky discovered that the Medinah Temple in Chicago, where the ILGWU was holding its annual convention in 1934, discriminated against blacks, he gaveled the convention to order and marched them out in dramatic protest. "It was just a case of supporting words by proper action," Dubinsky declared.

What socialists believed as faith, communists believed as ideology. Most Jews were not communists. But in the 1930s and 1940s, many communists were Jews. For them, communism offered the clearest alternative to capitalism amidst the wreck of the Great Depression and, with the exception of the brief period of the Hitler-Stalin pact, unswerving opposition to Nazism. Jewish support for communists would later collapse amidst a bitter debate over how much they had been misled. Many Jews would remain communist into the 1950s, gripped by a romantic notion of what was happening in the Soviet Union; others would date their disenchantment to the Hitler-Stalin pact. But in the 1920s and 1930s, communism posed the most radical alternative to a system that clearly oppressed the workers. Early on, the American Communist Party targeted blacks as the group most ripe for recruitment. For those Jews who adopted or flirted with communism, a commitment to blacks had to stand as the centerpiece of their beliefs. The communists were the first party to run a black on the national ticket, nominating James W. Ford for Vice President in 1932, 1936, and 1940. When the men known as the Scottsboro boys were accused of raping two white women in Alabama, the lawyer that rushed to defend them was Samuel Liebowitz, a Jew from Brooklyn, who became a folk hero among southern blacks. When the Communist Party turned its attention to organizing Harlem, a disproportionate number of the organizers were Jewish.

The upsurge in political activism among Jews was fed by religious changes as well. Even before the influx of Eastern

European Jews reshaped the Jewish landscape, a group of German-Jewish rabbis adopted an eight-point agenda that became the foundation of the 1885 Pittsburgh Platform, ushering in the Reform Movement in Judaism—Judaism's most liberal wing. The eighth point agreed to at the conference declared, "In full accordance with the spirit of Mosaic legislation . . . we deem it our duty to participate in the great task of modern times, to solve on the basis of justice and righteousness the problems presented by the contrasts and evils of the present organization of society." No other religious conference had ever gone so far to include the resolution of social problems in the creed of American Jews. A new generation of rabbis had put concern with social justice and the "prophetic tradition" of the Hebrew prophets at the center of the religion, de-emphasizing the legalistic tradition of obeying a myriad of laws. To be a good Jew, in this new wing of American Judaism, meant being concerned with social problems and social justice.

A Jew growing up in a Jewish neighborhood did not have to be a socialist or a communist to inhale the talk of socialism and equality that blew all around. It permeated life, creating a world view in which blacks were objects of sympathy rather than hate, potential allies rather than foes, people who could be helped and who could make Jews feel good for having helped them.

But feeling good was not sufficient reason to explain an alliance that linked Jewish union bosses and black workers, Jewish intellectuals and black intellectuals, the broad Jewish middle class and the struggle of blacks for equality. There were self-interested reasons, too.

Jews had come to America in the belief that it would be different, that there would be no anti-Semitism. Up until the 1880s, they were largely correct. Jews faced few legal barriers in the United States, although, to be sure, there were examples of social and economic discrimination. Then, in 1877, a hotel in Saratoga Springs refused to admit Joseph Seligman, a German-Jewish banker who had come to America penniless and worked his way to a fortune. Turning Seligman away underlined the social discrimination that until then had been well-understood but never so openly codified. Within a few years, discrimination against Jews had become widespread, with Jews shut out of housing in "better" neighborhoods and prevented from attending universities like Harvard, Yale, and Columbia because of quotas. In 1914, about 40 percent of the students at New York's Columbia University were Jewish. Fraternity brothers chanted:

> Oh, Harvard's run by millionaires
> And Yale is run by booze
> Cornell is run by farmers' sons,
> Columbia's run by Jews.
> So give a cheer for Baxter Street
> Another one for Pell
> And when the little sheenies die
> Their souls will go to hell.

By 1918, quotas at Columbia had brought the percentage of Jewish students down to 21 percent; throughout the 1920s the Jewish percentage hovered around 15 percent. Harvard and Yale soon followed Columbia's lead, with Yale establishing a Committee on the Limitation of Numbers and Harvard adopting a "Harvard Plan" that cut Jewish enrollment at Harvard from 21 to 10 percent. "Because of our Judaism, we must be prepared to give up some of the world's goods even as we must be prepared to make sacrifices because of other disadvantages with which we may happen to be born," Harry Austryn Wolfson, one of the first Jewish professors at Harvard, wrote gloomily in 1922. "All men are not born equal. Some are born blind, some deaf, some lame, and some are born Jews."

A revived Ku Klux Klan targeted blacks, Jews, and Catholics—"Koons, Kikes, and Katholics." In 1913, Leo Frank, a Jewish businessman in Georgia, became one of the few white men ever to be lynched in the South. Frank was accused of raping and killing a young girl. In a precedent-breaking move, a Georgia court allowed a black man to testify against a white. Frank was convicted. Inflamed by Tom Watson, a demagogic racist leader in the South, a mob broke into the jail where Frank was being held, dragged him out, and lynched him.

America, it seemed, might not be that different after all. The conservative wings of both the Democratic and Republican parties refused to renounce the violence of the Ku Klux Klan, in part because of the power and influence of southern senators. The pace of anti-Semitism increased. In the 1920s, Henry Ford's *Dearborn Independent* spewed forth anti-Semitism, and Ford was listed by a magazine as a potential presidential candidate.

What was different—historically so in light of the attitudes of Jews in America in the nineteenth century—was the response of Jews to this rise of anti-Semitism. At first, Jews responded much as they always had. They turned inward and began pooling their resources for the common defense. In 1906, as anti-Semitism grew in America and pogroms broke out in Russia, a group of wealthy German Jews formed the American Jewish Committee. A dozen years later, a group of Eastern European Jews formed the American Jewish Congress. In 1914, in the wake of the Frank lynching, the B'nai B'rith created the Anti-Defamation League. But very gradually the strategy of these organizations broadened and they, and other Jews, began to see links in their oppression with attacks and oppression of blacks.

In New York, the dominant newspaper of the immigrant Jewish community was the socialist, Yiddish *Forward*. Beginning around the time of Frank's lynching, the paper began writing extensively about blacks as victims of America's intolerance. It ran lengthy articles on the history of the slave trade and reminiscences by former slaves. The *Forward*'s editors took the word "lynch" and put it into Yiddish letters and proper Yiddish grammatical form. Following the East St. Louis riot in 1917 in which thirty-nine blacks were killed, the *Forward* compared the riot to the Kishinev pogrom in Russia in 1903, when more than fifty Jews were killed: "Kishinev and St. Louis—the same soil, the same people. It is a distance of four and a half thousand miles between these two cities and yet they are so close and so similar to each other. . . . Actually twin sisters, which could easily be mistaken for each other." Just before Memorial Day, 1927, the *Forward* asked indignantly: "Where is the spirit of freedom with which our America is always priding itself? And where is the holiness of the constitution which is so often mentioned? And Monday, the 30th of May, the American people decorated the graves of those who fell in the great battle to free the slaves in America and to free America from the stain and shame of slavery. The slaves are today not free and on America, the stain of the shame of slavery is still not evident."

Unlike much of the white press, the *Forward* and other Yiddish newspapers ran articles showing that the roots of black crime often lay in poverty and hopelessness. The *Forward* ran a moving feature on the mother of a black man convicted of murdering several policemen. She had "raised my children right and I hoped that he would be a respectable person. However, he went away to the army and there they taught him to shoot and to murder—nothing else could have been expected of him then."

In 1909, when the "call" was issued that led to the founding of the NAACP, several prominent Jews were among the signers, including Rabbi Stephen Wise, the leading Reform rabbi in the country. In the next thirty years, Jewish involvement with and contributions to the NAACP mushroomed. Joel E. Spingarn, an assimilated Jewish professor of English at Columbia, became the NAACP's chairman in 1914 and served off and on in that role until his death in 1939. A year later, W. E. B. Du Bois's autobiography was published, dedicated to Spingarn. Joel Spingarn's brother, Arthur Spingarn, headed the NAACP's legal fights, drawing on the expertise of the nation's leading Jewish legal scholar, Felix Frankfurter at Harvard. Louis Marshall, head of the American Jewish Committee, argued on behalf of the NAACP in the Supreme Court, attacking restrictive housing covenants that discriminated against blacks and Jews. At a time when the cause of black rights was far from popular, Jewish givers gave tens of thousands of dollars to keep the NAACP on its feet. In 1930, the onset of the Depression threatened the NAACP's future. William Rosenwald, son of Julius Rosenwald, the founder of Sears, Roebuck, offered to donate $1,000 annually for three years if four others agreed to match the gift. Four did, three of them Jews—Herbert Lehman and Felix Warburg, financiers, and Harold Guinzburg, head of the Viking Press—and one non-Jew, Edsel Ford.

Jewish philanthropists, especially Julius Rosenwald, became generous supporters of Booker T. Washington's Tuskegee Institute, appearing at fund-raisers for Washington in New York and building a network of Jewish donors. Jacob Schiff had Washington screen requests for money from other black supplicants. Rosenwald set up the Rosenwald Fund to dispense money to build black elementary schools in the South. Between 1912 and 1915, 300 schools were built; by 1932, the Rosenwald Fund had established 5,357 schools in the South, serving 663,615 students. By the Depression, an astonishing 25 to 40 percent of all black children in the South were being educated in schools built with Rosenwald money.

What bound these events together was a recognition on the part of Jews that they could not go it alone. Their appeals against racism and anti-Semitism often fell on deaf political ears. Jews were special, yes, but they were also one of the underdogs, one of several embattled ethnic groups. Their struggle for equality and fair treatment was linked to the struggles of blacks for greater opportunity. It was not a struggle of equals; Jews did not consider their plight equal to that of blacks. But they recognized in the black struggle for rights elements that could benefit them and conditions with which they could sympathize. By the 1930s, wrote one Jewish historian, Jews had come to consider themselves "one of the 'minorities,' that is, one of several groups to some degree discriminated against. Along with the Negroes, the Catholics, and many of the foreign-born, they were deprived by prejudice of the equal opportunities of American society." And, like those other groups, Jews by the 1930s had found a political home and a political program to overturn those injustices: Franklin Roosevelt and the New Deal of the Democratic Party.

The rise of anti-Semitism in the United States and the in-fusion of socialism and communism brought by Eastern European immigrants would probably have been enough to tilt most Jews to the causes of liberalism and see in blacks people worthy of pity and support. The rise of anti-Semitism in Germany and the cataclysm of the Holocaust reinforced that view. The Holocaust reshaped the Jewish view of the world. It was the culmination of centuries of oppression and expulsion: Jews expelled from England and France during the Middle Ages, confined to the ghetto of Venice, forced to wear yellow badges in France and Germany in the thirteenth century, expelled from Spain during the Inquisition, conscripted into military service at age twelve for twenty-five years by the Czar in Russia. In its inaugural issue in November 1945, *Commentary*, a publication of the American Jewish Committee that would become, in the next four decades, the most influential magazine of Jewish affairs, put the truth starkly, though its figures for the Holocaust were still low: "Jews live with this fact: 4,750,000 of 6,000,000 Jews of Europe have been murdered. Not killed in battle but slaughtered like cattle. . . . The kind of thinking and feeling that set loose this nightmare phenomenon still burns high in many countries, and lies latent in all. We have no gauge to measure the potentialities of this great Nazi secret weapon of World War II. But there are many—and they are not guided by personal hurt alone—who believe that here is a force that, in the political and social scene, can wreak destruction comparable to the atomic bomb itself."

What had happened in Germany could happen anywhere. As the twentieth-century's ultimate victim, Jews would more easily identify with other victims of oppression and injustice. The memories they carried with them after World War II made them all the more sensitive to cries of injustice—for once persecution started, many Jews remained convinced that it would end up directed at them.

Emerging from a trip through Jewish history made it clear that it had never been preordained that Jews would enroll in the civil rights movement. A constellation of factors—economic, political, social—provided fertile soil for religious ideas of social justice and opposition to oppression to take root. The teachings of the Old Testament—the exodus from Egypt, the exhortations of the prophets—predisposed Jews to activism. But Jews had turned to black causes out of sympathy fueled by the radical politics of Eastern European immigrants, by their own experience with discrimination, and by the horror of the Holocaust. That raised questions: What would happen as the sons and daughters of those Eastern European immigrants and union organizers benefited from educational opportunities and became upwardly mobile, becoming businessmen, lawyers, and doctors living in better neighborhoods? What would happen when discrimination against Jews abated and Jews became the most affluent and successful ethnic group in the country? What would happen when emotional investment in Israel replaced the trauma of the Holocaust as the focus of Jewish concern?

Such a skeptical view was useful. For, among blacks, while there was a strong history of positive feelings about Jews, there was also a strong history of ambivalence.

From "An Ante-Bellum Sermon" by Paul Laurence Dunbar, a black dialect poet, 1896

> Ol' pharaoh down in Egypt was the wust man evah
> bo'n.
> He had those Hebrew chillun down there wukkin in
> his corn. . . .
> The Lord got tired of his foolin' and said,
> I'll make him rue the houah
> I'll empty down upon him all the vials of my powah.
> An' he did.
> An' pharaoh's army wa'n't worth half a dime.
> You can trust the Lord, my chillun,
> He'll do it evah time.

I began my search into the black roots of the black-Jewish alliance with an article by James Baldwin in a 1948 issue of *Commentary*. Surveying the state of black-Jewish relations then, Baldwin concluded: "It seems unlikely that within this complicated structure any real and systematic cooperation can be achieved between Negroes and Jews. (This is in terms of the overall social problems and is not meant to imply that individual friendships are impossible or that they are valueless when they occur.) The structure of the American common-wealth has trapped both these minorities into attitudes of perpetual hostility. They do not dare trust each other—the Jew because he feels he must climb higher on the American social ladder and has, so far as he is concerned, nothing to gain from identification with any minority even more unloved than he; while the Negro is in the even less tenable position of not really daring to trust anyone."

This in 1948.

It was on plantations in the South that blacks first met Jews. Cut off from much of their own tradition and history, slaves learned Christianity from white preachers and quickly fused it with West African belief and practice—the call-and-response pattern of sermons, the singing and dancing of the audience. White preachers emphasized tales in the Bible that taught slaves to be obedient to their masters. But slave preachers spoke from a different text. They found more fertile ground in the Old Testament, in the stories of Jewish prophets railing against injustice and oppression, and of the children of Israel enslaved in a strange land.

The tale of the Exodus and the emancipation of the Jews resonated strongly. In 1822, in clandestine meetings in South Carolina, Denmark Vesey organized a rebellion of slaves. At every meeting he or one of his comrades would read from the Bible about how the children of Israel were delivered out of bondage in Egypt. Then they would sing:

When Israel was in Egypt's land
Let my people go
They worked so hard they could not stand

Let my people go
Go down, Moses, way down to Egypt land
Tell old Pharaoh
Let my people go.

"Crossing over Jordan into Canaan" was symbolic of the triumph of the oppressed people. The "Jordan waters" were "chilly and cold," as was the Ohio River, the last barrier slaves had to cross when fleeing North to freedom on the Underground Railroad. The story of the Jews enslaved in Egypt became the first protest story, Negro spirituals the first protest songs.

Black preachers and newspapers often extolled Jews as examples. Wrote one at the end of the nineteenth century: "The Israelites give us our finest object lesson in the possibilities growing out of thrift and economy. Examine the names upon our trade and financial emporiums and you will find the bulk of them suggestive of Jewish origin. The Jew has learned that money is taken by the world as a measure of worth. Can we not learn the same?" There were few blacks in the North in the 1930s who had not at least heard of Samuel Leibowitz, the Jewish lawyer from Brooklyn who was defending the Scottsboro boys and whose activities were covered in black newspapers like the *Chicago Defender*, the *Pittsburgh Courier*, and the *Afro*; or did not know about the Spingarn brothers who headed the NAACP and bestowed an annual Spingarn medal on black leaders, authors, and artists; or had not attended or did not know someone who attended one of the Rosenwald schools. At a time when the Ku Klux Klan and other night riders were lynching up to one hundred blacks a year, the image of Jews as somehow different from other white people stood out. The very names of black churches summoned up images of the Old Testament, of a wrathful God who would punish the wicked and free the oppressed: the A.M.E. Zion Church, the Mt. Zion Methodist Church, Martin Luther King's Ebenezer Baptist Church.

Blacks and Jews together. It was a powerful image—enslaved and oppressed blacks finding succor and hope in the biblical story of Jewish freedom. But side by side with this myth, often out of sight of whites, flourished another set of images, these far less complimentary to Jews.

In one of his earliest memories, St. Clair Drake, one of the country's leading sociologists, is walking down the road in Staunton, Virginia, in the Shenandoah Valley with his grandmother. It is a hot day, the sun beating down on the road. Drake is accompanying his grandmother to a school for white girls, where she works as a maid. They pass the house of one of only two Jewish families in town—a wealthy family that owns a chain of stores. The Jewish woman on the veranda invites Drake and his grandmother up for a glass of water. The two Jewish families are the only whites in town who allow a black on their veranda. Yet when Drake goes home, it is common for him and his family to talk about the Jewish family stores "Jewing" them.

"They'll cheat you. You got to be careful," people would tell him.

In many ways that was a paradigm for the way many blacks looked at Jews. Jews were both good and bad. They were some of the best friends blacks had. They were also some of their most humiliating exploiters. The contradictions often existed side by side.

Richard Wright, in his autobiographical tale of growing up in the South, *Black Boy*, wrote that "all of us black people who lived in the neighborhood hated Jews, not because they exploited us, but because we had been taught at home and in Sunday school that Jews were 'Christ-killers.'

"With the Jews thus singled out for us, we made them fair game for ridicule.

"We black children, seven, eight, and nine years of age, used to run to the Jew's store and shout:

Jew, Jew, Jew
What do you chew?

"Or we would form a long line and weave back and forth in front of the door, singing:

Jew, Jew
Two for five
That's what keeps
Jews alive

"Or we would chant:

Bloody Christ-killers
Never trust a Jew
Bloody Christ-killers
What won't a Jew do?"

There was even a competing anti-Jewish religious myth, popular among free-Negro churches in the northern cities before the Civil War. This took as its text a prophecy from the Book of Psalms: "Princes shall come out of Egypt, and Ethiopia shall soon stretch forth her hand unto God." The message here was that, before slavery, blacks were a people who lived in glorious and powerful kingdoms. So powerful were the Egyptians that they were able to enslave God's own chosen people, the Jews. There were seeds in this myth of black nationalism that would flower in the twentieth century under Marcus Garvey and Malcolm X. But more palpable was the sense of black pride these biblical stories of the Kingdom of Ethiopia projected. Negro spirituals that sang of the endurance of suffering and the promise of redemption—so admired by many whites—were considered by some blacks to be slave songs. In 1927, when St. Clair Drake began college at the Hampton Institute, an all-black school, he arrived to find the students on strike over several issues—among them the fact that every Sunday night students were expected to file into the campus auditorium and sing Negro spirituals for white townspeople in the balcony. The students found the performance demeaning.

While there were undercurrents of tension in black views of Jews in the South, overall the image was positive. There were few Jews in the South and most benefited by comparison to the other whites around. Starting around the time of World War I, the great migration of blacks to the North began, filling cities like Chicago, Detroit, and New York. In 1910, nine out of every ten blacks lived in the South and three out of every four lived in rural areas. By 1960, three-fourths of blacks lived in cities and half lived outside the old slave states. It was here, in the cities of the North, Midwest, and West, that many blacks met for the first time the Jews they had heard so much about in church.

The mixed feelings blacks drew from those encounters filled their writings and recollections. "The Jewish boys in high school were troubling because I could find no point of connection between them and the Jewish pawnbrokers and landlords and grocery store owners in Harlem," James Baldwin wrote of his childhood in Harlem in the 1920s and 1930s. "I knew that these people were Jews—God knows I was told it often enough—but I thought of them only as white. Jews, as such, until I got to high school, were all incarcerated in the Bible, and their names were Abraham, Moses, Daniel, Ezekiel, and Job, and Shadrach, Meshach, and Abednego. It was bewildering to find them so many miles and centuries out of Egypt, and so far from the fiery furnace." When St. Clair Drake's family moved to Pittsburgh, they were able to buy their first house in an all-white neighborhood with the help of a Jewish man. The man bought the house, then sold it to the Drakes for a dollar, breaking segregation. Blacks in northern ghettos insisted they preferred working for Jews. They were more courteous, less patronizing. Yet the wages were still low and conditions often insulting. In an article for a Harlem newspaper in 1933, two black women wrote of the "Bronx slave market" in which black women worked as maids for white, usually Jewish, families.

In 1935, when rioting broke out in Harlem, it was directed against Jewish merchants and stores. Roi Ottley, a black author, writing in 1943, charged that Jews had introduced the idea of installment buying into black life, inducing blacks to spend beyond their means, leading to a buildup of resentment and anger. Jewish-owned pawnshops, Ottley said, required blacks to leave a suit for a month for a two-dollar loan—and then charged an additional one-dollar storage fee. They drove a hard bargain.

Jews were different from white people. There was "Mr. Charlie," black slang for whites, and there was "Mr. Goldberg," black slang for Jews. At their worst, Jews were the conniving tricksters who took advantage of innocent blacks beaten down by the oppression of white society. They were like the driver on the plantation, the hated middleman who did the white man's dirty work.

Or Jews were insincere. Under the guise of "helping" blacks and being their "friend," Jews patronized blacks and exploited them. Jews would leave neighborhoods as blacks moved in. But they kept their businesses there: the apartment buildings they had bought, the stores they owned and ran. During the Depression, black activists in Harlem launched a "Don't Buy Where You Can't Work" campaign. Black leaders approached Blumstein's, the largest store in Harlem, which was owned by a Jewish family. Ottley reported that Blumstein "remained adamant to requests or to persuasion to employ Negroes as clerical workers and salesgirls. As a sponsor of Negro charitable institutions, and as the employer of Negro elevator operators, porters and maids, he explained that he had done his share for Negroes, and refuses to budge an inch in response to the demand for more jobs."

Such an attitude infuriated blacks. It reeked of condescension. Encounters between blacks and Jews always seemed to involve Jews reaching out and "helping" blacks, "teaching" them, "guiding" them. Many black intellectuals ended their flirtation with the Communist Party bitter not only at the communists but at Jews they felt had treated them condescendingly. "How can the average public school Negro be expected to understand the exigencies of the capitalist system as it applies to both Jew and Gentile in America . . . since both groups act strangely like Hitlerian Aryans . . . when it comes to colored folks?" asked Langston Hughes, bitter after a feud with Jewish communists.

Like Jewish attitudes toward blacks, black attitudes toward

Jews were not predetermined by history. There were roots of cooperation in black attitudes toward Jews—the shared feelings of being an oppressed people, the history of Jewish philanthropy, the embrace by many left-wing Jews of unpopular causes, the decency and liberalism shown by individual Jews towards blacks at a time when most whites shunned them. There were also roots of division—the persistence of an elder-brother mentality, resentment at Jewish overbearingness, bitterness at ghetto businesses, a belief that Jews failed to live up to their own moral standards. An alliance was not inevitable. Blacks could choose from a kaleidoscope of often contradictory images.

Why, then, as the civil rights movement gained popularity in the 1950s, were blacks prepared to accept Jews as allies?

Part of the answer was necessity. With a foot on your neck you don't argue with people who are going to help you. But another answer lay in the shifting cycles of black attitudes— the competing tendencies of cosmopolitanism and nationalism, of turning inward and reaching outward, of embracing white allies and scorning white help. All these were built around a central question: Could blacks trust white people?

The Civil War and Reconstruction kindled hopes among blacks that America was truly committed to an equal society. The coming of freedom literally provoked dancing in the streets. In Charleston, South Carolina, a giant procession of 4,000 black artisans, schoolchildren, and soldiers paraded through town to celebrate the onset of freedom. Similar parades erupted across the South as the Confederacy folded and retreated before the Union victors. Constitutions written by northerners gave blacks the right to vote in southern states, and blacks registered to vote across the South. "The southern whites accept them precisely as northern men in cities accept the ignorant Irish vote—not cheerfully, but with acquiescence in the inevitable; and when the strict color-line is once broken they are just as ready to conciliate the Negro as the northern politician to flatter the Irishman," one northern traveler wrote. That was probably overstated. But blacks were regularly elected to office in the South in the decades after the end of the Civil

War. Between 1876 and 1894, North Carolina elected fifty-two blacks to its state house of representatives. Between 1869 and 1901 the South always had at least one black member of Congress.

By 1877, however, northern interest in the rights of blacks had waned. The Freedman's Bureau, designed to aid blacks after slavery, had closed in 1870. Northern philanthropy to black educational institutions in the South declined. Northern schoolteachers who had headed south to help educate the freed slaves were driven out by threats of violence, including murder. In the Great Compromise of 1877, northern senators agreed to pull troops out of the South in exchange for southern support of the election of Rutherford B. Hayes. The South would be left alone to take care of its "Negro problem."

For blacks, the effect was catastrophic. Back under the control of southern whites, the state legislatures in the South set up the Jim Crow system, which segregated whites from blacks in streetcars, public restrooms, restaurants, even elevators. State by state, the right to vote was stripped from blacks by use of literacy and property qualifications—with loopholes that only whites could squeeze through, such as demonstrating "good character" to an all-white election board or proving that one's grandfather had been registered to vote. These laws decimated black voters. In 1896, for example, there were 130,334 blacks registered to vote in Louisiana. Eight years later there were fewer than 1,400.

Lynching and mob violence reached staggering proportions. "If it is necessary, every Negro in the state will be lynched. It will be done to maintain white supremacy," announced the governor of Mississippi in 1907. He meant what he said. Between 1889 and 1918, more than 3,000 blacks were lynched in the South, an average of 100 a year.

The Constitution offered little prospect for relief. In 1896, the Supreme Court delivered its decision in *Plessy* v. *Ferguson*, ruling that the doctrine of "separate but equal," upon which the Jim Crow system rested, was constitutional. Separate drinking fountains, railway cars, schools, and pools were all constitutional. Two years later, the Supreme Court upheld the poll taxes and literacy qualifications that had eviscerated the black vote in the South.

Racist literature and scholarship boomed. "Scientific" studies argued that blacks were biologically inferior and could not handle self-government. Titles included *The Negro a Beast*, published in 1900, and *The Negro, a Menace to American Civilization*, published seven years later. A popular southern trilogy by Thomas Dixon, which later served as the basis for D. W. Griffith's movie *Birth of a Nation*, romanticized the history of the Ku Klux Klan and portrayed black men who lived only to attack white women.

Under such a reign of terror and drawn by the promise of better-paying work in northern factories, thousands of blacks headed north, up the Mississippi on what was called the "Chicken Bone Express." At the height of the Great Migration, blacks were coming north at the rate of 500,000 a year, pouring into New York, Chicago, Detroit, Indianapolis, and Pittsburgh. Work drew most of them, especially when World War I broke out and northern factories needed labor to replace the soldiers who had been drafted.

Like the Civil War, World War I aroused in blacks a new hope that their rights would be restored and a new militancy in demanding them. More than 350,000 blacks entered the army. Many saw overseas duty. The blacks coming north for jobs in war industries were lured by high wages and the promise of prosperity. War propaganda underscored that the war was being fought as a "crusade for democracy."

The coming of peace smashed these hopes. In 1917 race riots pitting whites against blacks ripped apart Philadelphia and Chester, Pennsylvania, and East St. Louis, Illinois, where, in the most serious racial strife of the century, at least thirty-nine blacks were killed. But this was only a prelude to the violence of Red Summer, 1919. During the last six months of that year, twenty-five race riots erupted in American cities, most in the North. Returning white veterans were incensed that blacks had taken "their" jobs. They resented these interlopers who had moved into "their" cities. Mobs took over parts of cities for days, flogging, burning, and torturing black residents. In the first year following World War I, more than seventy blacks were lynched, several of them veterans still in uniform. Crossing the River Jordan had not led to the Promised Land, but to a land as dark as Egypt.

The roller-coaster nature of black history, of promises made, then snatched away, made blacks skeptical of the promises of whites to help them. Referring to the dilemma facing black leaders in the early twentieth century and in the years that followed, the black historian Vincent Harding wrote, "The struggle for, with, and against white allies was then, as it has always been since then, a crucial element in the black freedom movement." Seen in this light, black attitudes toward Jews had less to do with how blacks felt about Jews than how they felt about whites.

In 1852, more than 100 years before Malcolm X and the Black Panthers, Martin Delaney, the father of the black emigration movement, cast his vote for separatism. "No people can be free themselves who do not constitute part of the ruling element of the country in which they live," Delaney declared. ". . . The white races are but one-third of the population of the globe—or one of them to two of us—and it cannot much longer continue that two-thirds will passively submit to the universal domination of this one-third. The time has now fully arrived when the colored race is called upon by all the ties of common humanity, and all the claims of consummate justice, to go forward and take their position, and do battle in the struggle now being made for the redemption of the world."

By the early twentieth century, with the founding of the National Urban League and the NAACP, the tendency toward working with whites had come to the fore. W. E. B. Du Bois, the country's leading black intellectual and spokesman for most middle-class blacks as editor of the NAACP's *The Crisis* during the 1930s and 1940s, was uncompromising in his belief that blacks be treated equally, but he felt that blacks needed white allies who could give blacks access to power. Many of the whites Du Bois worked with in the NAACP were Jews, and he wrote frequently in *The Crisis* during the 1930s of the rise of anti-Semitism in Germany in the 1930s. "We may be expelled from the United States as the Jew is being expelled from Germany," he wrote in his autobiography, published in 1940. Zionism, the demand for the creation of a Jewish state, also fascinated black leaders in the years between the world wars. The announcement of the Balfour Declaration in 1917 with its promise of a Jewish homeland in Palestine galvanized blacks who believed that a black homeland could provide a similar refuge for blacks. "The African movement means to us what the Zionist movement must mean to the Jews, the centralization of race effort and the recognition of a racial fount," wrote Du Bois.

The strains of black nationalism blossomed again in the 1920s when Marcus Garvey and his United Negro Improvement Association mobilized people for his back-to-Africa movement. At its height, the U.N.I.A. was the largest organization ever established by blacks, and circulation of Garvey's newspaper far outstripped circulation of *The Crisis*. Garvey admired Jews in the abstract. He told a rally in 1920: "A new spirit, a new courage, has come to us simultaneously as it came to other people, of the world. It came to us at the same time it came to the Jew. When the Jew said, 'We shall have Palestine!' the same sentiment came to us when we said, 'We shall have Africa.' " But Garvey's movement was essentially separatist, with little room for whites.

Martin Luther King, his fellow southern ministers, and others who launched the civil rights movement embodied the resurgence of the cosmopolitan strain. World War II—like the Civil War and World War I before it—heightened black expectations. It was another war for freedom, against prejudice, for the wonders of democracy. The rhetoric that surrounded the war fueled black desires for integration and desegregation. The move to cities caused by the great migration was also having an effect, bringing blacks in closer touch with whites. A psychologist writing in 1943 observed:

Gone is the intensity of religious belief that their parents knew. The young people are not atheists, but they do not have the fervor and sincerity of belief in a future world. They are much more hurt by slights and minor insults than are their parents, because they do not put their faith in the promise of a heavenly victory. . . .

The steady trek of the rural Negro to cities, North and South, has changed the milieu of masses of Negroes from the rural peasant life to the industrial urban one. . . . In the city the Negro is influenced by the same advertisements, the same radio sketches, the same political bosses, the same parties (left or right), and all the other urban forces which influence the white man.

The Negro's goals for success are thus becoming increasingly the same as those of the white person; and these goals are primarily in the economic field, although those in other fields, such as art and athletics, are not to be minimized either. The securing of these goals is in this world rather than in a future one. They are attained through the competition and aggressive struggle so characteristic of our culture rather than through meekness and subservience.

King cast the demands of blacks as a challenge to America's conscience. Before World War II, black leaders had fallen into one of two categories. There were the intellectual leaders like Du Bois, who appealed to the black middle class but lacked a mass base among the poorer blacks. Then there were the charismatic leaders like Marcus Garvey, who could galvanize poor blacks but scared off many middle-class blacks, as well as most whites. King was a populist with a Ph.D. who reached to all levels of blacks and built connections to whites. He posed the black struggle for equality as a fulfillment of constitutional obligations rather than as a challenge to the established order. He appealed to the best in whites in order to get the most for blacks. "Our victory," King declared in the early months of the Montgomery bus boycott in 1956, "will not be a victory for Montgomery's Negroes alone. It will be a victory for justice, a victory for fair play, and a victory for democracy."

The ministers and sons of ministers who joined King in those early days—almost all the civil rights leaders in the 1950s, James Farmer noted in his autobiography, were either preachers themselves or "PK's," preacher's kids—drew from this middle-class tradition. They were southern, middle class, integrationist. They were complemented by King's most influential northern advisers like Bayard Rustin, who came from a tradition of socialism and the labor movement that emphasized the importance of ideology over race.

In such an atmosphere, when blacks were seeking cooperation from liberal whites, Jews were an obvious choice for allies. They were willing to help, and had access to money, influence, and intellectual circles. The ambivalent feelings toward Jews could be buried. The positive could be emphasized, negative stereotypes put aside while the two groups worked together for a broader goal.

But there was no guarantee that belief in the success of working with whites would not fade. Even as King was launching the boycott in Montgomery that became the first step in the civil rights movement, talking about patriotism and democracy, Malcolm X was recruiting people to a storefront mosque in Harlem spreading the nationalistic, separatist message of the Black Muslims.

The close of Invisible Man by Ralph Ellison, 1952

The hibernation is over. I must shake off the old skin and come up for breath. There's a stench in the air, which, from this distance underground might be the smell either of death or of spring—I hope of spring. But don't let me trick you, there is death in the smell of spring and in the smell of thee as in the smell of me. And if nothing more, invisibility has taught my nose to classify the stenches of death.

In going underground, I whipped it all except the mind, the mind. And the mind that has conceived a plan of living must never lose sight of the chaos against which that pattern was conceived. That goes for societies as well as for individuals. Thus, having tried to give pattern to the chaos which lives within the pattern of your certainties, I must come out, I must emerge. . . . A decision has been made. I'm shaking off the old skin and I'll leave it here in the hole. I'm coming out, no less invisible without it, but coming out nevertheless. And I suppose it's damn well time. Even hibernation can be overdone, come to think of it. Perhaps that's my greatest social crime. I've overstayed my hibernation, since there's a possibility that even an invisible man has a socially responsible role to play.

The murder of Chaney, Goodman, and Schwerner in the summer of 1964 was a powerful symbol, but—like many symbols—it masked a great deal of complexity. A confluence of events had brought blacks and Jews together. History, recent experiences in America, and the trauma of the Holocaust in Europe had shaped the Jewish vision as ally to the underdog. The message that King offered—that people be judged not on their skin color or religion, but on the content of their character and their merits—appealed to them. The rhetoric of World War II and the burgeoning Cold War persuaded black leaders that now was again the time to work with white allies. The alliance between blacks and Jews was not a natural one. It resembled an Indonesian gamelan symphony, in which each instrument plays its own tune, following its own score. For most of the time, the music sounds dissonant. Then, at certain moments, the music wells up as all the instruments blend together in harmonious symphony. But the instruments continue playing their separate scores. The dissonance can return.

Still, the impulse behind the cooperation of Jews and blacks was genuine, and so were the friendships and the relationships that grew out of the cooperation. After their son's body was found with Mickey Schwerner and Jim Chaney, Carolyn and Robert Goodman decided to help Chaney's mother and her youngest son move north from Mississippi. They helped find Fannie Chaney an apartment on Columbus Avenue, a few blocks from where the Goodmans lived, and helped her find a job. They raised scholarship money so her son Ben, who had met Andy over dinner the night before he disappeared, could go to Andy's old private school on New York's Upper West

Side. "We wanted to help that family as much as we could," Carolyn Goodman told me more than twenty years later. "We wanted to help make a difference in their lives."

The summer of 1964 was that kind of time. It was a time, some believed, when together you might change the world.

COOPERATION

2

Black and White Together: Paul Parks

Paul Parks liked to tell Martin Luther King this story.

The United States Army was still segregated in April 1945. Blacks fought in separate companies commanded by separate officers. Allied troops pushed east to Berlin and south toward Austria. General Dwight D. Eisenhower wanted to wrap up the war by June.

Parks didn't want to be there. A twenty-year-old sergeant from the poor, black part of Indianapolis, Parks had been plucked from class by a high school math teacher and groomed to enter Purdue to study as an engineer. He had been drafted, shipped to North Africa, then to England, then to Germany to participate in the invasion. Near the end of April, on the outskirts of Munich, Parks had settled down for the night when he received word that the next morning he and his troops would be the advance soldiers into a camp called Dachau. Parks assumed Dachau was a German army camp. He wondered why his unit was to be the first one in. They were support soldiers—an all-black platoon charged with building bridges and defusing mines—not combat troops.

Parks had known a handful of Jews before going overseas. But nothing prepared him for what he would see the next day.

Discussion of the camps had never come up in basic training or in any of the directives given rank-and-file GIs. The U.S. high command knew about the concentration camps. They had known about them since the summer of 1942. But despite the pleas of Jewish leaders, the Allies had not tried to bomb or liberate the camps during the war—a legacy of anti-Semitism in the State Department and British Foreign Office and Eisenhower's belief that defeating Germany was the Allies' most pressing priority. Within hours after liberating Dachau, the American high command would ship in medicine and food to the concentration-camp survivors. But the first priority was to clear away the dead bodies the Germans had left behind. Parks's black platoon, at the bottom of the army hierarchy, was the army's burial squad.

On April 29, 1945, Parks's platoon moved into Dachau with their large bulldozers. As they entered, Jews began drifting out of the barracks, looking like emaciated ghosts. They ran up and began to hug the black GIs. Most of the Jews, from Germany and Eastern Europe, had never seen a black man before. They assumed the soldiers were white soldiers dirty with mud or perhaps recruits from Madagascar. The blacks were stunned by what they saw. The ovens were still warm. Some soldiers became sick. Others were afraid to embrace the Jews for fear they might break.

After several hours, reinforcements arrived. As they distributed food and water to the prisoners, one of the inmates, a rabbi, came up to Parks. Parks sat down with him on the road.

"Why Jews?" Parks asked him. "What did they do? Did they fight the Germans? What did they do?"

The rabbi answered, "Nothing."

"It doesn't make sense," Parks responded. "Why were they killed?"

"They were killed because they were Jews," said the rabbi.

Parks sat by the road and thought. "I understand that," the twenty-year-old soldier said finally. "I understand that because I've seen people lynched just because they were black."

The first time Parks told Martin Luther King that story was in Atlanta in 1962. Parks had just come from a meeting of the social action committee of his church, the United Church of Christ, held in New Orleans. New Orleans was a segregated town. Parks went for a walk on Bourbon Street, but every time he tried to enter a club or restaurant they closed the door in his face. Andrew Young, one of King's top deputies, was in New Orleans as well, and the two men had tried unsuccessfully to persuade the hotels there to integrate their workers. Young wanted King to meet this engineer from Boston. Unlike some of the younger people who had been drawn to the more radical, student-run Student Nonviolent Coordinating Committee (SNCC), Parks was nearing forty and had come to the civil rights movement through his church ties. For Young, King, and others in the movement, Parks offered the skills necessary to be a negotiator and a facilitator, a member of the small teams of negotiators King would send in to meet with white businessmen and city officials in southern towns to present his demands. King was impressed with Parks at that first meeting. Soon Parks was commuting down South regularly from Boston, joining King in Mississippi, Alabama, and Louisiana.

Brochure distributed by the Ku Klux Klan, Mississippi, 1964

We are looking for, and enlisting ONLY: Sober, Intelligent, Courageous, Christian, American, White men who are consciously and fully aware of the basic FACT that their physical life and earthly destiny are absolutely bound up with the Survival of this Nation, under God. Our governmental principles are precisely those of the ORIGINAL U.S. Constitution. Our members are Christians who are anxious to preserve not only their souls for all Eternity, but who are MILITANTLY DETERMINED, God willing, to save their lives, and the Life of this Nation,

*in order that their descendants shall enjoy the same, full,
God-given blessings of True Liberty that we have been
permitted to enjoy up to now.*

*We do not accept Jews, because they reject Christ, and,
through the machinations of their International Banking
Cartel, are at the root-center of what we call "communism" today.*

*We do not accept Papists because they bow to a Roman
Dictator, in direct violation of the First Commandment,
and the True American Spirit of Responsible, Individual
Liberty.*

*We do not accept Turks, Mongols, Orientals, Negroes,
nor any other person whose native background or culture
is foreign to the Anglo Saxon system of Government by
responsible, FREE, individual Citizens.*

In another age, after the civil rights movement had given
birth to activist movements for many other ethnic groups,
Parks might have been an activist for American Indians. His
people were from central Florida and carried more Indian blood
in them than black blood. Parks's father was a Seminole Indian; his mother part Creek Indian and part black. They had
come from central Florida to Indiana at the end of World War
I, enticed by the promise of jobs at the steel foundries in
Marion. Soon after arriving, Parks's father had come down
with tuberculosis and they had had to move to Indianapolis
to be near the government Veterans Administration hospital.
At home, Parks's father often dressed him in moccasins and
other Indian clothes. But outside the family, they were considered black.

Growing up, what stuck with Parks the most was the driving
passion of his mother and her fight against lynching. Parks's
mother had been seven when she saw her first lynching in
Macon, Georgia, and had become involved in the NAACP's
drive to get Congress to pass a federal anti-lynching bill. The
lynchings weren't confined to the South; Parks's mother had
witnessed a lynching in Marion, too, when a young man she

knew was mistaken for someone else. He was lynched with two others. Parks's mother became involved in NAACP activities in Indiana. Looking back, Parks often reflected that he learned his bravery from his father and his activism from his mother.

Although Indiana had not joined the Confederacy, its "Black Code" before the Civil War was among the harshest in the North, and in the 1920s it became a hotbed of Ku Klux Klan activity. The rise of the Klan paralleled the rise of Indiana's black population. Between 1910 and 1930, the black population of Indiana doubled, with most blacks settling in Indianapolis—where they eventually made up 12 percent of the population—or around the steel mills in Gary. And so, too, by 1923 there were between 250,000 and 500,000 members of the Klan in Indiana, with Klaverns across the state. In the 1924 elections, Klan-backed candidates swept to victory. The Klan could count among its supporters the governor, half the members of the state house of representatives, and a large number of state senators. Although the official Klan newspaper declared the Klan's opposition to lynching, few believed it; it was a common sight for groups of white-robed Klansmen to march through black neighborhoods warning blacks to "stay in their place."

Indianapolis was a segregated city. Blacks chafed under the rules, sometimes angrily, sometimes desultorily. The leading Negro newspaper, the *Freeman*, conceded: "We have learned to forgo some rights that are common . . . because we know the price. We would gain but little in a way if certain places were thrown open to us. We have not insisted that hotels should entertain our race, or the theaters, rights that are clearly ours." The local NAACP successfully challenged a zoning ordinance that segregated neighborhoods into black and white, but blacks remained confined to all-Negro slums anyway. Indianapolis's high schools, however, had never been segregated. The first black student had gone there in 1872 and a steady stream had entered ever since. In 1927, however, bowing to pressure from white parents, the Indianapolis school committee ordered all black students to attend a newly constructed high school named after Crispus Attucks, thus ending the brief window of educational opportunity for blacks in Indianapolis. When it came time for Parks to go to high school, he went to Crispus Attucks.

For Jews, Indianapolis, like most midwestern cities, was a relatively easy and safe place to live. While the pace of Klan activities rattled the nerves of many, Klan-sponsored efforts to boycott Jewish businesses failed. Jews were a small minority—about 1 percent of the population—and a prosperous one. The poor and working-class Jewish community in Indianapolis disappeared quickly, replaced by a thriving community of white-collar workers, professionals, and storeowners. Gabe Segal owned a grocery store right down the street in Parks's neighborhood.

Parks was drawn to Segal in part because the family depended on him. During the Depression, Segal ran a tab for Parks's mother. He gave Parks a job—plucking chickens. But Parks also sensed that Segal was a kindred spirit. He and Segal both felt like outsiders: Segal because he was a Jew, Parks because he was part Indian and part black, an outsider in white society as well as in his own black neighborhood. One day Segal took him aside to explain the Star of David and the Hanukkah menorah. Parks felt a bond with these other outsiders, a single white family in Indianapolis's all-black ghetto—the family of Gabriel Segal, an orthodox Jew.

Parks was a bad kid at Crispus Attucks. He ran with gangs, fought constantly. Parks's Indian background made him an object of ridicule among his black schoolmates. They would bait him to prove his bravery, and he would fight. When someone pushed Parks, he never walked away. He always fought back. Finally, the kids left him alone and Parks gradually fell under the spell of a math teacher, a Phi Beta Kappa from Amherst, who gave him a job at his house on Saturdays and after school and paid him so he could buy some new clothes. One day the teacher pulled Parks aside.

"You're good in math," he told him. "You should be an engineer."

Parks was skeptical, but he soon found himself enrolled in

math courses. He excelled. He joined the debate team. And when graduation came, the math teacher had snared Parks a scholarship to attend Purdue.

It was 1941. America was about to enter a war against the Nazis, who had based their ideology on creation of a master race superior to all others. The war would pit America's democratic tradition against European fascism. But America's democratic values were not so democratic in practice. Purdue—reflecting the general feelings of society—rigidly segregated blacks from whites and accepted Jews only begrudgingly. It was raw discrimination, Parks found, worse even than the signs in Indianapolis that separated "white" drinking fountains from "colored." It was the kind of discrimination where you would look into the eyes of whites and they would just look away, as if you weren't there. Soon after arriving, Parks and the other black male students were solemnly informed that they were forbidden to go out with white women. Years later, Parks would remember vividly the fear that came over him one day his freshman year when he was in the campus bookstore and the campus beauty queen sneaked up behind him and put her arms around him.

"Oh, we're glad to have you on campus," she squealed.

Parks wriggled to get free. He kept thinking: The wrath of God is gonna come down on me. Jesus! The wrath of God. I wanna run and hide.

There were only ten black students on campus. Blacks could not live in the dormitories. They could not live in town in a white-owned rooming house. Deans and faculty discouraged blacks from entering engineering because, as one told Parks, "Purdue has always bragged about its ability to place its engineers, and there's no place for a black engineer." Parks moved into a cold-water flat in town, a forty-five-minute bus ride from classes. His grades suffered. More than most disciplines, engineering relied on group study, the ability of students to quiz and trade information with one another. Living off-campus in an apartment run by a black woman who gave him a room and three meals a day for five dollars a week, Parks could not find enough students to study with. He knew he had to be on campus his sophomore year. Then someone told him about International House.

Sitting on a corner lot in a big old Victorian structure, International House was Purdue's euphemism for Jewish student housing. Unofficial and subtle discrimination against Jews was in force at Purdue when Parks arrived, as it was in elite and competitive schools across the country. It was a movement that had begun on the East Coast at Ivy League schools around the time of World War I and swept westward. International House, run and supported by Purdue, was open to foreign students, Jews, and blacks.

Parks moved into International House his sophomore year. He soon discovered that Jews loved to debate. Miles Cranzler, a Jewish student in International House, invited him to discussion groups at the Purdue Hillel—the campus Jewish student society—where he and his housemates would debate the merits of Judaism versus Christianity. Most of Parks's friends at Purdue were Jews. Like most blacks, he was learning to make distinctions among whites. His friendships at Purdue confirmed his early dealings with Gabe Segal. Jews, Parks decided at Purdue, were the good guys.

In none of these encounters did Parks feel any special kinship with Jews as a people or as a black-Jewish coalition. They were just kids hanging around, trying to pass their courses and stay a step ahead of the school administration. Parks was busy with his own battles. Determined to live in a regular dormitory, he stood underneath a tree with a sign protesting the exclusion of blacks. No one aided him. He was harassed by faculty and administrators. One math teacher barred him from his class, saying he refused to teach blacks. In a laboratory, a professor called Parks to the front of class, put a solution containing quinine in his hand, and said: "When it starts getting a reaction, you dance a little jig for us." Though the solution burned, Parks refused to move until the professor sent him back to his seat, warning him, "I don't like smart alecs."

An assistant dean stopped the worst of the classroom harassment, but Parks had aroused the anger of the administration. In late 1942, as he reached draft age, Parks went to one of Purdue's deans with a standard request: He wanted a letter authorizing a college deferment. The dean gave him a sealed envelope. Parks took it down to the recruiting office and was promptly drafted. The dean had enclosed a letter recommending that Parks be drafted for military service immediately.

"You've caused nothing but trouble since you've been on this campus," the dean told Parks when Parks stormed into his office. "Maybe you'll learn something in the army."

"I'll be back," Parks said.

The dean responded: "That's not necessarily true. There are no guarantees."

World War II, like the Civil War and World War I before it, represented two wars for black soldiers—one war against the enemy; the other for acceptance by the country they were fighting for. The army was segregated; even the blood banks were kept separate. The years of the New Deal had seen a slight easing in hostility toward blacks. In Washington, blacks had an unusual but powerful champion in Eleanor Roosevelt, who was openly friendly with blacks and who in 1939 resigned from the Daughters of the American Revolution when the group refused to allow Marian Anderson to sing at Constitution Hall. Under Roosevelt's prodding, the Department of the Interior had allowed Anderson to give her concert from the steps of the Lincoln Memorial on Easter Sunday.

The migration of blacks northward, where their numbers made them a potentially strategic voting bloc, forced Democratic politicians to begin to pay more attention to the demands of black leaders. President Franklin Delano Roosevelt appointed blacks to oversee race relations in several federal departments: Mary McCleod Bethune was named director of Negro affairs for the National Youth Administration; William H. Hastie was named the first black federal judge, assigned to the district court in the Virgin Islands. The policies of the New Deal especially benefited blacks, since black unemployment was higher and more widespread than white unemployment. But the New Deal did not dent the country's long-established racial segregation. If a black tried to buy a home in a white community, the Federal Housing Administration refused to guarantee the mortgage. The United States Housing Authority built separate housing projects, one set for blacks, another set for whites. In 1941, as the country prepared for the most challenging war in its history, A. Philip Randolph, the black union leader, had to threaten a march on Washington of 50,000 to 100,000 blacks in order to get Roosevelt to set up a Fair Employment Practices Commission to pressure defense industries into hiring black workers.

It was in the army that Parks saw his first lynching. He and another black soldier had crossed the border into Mississippi from his base in Louisiana in a two-and-a-half-ton truck to get supplies. When Parks went into the store, leaving his companion in the truck, the white storeowner motioned to him quickly and said, "Don't go back out there, just come with us." He hid Parks underneath a porch at the side of the store. Parks watched as a group of whites took the black soldier who had accompanied him, attached him to the truck, and dragged him behind the truck up and down the road until he died. Parks sneaked back to base and told his superiors what had happened. But nothing was ever done. The black soldiers in Parks's unit wanted to cross the border again and assault the town; the army quickly transferred them.

The memory of that lynching stayed with Parks. He remembered it when he walked into Dachau, and he remembered it when he returned to Purdue, back to International House, where he resumed studying for his engineering degree and resumed his fight for integrated dormitories. This time, Parks was a changed man. Parks believed that black soldiers had gotten screwed. They were drafted just like everyone else, but when they fought they fought in segregated units and when they died they were buried in segregated graveyards. During the war, a reporter from *Stars and Stripes* had interviewed Parks, asking him why he fought. Parks replied: "If I fight with some valor I will have the right to fight for my rights back home." In Paris, Parks had marched in a tickertape parade, reveling in the roars of the crowds for a job well done. When Parks returned to Indianapolis, the taxi driver refused to take him home. He didn't go to the black part of town. Parks pulled out a gun and put it to the driver's head. "You don't look any different than anyone else I've been shooting," he said. The cabbie took him home.

A silent anger burned inside Parks. Nobody cared that he had fought in the war. Nobody cared about the ribbons. Shortly before he graduated, Parks won the fight to have blacks move into Purdue's dormitories. The governor ordered Purdue to admit five black girls into a previously all-white dormitory. Purdue acceded. It put the five girls in a room meant for two.

After graduation, Parks's fights in Indiana were over. He moved to Boston, where he had been offered a job as an engineer, married, and began a family. But the anger he felt at segregation and his own second-class status ate at him. When his son was born in 1948 the anger welled up. You have no right to do this, he told himself, to bring a kid into a segregated world. He had to catch himself and staunch the bitterness: How sad, he would say later, to feel the birth of a son as a tragedy.

Parks's feistiness, his obstinacy, his refusal to back down when it came to asserting his rights, mirrored a broader change taking place in the black psyche. The galvanizing force was the Supreme Court's *Brown* v. *Board of Education of Topeka* decision in May 1954—the decision that abolished segregated schools. The decision connected the fight for racial justice with the American dream of education as a way to a better life. The consequences of the decision reached into every black home in the country. And, for the first time, it shifted the weight of the government behind the black struggle instead of on top of it, weighing it down. Parks had done some research for Thurgood Marshall, the NAACP Legal Defense Fund lawyer who had argued the case, and sat in on the arguments before the Supreme Court in 1952. When he heard about the decision, he was in Boston, and his mind raced back to a visit he and his family had made to Baltimore that year. It was their first trip as a family to a segregated city, and the restrooms in

the amusement park were marked "White" and "Colored."
Every time their children had to go to the bathroom, Parks
stood in front of the "Colored" sign so they wouldn't see it.
"I don't want them to be degraded," he told his wife. The
desegregation decision, Parks believed, meant the death of
segregation. It might be a long fight. But for the first time the
Supreme Court had said segregation was wrong. The law, Parks
thought, is now on our side.

Working for a series of engineering firms and raising his
family occupied most of Parks's time in Boston in the late
1950s. But slowly, inexorably, he found himself pulled toward
the local civil rights struggle. To some of his friends, Parks
had the air of a man who stumbled into history. He had walked
into Dachau an unsuspecting soldier of twenty, and there were
other stories that Parks told that added to this image: He had
first met Marshall, the great civil rights lawyer and later the
first black Supreme Court Justice, lying on his back in front
of a segregated movie theater in West Lafayette, Indiana. Parks
had tried to buy a seat to an afternoon show. When the manager insisted on putting him in the balcony, Parks had simply
flopped his large body down on the sidewalk and refused to
move. As the police prepared to carry him away, his mother
had run to a nearby YMCA, where Marshall was speaking,
and corraled the famous lawyer to bail her son out of jail. The
case led to an easing of Indiana's segregation of movie theaters.

But Parks's decision to join the civil rights movement was
conscious and deliberate. In Boston, as the decade of the 1950s
ended and the 1960s began, Parks joined the NAACP and
worked on the education committee that was struggling to
prove that Boston's schools were segregated; victory would
come a dozen years later when a federal court ordered the
schools desegregated. He supported a black candidate for election to the Boston School Committee. Although he lived in
the black neighborhood of Roxbury, Parks joined a fair-hous-
ing group in Newton, a suburb with a large Jewish population,
and began going out on evenings looking for houses with a
Jewish couple to test for prejudice in home sales.

Here again, he found, Jews were kindred spirits. They were

not an influential group in Boston. Boston was a city where power tended to be lodged in the Brahmins or the Irish politicians. Yet in lobbying for school integration, in fighting for educational reform, in fighting discrimination in housing, Parks found that over and over again his closest white allies were Jews. "The only white folks who are with us in the front line," he told a friend at one point, "are Jewish."

Down South, the pace of the civil rights struggle was increasing. Parks was asked by his church to attend the national social action meeting in New Orleans and there met Andrew Young, who introduced him to King. Parks had only read about King and admired him from afar. But the fit between King and this forty-year-old army veteran who had been fighting for integration most of his life and considered Jews and liberals among his closest allies was natural. By 1962 the civil rights movement—and King as its leading spokesman—had emerged as a struggle that was deeply patriotic, committed to overturning injustice, and eager for white allies.

Alice Walker, Winter 1966–67

Six years ago, after half-heartedly watching my mother's soap operas and wondering whether there wasn't something more to be asked of life, the Civil Rights Movement came into my life. Like a good omen for the future, the face of Dr. Martin Luther King, Jr., was the first black face I saw on our new television screen. And, as in a fairy tale, my soul was stirred by the meaning for me of his mission—at the time he was being rather ignominiously dumped into a police van for having led a protest march in Alabama—and I fell in love with the sober and determined face of the Movement. The singing of "We Shall Overcome"—that song betrayed by nonbelievers in it—rang for the first time in my ears. The influence that my mother's soap operas might have had on me became impossible. The life of Dr. King, seeming bigger, and more miraculous than the man himself, because of

*all he had done and suffered, offered a pattern of strength
and sincerity I felt I could trust. He had suffered much
because of his simple belief in nonviolence, love, and
brotherhood. Perhaps the majority of men could not be
reached through these beliefs, but because Dr. King kept
trying to reach them in spite of danger to himself and
his family, I saw in him the hero for whom I had waited
so long.*

What was so striking about the civil rights fight, looking
back, was how it galvanized ordinary people. The movement,
as it became known, began with a bus boycott in Montgomery
in December 1955, when Rosa Parks, a tailor's assistant at a
department store and onetime secretary of the local NAACP,
refused to give up her seat at the front of a bus to a white man
and move to the back of the bus. The black leadership of
Montgomery had been looking for a way to end segregated
seating on buses for some time. With the arrest of Parks, they
found their chance. In searching for a leader of the protest,
E. D. Nixon, a local black leader, placed phone calls to three
local ministers. The third was Martin Luther King, Jr., a twenty-
six-year-old preacher just out of seminary who at first hesitated, then agreed to head the Montgomery Improvement Association and lead the boycott. The boycott lasted more than
a year; the Montgomery Improvement Association arranged
car pools to bring black workers to and from work; domestics
walked to their jobs in white neighborhoods; employers were
forced to pick up and drop off black employees themselves.
On November 13, the Supreme Court ruled that segregation
of buses in Montgomery was unconstitutional. In a final stab
at preventing integration, segregationists challenged the ruling, but the Supreme Court stood fast and on December 21,
1956, King and his followers ended the boycott by putting
their fares in the bus change machines and sitting in the front.

The following year, King and other ministers met in Atlanta
to establish the Southern Christian Leadership Conference to

coordinate protests throughout the South. But it wasn't until 1960, on a Monday afternoon in February, that the movement received its greatest boost, from an unexpected quarter. Four black students from North Carolina A&T College sat down at a lunch counter in the Woolworth's in Greensboro, North Carolina, and asked for a cup of coffee. They were refused service and arrested. Overnight, the movement caught fire in both the South and the North. Students in Nashville and other cities began flooding lunch counters and starting boycotts. Sympathy picket lines sprang up at Woolworth and Kress stores up North. Soon the Congress of Racial Equality, CORE, was launching freedom rides across the South, sending groups of a dozen or so blacks and whites on Greyhound buses to challenge the segregation of bus waiting rooms. By 1963, at the height of civil rights activity, there were 930 public demonstrations taking place in 115 cities in eleven southern states. More than 20,000 people were arrested in 1963 alone, including, again and again, the leaders of the protest movement: King, his deputy Ralph Abernathy, CORE's James Farmer, and the head of SNCC, John Lewis.

The movement defied southern attempts to terrorize it out of existence. Virtually every senator from the South pledged opposition to the Supreme Court's desegregation order in the "Southern Manifesto" issued in 1955. In 1957, President Eisenhower had to use federal troops to desegregate schools in Little Rock. School officials shut down the school system rather than comply. Members of the Ku Klux Klan and other extremist organizations beat up freedom riders, demonstrators, and blacks trying to register to vote. In 1963, ten people died in civil rights—related violence, and there were thirty-five bombings. Still, the movement kept growing.

From the very start of the movement, in Montgomery, Jews had been involved, first as supporters and fund-raisers, then as lawyers, advisers, and speechwriters. For blacks involved in civil rights, Jews were not an arcane group. They were around and they were helpful.

Soon after the bus boycott began in Montgomery, supporters organized a benefit rally in Madison Square Garden that featured Charles Zimmerman, a prominent Jewish labor leader with the International Ladies' Garment Workers' Union, together with Eleanor Roosevelt, Roy Wilkins, A. Philip Randolph, and Tallulah Bankhead. Jews had always been financial supporters of groups like the NAACP, but with Montgomery and the sit-ins, support spiraled. By the mid-1960s, Jewish contributions made up three-quarters of the money raised by SNCC, CORE, and SCLC. So important were contributions from Jews to SCLC, Jesse Jackson recalled later, that for a time King's advisers debated whether they should call the group simply the Southern Leadership Conference, eliminating the reference to "Christian." In phone conversations with King, Bayard Rustin, one of King's top advisers, would remind him to include references in his speeches to the "*Judeo*-Christian tradition."

King drew powerfully on the images of Jews in the Old Testament, telling audiences, "As sure as Moses got the children of Israel across the Red Sea, we can stick together and win." Traveling around the country, CORE's James Farmer repeated what his assistant Marvin Rich, a Jewish civil rights worker from St. Louis, referred to as "that quote," a centuries-old quotation from the Jewish sage Rabbi Hillel, which lifted audiences, especially Jewish audiences, to their feet: "If I am not for myself, who will be for me? But if I am only for myself, what am I? And if not now, when?"

Stanley Levison, a Jewish New York businessman, began as a fund-raiser for King. Within a few years he had emerged, in the words of King's biographer, David Garrow, as one of King's "closest personal advisers," doing a myriad of tasks: drafting speeches and articles, fund-raising, overseeing King's tax returns, helping formulate strategies and tactics. "There were two people Martin talked to and listened to [in the mid-1960s] before he made a firm decision," an aide to King told Garrow, "Andy [Young] and Stanley." Similarly, in the late 1950s and early 1960s, the aides King relied on most were Levison and Bayard Rustin. So crucial was Levison's help that when the FBI and President Kennedy confronted King in 1963 with evidence that Levison had been a member of the Communist

Party and threatened to expose the information and tar the civil rights movement, King refused to cut his ties with Levison, continuing to consult with him through intermediaries and gradually bringing him back into his inner circle.

Rich, whose wife was black, had become an early supporter and then key aide to James Farmer at CORE, along with Alan Gartner, who came from a liberal Jewish Republican family in New York and, at one point, was Farmer's choice to become the president of CORE. Howard Zinn, a Jewish professor at Spelman College in Atlanta, became an adviser to SNCC, the most radical civil rights organization.

Several of SNCC's key members, including Stokely Carmichael and Robert Moses, had come to the civil rights movement bringing extensive personal contacts with New York's radical Jewish community. Moses, who was one of the movement's most charismatic leaders and the director of Freedom Summer, had gone to the Jewish socialist camp, Camp Wo-Chi-Ca, as a child and befriended many Jews from radical and socialist homes. Stokely Carmichael had attended the Bronx High School of Science in New York, where most of the students were Jewish, and several of his friends were the sons of Jewish radicals. Carmichael's best friend in high school was John Dennis, son of a Communist Party leader; his first demonstration was a pro-Israel rally held in front of the United Nations by the Young Socialist League. "Someone had said something anti-Semitic," Carmichael told fellow SNCC member Clayborne Carson in 1965. "I don't remember what." Carmichael wanted to go to Brandeis and become a teacher, like so many of his Jewish classmates. But his parents convinced him to go to an all-black college in the South, and it was there that he fell into the civil rights movement.

The style of the civil rights movement was one that encouraged alliances. An aura of patriotism suffused these early days of the movement. That was one of the reasons the struggle attracted so much white support in the North. Over and over again, protesters emphasized that they wanted their constitutional rights, not revolutionary rights. "All I want is to come in and place my order and be served and leave a tip if I

feel like it," one of the leaders of the student sit-ins in Charlotte, North Carolina, declared in 1960. Diane Nash, a leader
of the sit-ins in Nashville, predicted that if blacks were given
equal educational opportunities, "maybe some day a Negro
will invent one of our missiles." Always neatly dressed, the
black protesters refused to fight back when arrested. The
churches were their base, hymns and songs their rallying cry.

Part of this was no doubt tactical. Julius Lester, a member
of SNCC who would play a key role in the Ocean Hill–
Brownsville school controversy in New York in 1968, suggested to me that much of the patriotic rhetoric was just "smart
politics." Civil rights workers knew they had to wrap themselves in the Constitution and the Bible to get support. But
the movement also projected an image that genuinely tapped
into the patriotism of the country and spoke to the optimistic
idealism that President Kennedy had invoked in his inaugural
address. It was an inclusive movement. King encouraged Catholics, Jews, Protestants, blacks, and whites to join in protesting
segregation. Southern opponents of civil rights tried to portray
the demonstrators as locked in the grip of communists and
"outside agitators." But the rhetoric of civil rights—of love
and nonviolence, integration and equality—belied those charges
and struck a chord with liberal whites. "If we are wrong, then
the Constitution is wrong," King told supporters during the
Montgomery bus boycott. "If we are wrong then the Bible is
wrong. If we are wrong, then Almighty God is wrong."

As the sit-ins spread across the South, a reporter at a press
conference in New York asked Harlem Congressman Adam
Clayton Powell if he was calling on all blacks to boycott northern branches of stores such as Woolworth's.

"Oh, no," Powell replied, "I'm advocating that American
citizens interested in democracy stay out of these stores."

Paul Parks embraced the chance to work directly for King
in the time he could take off from his engineering job. Soon,
he was sent to Magnolia, Mississippi, where King had been
leading demonstrations to desegregate local restaurants. After
King left, Parks went in to negotiate. Parks thought he had

an agreement with the local sheriff to allow a set number of blacks to eat at the "white" restaurants. But when blacks began eating at the restaurants, the sheriff arrested them all and threw them out of town. Parks was angry: If people attacked him, they were in trouble. But King told him to cool his anger. "Never stop negotiating," he told Parks. "Gandhi was always negotiating. You should never stop negotiating. The idea of bringing people out to demonstrate is to negotiate."

As he flew in and out of the South between 1962 and 1964, Parks found once again—as in Boston—that Jews were often his allies. There was Allard Lowenstein, who was organizing "freedom votes," black voters in the South. The first time Parks met Lowenstein, he thought him a pompous ass. The more he got to know him, the more Parks respected Lowenstein as a sensitive, decent person who worked excellently with black kids. Joseph L. Rauh, a Jewish lawyer with deep connections to the labor movement and the liberal wing of the Democratic Party, got Parks to join Americans for Democratic Action. Jack Greenberg, head of the NAACP Legal Defense Fund, more than once had to bail Parks out of jail. Rauh, Greenberg, Lowenstein—they struck Parks as some of the most honest people he had ever met. They would not back off from anybody.

In Boston, Parks became an emissary from King to Kivie Kaplan, the Jewish president of the NAACP and a major contributor to SCLC and the NAACP. Parks was impressed with the money Kaplan gave, but he was also impressed with the fact that Kaplan, a millionaire, would come to civil rights meetings and linger over dinner with Parks for hours, talking about the movement and discrimination. This man was not only giving his money; he was, more importantly, giving of himself.

And Lord, how those Jews could talk. They debated and argued. Though there were only a few of them at any office or in any rally, they seemed at times to dominate the movement. Down South, Parks referred to them as "list makers," the ones who sat in storefronts and makeshift offices coordinating demonstrations and sit-ins while blacks filed in and out from their work on the street.

In less soaring language than King's, Parks felt the need for allies. He had grown up in a town where blacks made up only 12 percent of the population; in Boston they were less than 20 percent. That made Parks especially sensitive to the need to forge coalitions to win victories, Linda Kamm, one of Parks's Jewish friends, believed. There was no way blacks in Boston could accomplish much on their own. As a boy, Parks had been told by his father how the Seminoles had formed alliances with the Creeks to fight for their land. "You can't win the battles by yourself," his father had said. "You need allies."

And so in August 1963, Parks made his way to Washington, D.C., to attend the March on Washington. In the brutal heat he stood in the crowd in front of the Lincoln Memorial and heard King deliver his "I Have a Dream" speech. Parks wouldn't have missed the march for anything. It was exciting, meeting people from all over the country, people who were involved, committed. At the end, Parks joined hands with others and, swaying gently from side to side, sang the anthem of the movement, "We Shall Overcome," with its chorus, "Black and white together."

Perhaps because of his work with Jews in Boston, perhaps because of his experiences at Purdue, perhaps because of his experiences at Dachau, Parks felt the alliance between blacks and Jews more keenly than many other blacks I talked with. They certainly saw an alliance between blacks and white liberals, many of whom happened to be Jews. But Parks believed from early on that Jews were playing a special role.

The murders of Schwerner, Chaney, and Goodman depressed and angered him. Schwerner had been one of those "list makers," someone who by force of energy and personality seemed to radiate commitment and action. Goodman had been a college kid moved to come south for the summer to fight for black rights. Chaney had been a dedicated worker. Parks was sitting in the back of a church in Selma, Alabama, in the summer of 1964 when he heard about the murders. While newspaper reports at the time emphasized that a black and two whites had been murdered, Parks saw things differently. He thought back to the way his mother told him the Ku Klux Klan had always targeted "Koons, Kikes, and Katholics." The symbolism of this murder was apparent. The South, Parks believed, was sending a message: These Jews are coming here stirring things up and causing trouble just like the blacks. The Klan is going to teach both of them a lesson.

Abraham Wood, a Birmingham minister, recalling the months in Alabama in 1963, when a bomb went off at the motel where Martin Luther King was staying in Birmingham, and, later, a bomb went off at the Sixteenth Street Church, killing four black girls

---

That was a terrible night [when King's motel was bombed], when blacks went wild. I knew then that we were not going to be able to hold this element in check. And then afterwards, when the Sixteenth Street bombings took place and I went to the scene, dashed to that scene . . . I found a group of young blacks with a pile of rocks and every car that passed with a white driver in it, they were tearing it up. Of course, I went there and I said, "Brethren, don't, don't, don't do this, this isn't the way." Angry mood. "All right, you're one of 'em, you're with 'em." No talking to them . . . not going to be reasoned with, you see. So I had to go away from there. . . . I said to myself, "Not going to be long till this thing is going to take a new turn." You see, that's another element coming in, with "Burn, baby, burn" and this kind of thing.

What I saw at Sixteenth Street, what I saw at the motel, was the forerunner of what happened. Later it was "Burn, baby, burn," and Carmichael. That came later and I saw it coming. I saw it coming.

Parks's feelings about the deaths of Schwerner, Chancy, and Goodman captured the belief of many that the alliance between blacks and Jews was strong and unshakeable. But even as the bodies of the three civil rights workers were being dug up, tensions were growing that would soon rip the alliance apart.

The main issue centered on the role of whites in the movement, especially white liberals. During the planning meeting for Freedom Summer in 1963, Moses and others advocated that white students come south to help in voter registration drives. Some blacks objected, saying whites would automatically take leadership roles. But Moses successfully pushed the importance of coalitions and alliances, arguing "to have white people working along side of you, so that it changes the whole complexion of what you are doing, so it isn't any longer Negro fighting white, it's a question of rational people against irrational people."

But factions inside SNCC and elsewhere felt that it was time for whites to step aside. In the fall of 1962, Loren Miller, a vice president of the NAACP, had bid "Farewell to Liberals" in an article in *The Nation*, a magazine whose subscribers included many whites who had supported and given money to civil rights: "Profoundly influenced by the overthrow of white colonialism in Asia and Africa, [young Negro militants] not only want Freedom Now, but insist on substituting a grand strategy for the liberal tactic of fighting one battle at a time. They are determined to plot the strategy and dictate the tactics of the campaign. . . . Their message is plain: To liberals a fond farewell, with thanks for services rendered, until you are ready to re-enlist as foot soldiers and subordinates in a Negro-led, Negro-officered army under the banner of Freedom Now." By 1964, SNCC's executive director James Forman was openly complaining about the "white liberal-labor syndrome and its black sellouts."

This tension over white participation in the civil rights movement and the debate over "liberal tactics" versus a more militant strategy hovered over Freedom Summer. There were moving stories of blacks and whites getting to know each other, of black families appreciating the help and sacrifices of the northern white volunteers. But northern white students were the object of suspicion and jealousy from some of their black co-workers. They were excluded from social gatherings. Their motivations were questioned, and a ripple of jealousy surrounded interracial dates and affairs.

The violence of the Ku Klux Klan and the nightriders was also taking its toll on blacks, hardening them. While searching for the bodies of the three civil rights workers, federal agents found several unidentified bodies of blacks, including one of a fourteen-year-old black boy wearing a CORE T-shirt. Blacks had welcomed white civil rights volunteers in the belief that their presence would attract the nation's attention. But the country's outrage at the disappearance of Schwerner, Chaney, and Goodman did not ease the fact that few up North had paid attention while black protesters were being killed during the past eight years.

The question of tactics and the role of liberals came to a head at the end of the summer when the Mississippi Freedom Democratic Party headed for Atlantic City for the Democratic Convention. Creation of the Freedom Democratic Party was one of the goals of Freedom Summer. More than 80,000 blacks joined the party, which then elected an integrated slate of delegates to challenge the all-white Mississippi delegation at the Democratic Convention. Spearheaded by the gripping testimony of Fannie Lou Hamer, the delegates from the Freedom delegation threatened a floor fight that might end with the regular Mississippi delegation being ousted. President Lyndon Johnson, fearing a southern backlash, pressured white backers of the Freedom party, including civil rights attorney Joseph Rauh, to work out a compromise. The compromise—imposed by Johnson—allowed the seating of two black delegates in an at-large capacity in addition to the regular Mississippi delegates. The Freedom delegation rejected the offer and left Atlantic City.

Parks believed the compromise was necessary. Earlier that summer he had been part of a large group of black leaders that met with Lyndon Johnson to discuss passage of the 1964 Civil Rights Act. Johnson minced no words. "I'll get this bill passed," he told the group, "if you deliver Negro votes to me in November." The group was rattled by Johnson's brass-knuckles

approach and adjourned to caucus. Parks argued for them to
agree. "If we're prostitutes to get this bill passed," he said,
"we're prostitutes." The group told Johnson they would work
for him in November.

John Lewis, chairman of the Student Non-Violent Coordinating Committee, Spring 1964

*Something is happening to people in the Southern Negro
Community. They're identifying with people because of
color. . . . They're conscious of things that happen in Cuba,
in Latin America and in Africa. Even in SNCC, we talk
about integration, about the beloved community, but
there have been great changes going on. There's been a
radical change in our people since 1960; the way they
dress, the music they listen to, their natural hairdos—
all of them want to go to Africa. . . . I think people are
searching for a sense of identity, and they're finding it.*

The Freedom Democratic Party returned to Mississippi bitter and angry. Organizers planned a "counter-election" in November which they hoped would elect integrationists to
Congress and unseat the regular congressmen with a court
challenge. Though they felt they had been sold out in Atlantic
City, much of the anger was still directed at "the system,"
not at whites. The Freedom Democratic Party enlisted Morton
Stavis, a Jewish lawyer, to help with the election effort; when
Stavis issued a call for lawyers to come south to help, three-
quarters of the more than 100 who responded were Jews.

But the cleavages exposed during Freedom Summer began
to widen and deepen in the next two years. In 1963, Dotty
Miller, a Jewish graduate of Queens College who had gone to
work for SNCC, had met her first black Muslim in Atlanta.
The Muslim came into SNCC's office and began denouncing
the presence of Jews in the civil rights movement. "The only

thing wrong with Hitler was that he didn't burn up all the Jews," the Muslim said. At the time, Miller felt, he was clearly trying to turn SNCC into a black nationalist organization. But no one paid him much mind. The Muslims were a tiny group. No one in Atlanta took them seriously.

By 1965, however, the Muslims, and their best-known spokesman, Malcolm X, were getting more attention.

It was Malcolm X who symbolized and gave voice to the frustrations and despair of northern ghettos. Malcolm spoke truth to power, a truth carved out of the same ghetto life. Malcolm's father, a follower of Marcus Garvey, had been killed by Klansmen and his mother had been institutionalized. Moving to Boston, then to New York and Harlem, Malcolm X— then known as Malcolm Little—had hustled and run a small armed-robbery gang, ending up in prison. After converting to the Nation of Islam, he became the most effective preacher the Black Muslims had.

By the mid-1960s the influence of the Nation of Islam among blacks, especially blacks interested in civil rights, had grown far in excess of the 40,000 or so members that Malcolm's preaching had attracted to the Nation. Malcolm X denounced the nonviolent civil rights demonstrations in the South, "this mealy-mouth, beg-in, wait-in, plead-in kind of action." The Man, the white man, was the enemy; the Man was the Devil. Malcolm urged blacks to abandon the term "Negro." It was a slave name. He insisted they be called black. He urged blacks to identify with people of color in other countries, shifting the terms of debate from one where blacks were a minority in the United States to one where they, along with Africans and Asians, were a majority of the people in the world.

King was the voice that white Americans heard as embodying the dream of an integrated America. Malcolm X was the voice of northern ghetto frustration. Other black leaders urged him to quiet down, to dampen his emotions. He responded: "When a man is hanging on a tree and he cries out, should he cry out unemotionally? When a man is sitting on a hot stove and he tells you how it feels to be there, is he supposed to speak without emotion? This is what you tell black people in this country when they begin to cry out against the injustices that they're suffering. As long as they describe these injustices in a way that makes you believe you have another hundred years to rectify the situation, then you don't call that emotion. But when a man is on a hot stove, he says, 'I'm coming up. I'm getting up.' Violently or nonviolently doesn't even enter into the picture—I'm coming up, do you understand?''

Within SNCC itself, a faction favoring black separatism was growing stronger. In CORE, younger and more militant members blocked efforts by Farmer to name one of his Jewish advisers president of CORE, insisting the post be filled by a black. The nonviolent preachings of Martin Luther King were losing their impact. Many blacks, especially younger ones, were rejecting King's turn-the-other-cheek brand of Christianity.

Both Parks and King were troubled by this.

In April 1965 King came to Boston and met with blacks in the basement of a church in the city's poor, black South End. Parks knew how tough the problems were in Boston. Entire parts of the city were considered off-limits to blacks. For two years, Parks and other civil rights leaders had tried fruitlessly to persuade the city school committee to end de facto segregation in the city's schools. The young black activists in town were angry. They admired Malcolm X, not King. They talked of setting up a separate republic, or returning to Africa.

"I see the destruction of all the things I want to do because there are forces that are trying to break up cooperation between blacks and whites," King told the meeting. "We must continue to build those bridges. We must continue to work beside white people."

Parks nodded in agreement. "Unless we have coalitions, we're dead."

But the younger blacks in the room would have none of it. "We have to go back to Africa," one shouted.

"You'd starve to death," Parks shot back. "The only hope we have is to make it where we are now."

The movement still seemed capable of success. In March

1965, King led his followers on a fifty-mile march from Selma, Alabama, to Montgomery to demand voting rights. Lyndon Johnson proposed a comprehensive voting rights act to Congress. In his Texas drawl, before a national television audience, Johnson embraced the anthem of the movement: "Their cause must be our cause, too. Because it's not just Negroes, but it's really all of us who must overcome the crippling legacy of bigotry and injustice. And we shall overcome." On August 6, 1965, Johnson signed the Voting Rights Act. James Bevel, an aide to King, declared: "There is no more civil rights movement. President Johnson signed it out of existence when he signed the voting rights bill."

Five days after the signing of the Voting Rights Act, Watts, the poor black ghetto in Los Angeles, exploded in rioting.

By the time the National Guard restored order, thirty-four people were dead, and police estimated the damage at $35 million. It was the worst riot in America in over twenty years.

Watts underscored what had been true for several years, a growing schism in the movement between middle-class moderates like Parks and the poor, younger, more militant blacks, locked in urban ghettos, bothered by talk of accommodation and compromise.

An uglier side was emerging among whites, too. Six months after Watts, King decided to move his civil rights struggle north. He settled on Chicago as the site of his first northern campaign, moving into a slum apartment on the city's West Side. In the summer of 1966, he announced he would march through Marquette Park, an all-white working-class neighborhood, to symbolize black demands for open housing. Parks flew out to Chicago to march with King and saw something he had not seen in over twenty years: Nazi banners. Thousands of whites surrounded the marchers, some waving swastikas, screaming, spitting. A brick flew out of the crowd and struck King on the head. That night, after the march was over, Parks went to King's motel room and talked about what had happened. "I know where this leads," Parks said. Once again, as King listened, he told the story of a young black soldier walking into Dachau.

While that was a powerful image it was also, increasingly, out of date. In a movement that was demanding to be black-led, there was no room for whites and, by corollary, no room for Jews. In December 1966, Bobby Seale and Huey Newton formed the Black Panther Party in Oakland, California, quickly becoming a magnet for publicity with their demands for black control of black neighborhoods and their insistence that blacks arm themselves for self-defense. In the midst of his demonstration in Chicago, King had flown south to Mississippi to lead a demonstration to protest the shooting of James Meredith, who four years before had been the first black to enroll at the University of Mississippi. But he watched helplessly as the march was taken over by Carmichael, the newly elected chairman of SNCC, who galvanized a crowd in Greenwood, Mississippi, with his call for Black Power.

"The only way we gonna stop them white men from whuppin' us is to take over," Carmichael told the crowd, his clenched fist raised high. "We been saying freedom for six years and we ain't got nothin'. What we gonna start saying now is Black Power!"

The crowd cheered. "Black Power!" they roared back.

An aide to Carmichael leapt to the platform and led the chants.

"What do you want?"

"Black Power!"

"What do you want?"

"Black Power!"

"What do you want? Black Power! Black Power! Black Power!"

Parks believed King was losing control of the movement to the young turks. He watched as King began paying more and more attention to the movement against the war in Vietnam. He believed the growing militancy among blacks explained part of King's motivation. King was losing his base. Many younger blacks would no longer listen to him.

The following summer of 1967 was a time of growing national black militance, ghetto riots, and challenges to the Johnson administration. During the summer, H. Rap Brown, succeeding Carmichael as head of SNCC, was indicted for arson after telling a crowd in Cambridge, Maryland: "If America don't come around, we're going to burn it down, brother. We are going to burn it down if we don't get our share of it." An hour later rioting broke out, and Brown was wounded by police. In its summer convention, the NAACP disassociated itself from the "Black Power" slogan, but both SNCC and CORE embraced it, and the rhetoric of violence and confrontation escalated. In July, Newark, New Jersey, exploded in rioting, with violence consuming the black neighborhoods for five days, killing 27, injuring 1,500, and sending 1,300 to jail. A week later, the worst riot in American history leveled entire blocks of Detroit. Federal troops were called in to bring the situation under control. By the time rioting had ended, forty-three people had died. News reports and white politicians called the disturbances "riots." For many black leaders they were something more: insurrections and rebellions of an embattled people trapped by white society.

It was clear that the civil rights struggle was taking a more militant and more anti-white turn. But what was emerging as well was a special animus against Jews.

It began with scattered comments. During the first riot in Harlem in 1964, many Jewish-owned stores had been attacked and looted and the anti-Semitism expressed by some of the rioters had shocked the mainstream civil rights leadership. In May 1967, H. Rap Brown captured headlines by saying, after police fired into a demonstration by SNCC workers, "If America chooses to play Nazis, black folks ain't going to play Jews." As Jewish involvement in civil rights issues in Boston increased, some blacks began coming to Parks, saying, "Hey, Jews are coming to help us, we need their money. We need their support. But I have some problems with them." The biggest problem was that several Jews were the large landlords in the black ghetto of Roxbury and had a reputation for rent gouging and overcharging.

"How can you work with Jews when Maurice Gordon [a notorious slumlord] exploits people?" a young black asked Parks at a school integration meeting.

"I don't like Maurice Gordon," Parks said. "I lived in one

of his houses in Roxbury. I know what he's about. But I don't classify him based on his Jewishness. He is an evil old man." In a meeting with King that Parks attended, a black civil rights worker began complaining that Jews were taking over the civil rights movement. King laced into him, saying, "There is no such thing. Many Jews have done more than anyone in this room to help blacks."

In the summer of 1967, in the aftermath of the Arab-Israeli Six-Day War, SNCC issued a leaflet filled with attacks on Israel and caricatures of Jews. For almost a year, SNCC had been expanding its interest in international affairs, part of the growing attraction to many blacks of linking their struggle with "liberation" and anti-colonial movements overseas. In June 1967, in the midst of Israel's Six-Day War with the Arab countries, SNCC's leaders asked the editor of the group's newsletter, Ethel Minor, to write a report on the background of the Arab-Israeli conflict. Minor had once been a member of the Nation of Islam and had been close to Palestinians in college. There were some in SNCC who worried about the group taking a position on the Arab-Israeli War at all, since many of SNCC's contributors were Jews. But others believed that SNCC had to speak out.

The result, published in the *SNCC Newsletter*, was a collection of anti-Semitic articles and cartoons that stirred a storm of controversy and marked a watershed in the already floundering black-Jewish alliance in the civil rights movement. "Zionists conquered the Arab homes and land through terror, force, and massacres," the newsletter said. A photograph of Israelis shooting a group of Arabs lined up against the wall carried the caption, "This is the Gaza Strip, Palestine, not Dachau, Germany." A cartoon showed Moshe Dayan with dollar signs on his epaulets; another, the boxer Muhammad Ali with a noose around his neck held by a hand marked with the Star of David and a dollar sign.

Letters of resignation and denunciation from Jewish supporters of SNCC poured into the group's offices. SNCC officials at first insisted that the newsletter did not represent the group's official views, but it soon became clear that it did, and also represented the views of some of the most charismatic black leaders. In a tour through Arab countries later in the year, Carmichael, who had stepped down as SNCC chairman in May, repeatedly denounced "Zionist aggression." The magazine of the Black Panthers chortled:

> We're gonna burn their towns and that ain't all.
> We're gonna piss upon the Wailing Wall
> And then we'll get Kosygin and DeGaulle.
> That will be ecstasy, killing every Jew we see.

In the uproar that followed publication of the SNCC leaflet, the moderate, pro-Israel words of black leaders like Bayard Rustin, Whitney Young, and King were drowned out. Increasingly, many Jews, and many whites, believed it was people like Carmichael who spoke for black America. But the rush of anger, of charges and counter-charges, failed to answer the most important question: Why the Jews?

There were several reasons. One was the growing frustration of blacks with the failed promises of civil rights. Blacks had struggled nonviolently for more than a decade, but poverty still gripped the ghetto and most black children still went to segregated schools. Jews were a part of the liberal coalition that had promised so much. Blacks were angry and frustrated, and they struck out—hitting those closest to them, the Jews.

A number of black intellectuals had also become convinced that the participation of white liberals and radicals in civil rights struggles over the years had stunted black intellectual development. Jews had indeed dominated many meetings of civil rights workers in the South. They talked faster, argued better. In 1967, Harold Cruse published *The Crisis of the Negro Intellectual*, which argued that Jews, with their emphasis on integration and assimilation, had blocked the growth of black nationalism and black independence. Without necessarily agreeing that Jews had deliberately stifled black leadership, many blacks, especially younger blacks, could agree that it was time for blacks to run their own organizations and their own struggle.

The makeup of the civil rights leadership had also changed.

From the southern-based ministers like King and sons of ministers like Farmer, control had shifted to northern blacks like Carmichael, Floyd McKissick, the Black Muslims, and others who carried ambivalent and often hostile views toward Jews bred out of experiences and stories of Jewish landlords and storeowners.

But overlying all of this was a belief that Jews had somehow failed to live up to their own high standards. Many blacks were mad at whites. But they felt betrayed by Jews. The Jewish shopkeeper in Harlem, the Jewish landlord, the Jewish pawnbroker, "is singled out by Negroes not because he acts differently from other white men, but because he doesn't," James Baldwin wrote in *The New York Times Magazine* in 1967. "His major distinction is given him by that history of Christendom, which has so successfully victimized both Negroes and Jews. And he is playing in Harlem the role assigned him by Christians long ago: He is doing their dirty work." Blacks had grown up with the story of the Exodus. They had known of the Rosenwald schools and the Spingarns who headed the NAACP. The Jews at the center of the civil rights movement had been activists, liberals, radicals. Consciously or unconsciously, blacks had expected a great deal from Jews. And the Jews had let them down.

Paul Parks was upset with the growth of anti-white and anti-Semitic attitudes among blacks. He believed the civil rights movement was dying. He had risen to become vice president of the Boston branch of the NAACP, and in speech after speech through 1967 he denounced black separatism. There is no way we can turn our backs on our allies, he told audiences. Just count the numbers. The movement will die without white support.

But those ideas were losing influence. In October 1963, two months after the March on Washington, a poll in *Newsweek* showed that 88 percent of blacks rated King as their top leader, followed by Jackie Robinson and James Meredith. By 1967, Americans no longer ranked King in the top ten. Parks, too, knew that he was losing touch with the younger, more militant blacks. In November 1967, he took a job with Boston's new mayor, Kevin White, to run the anti-poverty Model Cities program. He still believed fervently in school desegregation and integration. He continued to live in Roxbury, the city's poor black neighborhood, and counseled and worked with young people. But he became more and more distanced from the civil rights movement as it became more and more radical.

The night King was assassinated, Parks was still at work, at his desk. A call came from the mayor asking him to go to Blue Hill Avenue, in the heart of Roxbury. A riot was starting. Over the years, Parks had become friendly with George Rosen, a Jewish man who owned a hardware store on Blue Hill Avenue and had remained—like many Jewish storeowners—as the neighborhood changed from predominantly Jewish to predominantly black. When Parks arrived on the scene, black teenagers were looting stores up and down the street, yelling anti-Semitic slogans. Parks stood in front of Rosen's hardware store and faced them down, protecting it. As the teenagers went running by, continuing their looting and yelling, he said to himself: "No one is listening. This doesn't make any sense."

From the Report of the National Advisory Commission on Civil Disorders (the Kerner Commission), March 1968

This is our basic conclusion: Our nation is moving toward two societies, one black and one white—separate and unequal.

Reaction to last summer's disorders has quickened the movement and deepened the division. Discrimination and segregation have long permeated much of American life; they now threaten the future of every American.

The deepening racial division is not inevitable. The movement apart can be reversed. Choice is still possible. Our principal task is to define the choice and to press for a national resolution.

To pursue our present course will involve the contin-

*uing polarization of the American community and, ul-
timately, the destruction of basic democratic values.*

My conversations with Parks focused on his activities up
to 1968. But he would achieve his greatest prominence in the
years that followed. Parks would continue his fight for integrated schools and win the battle in 1975 when a federal judge
ordered busing to desegregate the school system. In the wake
of the desegregation order, the governor of Massachusetts named
Parks state secretary of education. He served until 1978, when
he returned to engineering, becoming a consultant.

Parks remained close to Jews. He traveled to Israel four
times and spoke frequently to Jewish groups commemorating
the Holocaust. On the wall of his office he kept a certificate
from a Holocaust survivors' association. It formally acknowledged his role as a liberator, in 1945, of one of the concentration camps.

3

"Not a Negro Cause But a Human Cause": Jack Greenberg

Jack Greenberg always insisted—and he was right—that it was never preordained that Jews would enlist in the civil rights struggles of the 1950s and 1960s or embrace the liberalism of the New Deal, the Great Society, and the Democratic Party. Reading from a prayer book and being exposed to Jewish values did not guarantee a political commitment to helping blacks or other minorities. Jews, like anyone else, had joined the civil rights movement as individuals. To understand why someone voted a certain way or devoted his or her life to a certain cause, Greenberg felt, required a full understanding of his family and the way he was taught to think, and of the experiences that had shaped his life.

That was true, but it was also true that, reaching back to the founding of the NAACP in 1909, Jews had played a far more prominent role than other whites in the fight for civil rights. Where there was a black-white alliance for civil rights and integration in the 1960s, it was often a black-Jewish alliance. Just a look at the top leadership of the civil rights organizations made that clear. King's top white adviser was

Stanley Levison, a Jewish lawyer whom the FBI believed was a communist agent but whom King relied on to handle his finances, edit his books, and give counsel during some of the most crucial crises facing the movement. The president of the NAACP and one of King's top contributors was Kivie Kaplan, a retired Boston businessman who—personally and through friends—gave hundreds of thousands of dollars, often after a hurried phone call from King or one of his lieutenants. Over at CORE, James Farmer's top fund-raiser and a key speech writer was Marvin Rich, later succeeded by another Jewish civil rights advocate, Alan Gartner. Jews made up more than half the white lawyers who went south to defend civil rights protesters. They made up half to three-quarters of the contributors to civil rights organizations, even to the more radical organizations, like SNCC. They were prominent among journalists who wrote about civil rights, and in polls and elections, they consistently backed civil rights and candidates who endorsed civil rights. In late 1964, pollsters asked a sample of blacks whether they thought Jews were more in favor of civil rights for blacks than other whites. Forty-five percent said they thought Jews were more in favor, while 35 percent said Jewish support was the same as other whites. Only 3 percent said Jewish support was less.

Blacks recognized there was something different about Jews. In talking with Greenberg and other Jews involved in the civil rights movement, I wanted to find out what it was. In the tapestry of their stories I hoped to find out why Jews had plunged so deeply into the civil rights movement and why it had touched them so deeply.

Ebbets Field, 1947: Joel Oppenheimer, recalling the first time he saw Jackie Robinson play

---

For years we used to hear stories about this fantastic black pitcher who once was supposed to have struck out all the Yankees. We didn't know his name—it was Satchel Paige—but we had heard about all the great black ball-

players and how they weren't allowed to play, and so for
me Jackie was all those guys rolled into one, and he was
going to lead my Dodgers to glory.

During the game Jackie made a good play in the field,
at which point everyone was yelling, "Jackie, Jackie,
Jackie," and I was yelling with them. And suddenly I
realized that behind me someone was yelling, "Yonkel,
Yonkel, Yonkel," which is Yiddish for Jackie. With great
wonderment and pleasure, I realized that here was this
little Jewish tailor—I always assumed he was a tailor—
the only white face in a crowd of blacks aside from me,
and he's yelling, "Yonkel, Yonkel, Yonkel." It was a very
moving moment.

One of the first civil rights lawyers I met had bowed out of
civil rights work several years before, exchanging the plane
trips to small-town airports in the South and the last-minute
rush to file briefs for the calmer life of a law school professor.
There were pictures on his walls of the lawyers he worked
with at the NAACP Legal Defense and Education Fund, black
and white, including Greenberg, who ran the fund for over
twenty-five years. I asked him why he joined the Legal Defense
Fund in 1961 at the height of the Freedom Rides. He talked
of the opportunities for social change and the drama of the
civil rights movement, the chance to do good in the world.
He is Jewish—not very religious; an ethical, secular Jew he
called himself—but he didn't think religion had anything to
do with his becoming a civil rights lawyer. Oh, perhaps in an
abstract way, Jews are people of the book, and law, therefore,
has some connection to Jews.

Gradually, the talk turned to Jackie Robinson, the first black
baseball player, who broke into the majors with the Brooklyn
Dodgers in 1947, when the lawyer was ten years old and living
in Queens.

Jackie Robinson?

"I'm thinking back now. The fans in the Brooklyn Dodgers
stands were not blacks but Jews. . . . And the Dodgers, the

Dodgers were the institutionalized underdogs." He mused some more. "The more adventurous part of the American dream—baseball is part of it. If you were Jewish at that time your identity had to be Yeshiva boys or go the communist route. Who were the great Jewish sports heroes? Hank Greenberg? Robinson is the perfect magnet for all these feelings. He is the first. He was an extraordinary player. He was adopted as the surrogate hero by many of us growing up at the time. He was the way we saw ourselves triumphing against the forces of bigotry and ignorance. He did it with tremendous poise and dignity. He had enormous inner reserves and was able to marshal them in terms of a long-term goal. The Dodgers had never won a World Series. He arrived and they moved closer and closer and they got it." That image stayed with me as I began my conversations with Jews involved in civil rights.

The year Jackie Robinson broke into the majors, Jack Greenberg was finishing up his last year at Columbia Law School. He had been born in 1925 and grew up in the Bensonhurst section of Brooklyn and in a neighborhood near Bronx Park, in Jewish neighborhoods where socialism and communism blew around like a steady breeze. Greenberg did not consider himself an observant Jew. He had been bar mitzvahed; his brother, Dan, had not. He seldom went to synagogue and did not participate in the myriad of Jewish groups—political and social—that flourished in New York. Greenberg's father was an accountant. He loved to argue and relished taking the opposite side of an argument just to provoke debate. That prevented him from adopting the Zionist socialism that was the ideology of choice among many Brooklyn Jews in the 1930s and 1940s. Rooted in the immigrant ideology many of these Jews had brought over with them from Eastern Europe, the Zionist socialists believed in creating a socialist homeland for the Jews, a workers' paradise in the Middle East. Other neighbors and friends of Greenberg's family stood even further left and embraced communism, even after the Hitler-Stalin pact that allied Stalin with the Nazis in 1939. Greenberg's family were not themselves socialists or communists. But many of

their friends and neighbors were. Greenberg said he saw his
father as an insider with an outsider's perspective.

Greenberg didn't know many blacks growing up in Brooklyn. He read about segregation in the newspapers and studied
it in school. But he did not get to know anyone black very
well until he went to college at Columbia and, as a member
of the navy reserve, served as lieutenant in the Pacific on a
landing ship. There were eleven men on board: seven officers
and four stewards, who acted as servants to the officers. The
officers were white; the stewards black. Greenberg became
friendly with one of the stewards, a talented carpenter who
built a desk for Greenberg out of plywood. Greenberg disliked
the whole notion of servants and asked the captain if the
carpenter could get another job on board. The captain said
nothing could be done, and he was right. The navy was still
segregated.

With his father an accountant, there was some hope that
Greenberg would follow in his footsteps, or perhaps get a com-
bined degree in accounting and law. Columbia, and the legal
profession in New York, were still shaking off the anti-Semitism that had gripped the college and the power structure
since the establishment of quotas during the First World War.
A decade before Greenberg graduated from Columbia, Morton
Stavis, a Jewish lawyer and Columbia Law School graduate,
made the rounds of Wall Street law firms seeking interviews
for jobs. The receptionists typically separated Jewish students
like Stavis from Gentile applicants when they came in for
interviews. At one law firm, Stavis was shunted to the one
Jewish lawyer in the office. The lawyer informed Stavis that
he should try to get a job at one of the "Jewish" law firms in
town. Greenberg did not feel such overt anti-Semitism during
his years at Columbia, but some of his professors knew better.
As late as 1956 Greenberg's mentor at Columbia, Professor
Walter Gellhorn, was wary about recommending Jewish students when fielding requests from certain prominent New
York law firms.

Unlike many of his classmates, Greenberg was not attracted

to corporate law or major firms on Wall Street. He had excelled at Columbia, but the course that intrigued him most was a seminar taught by Gellhorn, called "The Legal Survey," which involved researching and writing memoranda for civil liberties groups that lacked large legal staffs, like the American Civil Liberties Union and the Japanese-American Citizens' League. Greenberg wanted to work for a civil liberties group after he graduated. There were no jobs. Even Gellhorn, who was a director of the ACLU, couldn't find an opening. Disappointed, Greenberg went to work as a researcher for the New York State Law Revision Commission, where he reviewed old New York State laws and proposed changes. He asked Gellhorn to keep his ears open if anything turned up.

Gellhorn admired Greenberg's work. One day he received a call from Thurgood Marshall, then head of the NAACP Legal Defense and Education Fund. Marshall was already considered the leading black lawyer in the country. With a small staff of three black lawyers, Marshall was leading the fight to chip away at the web of laws that segregated blacks from whites in the South in schools, on trains, in bathrooms, at water fountains. His picture was pinned to the wall of many a black home as proof that a black man could argue before the Supreme Court. Marshall had occasionally used Gellhorn's students for research. He was now looking for another assistant to help with the Fund's work. Could Gellhorn suggest someone?

"Thurgood, I can think of a very good person if you people weren't so damned discriminatory," said Gellhorn, his voice deadpan. "If you weren't racially biased I could suggest a good person to you."

Marshall laughed. "Well," he said, "I'll try to overcome my prejudice if you want to send someone to me to be interviewed."

Gellhorn called Greenberg and sent him down to the Fund's cramped offices in NAACP headquarters near the New York Public Library. Marshall offered Greenberg a job as a staff lawyer and Greenberg signed on.

The NAACP Legal Defense Fund, like its parent organization, had a long history of involvement and alliances with liberal Jews. In 1911, soon after the NAACP set up its first office in Harlem, it established a legal vigilance committee headed by Arthur Spingarn, the Jewish lawyer who was the brother of Joel Spingarn, one of the NAACP's founders. Under Arthur Spingarn, the committee sought out and defended blacks who had been brutalized by the police. The year of the stock market crash, 1929, the NAACP retained another Jewish lawyer, Nathan Margold, to write a blueprint for improving black rights. The book-length report argued for an attack on segregated schools and the "separate but equal" doctrine enshrined by the Supreme Court in 1896. That doctrine was the legal foundation of segregation in the South. Margold called for an attack on segregation based on the argument that black schools in the South were, in fact, not equal but woefully under-funded and inadequate. The Margold report became the bible of the NAACP's legal efforts. After the NAACP created a separate Legal Defense Fund in 1939 for tax reasons, the Margold report became its bible, too.

In these early years, the NAACP relied heavily on white lawyers. There were few black lawyers around. In 1929, out of a population of 12 million blacks, there were only 1,100 black lawyers, fewer than 100 of whom had graduated from the country's top law schools. By the time Greenberg arrived at the Fund, its leader, Thurgood Marshall, was black, and so was Marshall's deputy, Robert Carter, as well as its two other staff lawyers. The Fund recruited top black legal talent. The cramped office produced an extraordinary alumni association. Of the four black lawyers that Greenberg joined in 1949, one (Marshall) became a Supreme Court Justice, two (Constance Motley, Robert Carter) became federal judges, and a fourth (Franklin Williams) became ambassador to Ghana.

After writing a memo on using three-judge panels to decide segregation cases, Greenberg was thrown into the fray, assigned to work with Robert Carter on an upcoming trial that would test segregation laws in Topeka, Kansas. The trial pitted

Oliver Brown and several other black parents against the local board of education. Under the name *Brown* v. *Board of Education*, the case would lead to the landmark 1954 Supreme Court decision ordering the desegregation of the nation's schools. But in June 1951, that decision was still several years away. Flying out to Topeka, Carter and Greenberg readied themselves for the local trial and prepared to meet another Brown—Esther Brown.

Esther Brown was a Jewish housewife in her thirties who lived in a suburb of Kansas City, Kansas. Driving her black maid home along the dirt roads leading to the black section of South Park, Kansas, Brown would become upset at the dilapidated state of the local black school—a squalid building without plumbing. When her maid asked her one day in 1948 how she thought the black residents of South Park should vote on an upcoming bond issue to build a new white school for $90,000, Brown said they should oppose it until their own school was fixed up. She then offered to argue the case before the South Park school board. When the bond issue passed anyway, Brown took the case of the black residents to a meeting of white parents in South Park.

Brown was no podium-thumping radical. "Look, I don't represent these people," she told the white parents. "One of them works for me and I've seen the conditions of their school. I know none of you would want your children educated under such circumstances. They're not asking for integration—just a fair shake." The whites hooted her down and told her to "go back where you came from." After that, Brown told author Richard Kluger years later, "I was a changed woman." Brown hired a black lawyer and got him to file suit on behalf of her maid and other black parents. Black parents organized a boycott of their segregated school. Brown helped them set up private schools in local churches, and traveled around Kansas to raise money for the lawsuit. Retribution was swift: Brown's husband was fired from his job; a cross was burned on her lawn. Brown persevered. She contacted the Legal Defense Fund office in New York and, with the help of Fund lawyer Franklin Williams, the parents won their case and black children were ordered to attend the white school. The day the children went to school for the first time, Brown made sure they were all wearing new clothes. She bought dresses for the girls, new shirts for the boys.

Brown then moved her crusade to Topeka, where she worked with the local NAACP to file the suit that would become *Brown* v. *Board of Education*. When Jack Greenberg and Robert Carter arrived in Topeka in June 1951, Brown made their hotel arrangements—a complicated matter since hotels in Topeka were segregated—and, more important, approached the local Jewish Community Relations Bureau, a group concerned with interracial issues, to help the New York lawyers find expert witnesses who could bolster their contention that segregation damaged the self-esteem and education of black children. Expert witnesses were crucial because the NAACP wanted to prove segregation in and of itself was harmful to black children, that it made them feel inferior. Carter and Greenberg's star witness in the case was Kenneth Clark, a black New York psychologist who was asked to collaborate with the NAACP after delivering a paper on segregation and black children to the White House Conference on Children in 1950—a paper funded and written under the auspices of the American Jewish Committee. The Topeka Jewish Community Relations Bureau tracked down some midwestern professors to help with the *Brown* case, and Clark's testimony ended up being crucial in convincing the Supreme Court to abolish segregation.

The supportive involvement of Jews and Jewish organizations in Topeka—from the courage and activism of Esther Brown to the initial funding given Kenneth Clark by the American Jewish Committee—mirrored what was happening nationally. In 1946, only months after the discovery of the Nazi death camps, a poll showed that 22 percent of the American people considered Jews to be a "menace to America." By 1950, the percentage had dropped to 5 percent, but few Jews, or Jewish organizations, believed attitudes had really changed—only gone underground. In cities across the country, Jewish organizations lobbied state legislatures and sued in courts to promote fair housing laws and fair employment laws banning discrimination. In San Francisco, a group of black and Jewish leaders, with a smattering of Catholic and Protestant clerics, met weekly in the offices of the Jewish Community Relations Council to plot strategy that led to the creation of the San Francisco Human Rights Commission. In 1954, the American Jewish Committee filed the first brief, in Englewood, New Jersey, against de facto school segregation in the North. A 1958 New York City law, pushed by Jewish organizations, banned discrimination in the sale or rental of housing. The Legal Defense Fund's Carter, who worked with Jewish groups constantly, welcomed and was acutely aware of their support. At a time when few people were willing to back the NAACP in its fight against segregated schools, he felt, Jews and Jewish groups were stepping forward.

Greenberg and Carter lost the battle in Topeka, but the Legal Defense Fund won the war. A local judge ruled that segregation in the Topeka schools was legal. But in reviewing the *Brown* v. *Board of Education* case and four related cases, the Supreme Court overturned a century of segregation. In one of the related cases, Greenberg had hustled to Delaware and won a landmark decision, persuading a judge to issue the first court-ordered integration decision in history. The state of Delaware had appealed the decision and Greenberg had argued the case before the Supreme Court, winning again.

At twenty-eight, Greenberg was a man on the move. He had argued and won a case before the Supreme Court and participated in a landmark civil rights case. Whenever he traveled to Washington to argue before the Supreme Court, his younger brother, Dan, who was working for a newspaper in Delaware, would try to come into town to watch him. Jack had remarkable poise, and he was one of the youngest people in the room. Many lawyers were arguing before the Supreme Court at the culmination of their careers; Jack's was just beginning. After one case, word came back that Justice Felix Frankfurter, one of the most learned justices on the court, had called one of his clerks over and asked, impressed, just who this Jack Greenberg was.

There was little time to relax after the *Brown* victory. In the months following the *Brown* v. *Board of Education* decision, the South confirmed its reputation for intransigence and hostility to blacks assuming even a shred of equality. Soon after the decision, all but one of the southern senators signed a manifesto pledging to resist desegregation. When the courts tried to desegregate schools in Little Rock, Arkansas, screaming parents blockaded the school, forcing them to be closed down for a year. It was guerrilla warfare as blacks in town after town had to go to court to desegregate their local schools.

The more Greenberg learned about the treatment of blacks in the late 1950s as he traveled the country for the Legal Defense Fund, the more incensed he became. The war against Germany had also been a war against racism, and the gross barriers subjugating blacks—the separate motels, separate restrooms, separate schools, separate lives—flew in the face of the Constitution. It was the combination of the gross and the petty that seemed to incense Greenberg most. As late as 1944, before the Supreme Court abolished all-white primaries in the South, not a single black held public office in the South, with the exception of a few border states. Forced by the courts to register blacks, southern registrars then stymied them with questions such as, "How many bubbles in a bar of soap?" In 1957 Greenberg came across an ad in the black newspaper, *Chicago Defender,* that, in its straightforward marketing, captured the humiliation of being black in America.

> Travel without embarrassment. . . . Would you like a vacation in
> *any* of the 48 states—minus rebuffs? Are you ready for any high-
> way emergency—even in a hostile town?
> [Join] Tourist Motor Club.

The ad offered a list of motels and restaurants that wouldn't turn away black customers.

Greenberg believed that by fighting segregation of blacks, he was also fighting discrimination against Jews. You could not compare the treatment of blacks and Jews in this country. Greenberg knew that. Jews were far better off. But it was also true that blacks and Jews were often beaten with the same stick, that housing rules that kept out one kept out the other, that people who didn't like one usually didn't like the other. A society in which someone's color or creed didn't matter meant a climate that would benefit both blacks and Jews. Ending discrimination meant erasing the blot on the Constitution that the country's treatment of blacks represented.

To his colleagues, Greenberg buried these convictions beneath a cool, aloof exterior. Throughout the 1950s he struck many at the NAACP as not "Jewish" at all—if Jewish meant an impassioned, expressive foe of injustice like Herbert Hill, the NAACP's labor director, who had graduated from an orthodox Jewish Yeshiva and spoke tirelessly before black churches, bearing down on issues with an enthusiasm and passion that overwhelmed and exhausted his opponents. Nor did Greenberg radiate the warmth of Jews like Allard Lowenstein, who would travel among rural southerners in the South in the 1960s getting them to register to vote, speaking to them with a "soul" that suggested a deep-felt empathy and understanding. Greenberg was a tough-minded New Yorker, businesslike and direct, who found sloganeering and grandstand displays of emotion distasteful. "A case can hardly be won by the lawyer who runs into court shouting slogans, preaching morality and history," Greenberg wrote years after joining the Legal Defense Fund. "All the lawyer's conventional jobs must be done. But although they can brief or argue historical considerations, so that courts will be properly informed, there are inherent limits to what lawyers can achieve. . . . All the lawyer can realistically do is marshal the evidence of what the claims of history may be and present them to the court." The best way to serve the cause of Negro rights, Greenberg believed, was by being the best lawyer possible.

James Farmer, head of the Congress of Racial Equality, 1962

When the Freedom Riders left from Montgomery, Alabama, to ride into the conscience of America and into Jackson, Mississippi, there were many persons who said to us:

"Don't go into Mississippi, go any place you like, go to the Union of South Africa, but stay out of Mississippi. . . . What you found in Alabama will be nothing compared to what you will meet in Mississippi."

I remember being told a story by one minister who urged us not to go.

He said: "Once upon a time there was a Negro who had lived in Mississippi, lived for a long time running from county to county. Finally he left the state, and left it pretty fast, as Dick Gregory would put it, not by Greyhound but by bloodhound, and he went to Illinois to live, in Chicago. And unable to find a job there, after several weeks of walking the street unemployed, he sat down and asked God what he should do.

God said, "Go back to Mississippi."

He said, "Lord, surely you don't mean it, you're jesting. You don't mean for me to go back to Mississippi. There is segregation there!"

The Lord said, "Go back to Mississippi."

The man looked up and said, "Very well, Lord, if you insist, I will do it, I will go. But will you go with me?"

The Lord said: "As far as Cincinnati."

Like many professional civil rights workers, Greenberg was unprepared for the sit-ins and waves of protests launched by Martin Luther King, CORE, SNCC, and other black groups that engulfed the South beginning in 1960. He had been focusing on desegregation cases, taking the Supreme Court case and making it apply everywhere. Suddenly, black and white Freedom Riders were boarding buses to Alabama and being beaten by mobs in Anniston as they tried to enter the "Whites Only" waiting room. King was issuing appeals of conscience asking northern whites to come south to join in the struggle. He was pledging to fill the jails of Birmingham, Alabama; St. Augustine, Florida; Albany, Georgia; and Jackson, Mississippi. Suddenly, the South was the center of the world, and lawyers were needed at the front.

The Jewish response to the outbreak of demonstrations in the South was striking in both its breadth and its depth. Fund-raisers from the Federation of Jewish Philanthropies began visiting CORE's headquarters opposite New York's City Hall once a week to brief James Farmer on how to make individual solicitations of large givers. Black and Jewish lawyers began meeting in the office of the Leadership Conference on Civil Rights, a building owned by the Union of American Hebrew Congregations, to begin drafting the laws that would become the Civil Rights Act of 1964 and the Voting Rights Act of 1965. Jewish contributions to civil rights organizations swelled; historians reviewing the records years later estimated that between half and three-quarters of the contributions to the NAACP, SCLC, SNCC, and CORE came from Jewish givers; more than half the white Freedom Riders were Jews, as were almost two-thirds of the white volunteers like Schwerner and Goodman who headed south for Freedom Summer. When Henry Schwartzchild, a veteran of the Freedom Rides and a former official of the Anti-Defamation League, organized a group of lawyers to go down South to defend protesters during Freedom Summer in 1964, he began with a list of lawyers provided by the American Jewish Committee. In 1965, when King asked members of the clergy to come to Selma, Alabama, to show support for black voting rights, several rabbis attending a rabbinical conference chartered a plane to fly south. In the front ranks, Rabbi Abraham Joshua Heschel, one of the most learned and respected rabbis in the country, locked arms with King and led the march across the Pettus Bridge toward Montgomery.

With the exception of rabbis like Heschel, few Jews cast their involvement in the movement in overtly Jewish terms. For some Jews there was a line that ran from the Kishinev— site of the Russian pogroms in the early twentieth century— through Auschwitz to Birmingham. Schwartzchild, a refugee from Nazi Germany, told friends he dated his involvement from the years following World War II. Returning to Germany to help the American army interrogate Germans, Schwartz-child resolved he would never be a "good German" standing by in the face of evil. "There was no doubt in any of our minds that we were risking our lives to achieve the very American goal of integration because our kinsmen had been slaughtered in Lithuania, Poland, and Germany," wrote Paul Cowan, a Jew from a highly assimilated family, reflecting on his family's commitment to civil rights. But most Jews spoke of their involvement as Carolyn Goodman had spoken of her son An-drew's or the civil rights lawyer had spoken of his or, indeed, Greenberg spoke of his: They were liberals; it was the right thing to do.

Yet while these Jews did not get involved because they were Jewish, there was something very Jewish about their getting involved.

Jews felt at home in a nation that spoke of equality. America in the 1950s was a country with its arteries clogged by prej-udice. Fresh from a war against Nazism and locked in a strug-gle with the Soviet Union in which each side proclaimed that its was the superior society, America was wracked by contra-dictions. It had fought an anti-racist war but its blacks could not eat in lunchrooms in the South. It trumpeted a society superior to communism, but blacks could not vote in southern states and attended substandard, segregated schools. Even gov-ernment officials were uncomfortable with the contradictions. In a brief filed with the Supreme Court in 1952 advocating desegregation of public schools, the Attorney General wrote: "It is in the context of the present world struggle between freedom and tyranny that the problem of racial discrimination must be viewed. . . . Racial discrimination furnishes grist for the Communist propaganda mills, and it raises doubt even among friendly nations as to the intensity of our devotion to the democratic faith." The brief went on to quote the Secretary of State: "The segregation of school children on a racial basis is one of the practices in the United States which has been singled out for hostile foreign comment in the United Nations and elsewhere. Other peoples cannot understand how such a practice can exist in a country which professes to be a staunch supporter of freedom, justice, and democracy."

The civil rights movement offered a point where Jewish self-interest and Jewish morality (though not, of course, only Jewish morality) intersected. Jews knew that—on their merits—they could make it with everyone else. A society opposed to discrimination was one where Jews could thrive. Tolerance would allow them to grow and prosper. This is what the lawyer had meant, I believe, when he talked about Jackie Robinson. Robinson represented the triumph of liberalism, of someone so good he had to be admitted to the major leagues—and then the Dodgers went on to win the pennant. Liberalism meant harnessing the energies of the country, striking down barriers so the country could call on all its resources and triumph.

The South made choosing sides easy. The battles in the South were over what Greenberg would later call American apartheid, the separation of blacks into separate schools, separate waiting rooms, separate lunch counters, separate lives. Jews arriving in this country in the early twentieth century had often spoken of "their America"—the great part of the country out there reserved for the Christians, wanting no part of people like Jews. The South in the 1950s was truly "their America"—home to the Ku Klux Klan, the night riders with their burning crosses and white robes. Leo Frank had been lynched in Georgia, and for years afterward the Yiddish *Forward* in New York reported the number of lynchings in that state, testimony to the South's barbarism and brutality. In 1957, Rabbi Jacob Rothschild of Atlanta signed a clerical statement calling for desegregation. The next year his synagogue was dynamited. A wave of bombings followed in the next eight months against Jewish community centers in five southern cities. Southern segregationists, Jews knew, were no friends of theirs.

Looking back, it would be easy to see the Jewish response to civil rights as driven largely by self-interest—wrapped perhaps in the cloak of idealism and altruism. Jews benefited enormously from the terrain shaped by the civil rights movement. Jews were the first to use anti-discrimination laws to gain access to restricted apartment buildings in large cities. The growing tide of tolerance left by the civil rights movement opened opportunities for Jews as well as for blacks in law firms, corporations, and universities. But to focus on self-interest as a motive was to miss the passion and excitement that enveloped Jews, like other whites, and like blacks, as the movement swept forward. The civil rights movement spoke to the Jewish head, but it also spoke to Jewish hearts.

Michael Walzer was a graduate student at Brandeis when Irving Howe, the editor of *Dissent* magazine, asked him to go south in 1960 to write about the growing student civil rights movement. He entered a small Baptist church in Montgomery, Alabama, and listened to a story that he knew well from his own Jewish training and his own scholarly work, the story of the Exodus. "There on the pulpit," Walzer wrote later, "the preacher, whose name I have long forgotten, acted out the 'going out' from Egypt and expounded its contemporary analogues [for the political struggle of southern blacks]: He cringed under the lash, challenged the pharaoh, hesitated fearfully at the sea, accepted the covenant and the law at the foot of the mountain." It was, Walzer said, the most extraordinary sermon he had ever heard.

John F. Kennedy, June 1963

We are confronted primarily with a moral issue. It is as old as the scriptures and is as clear as the American Constitution. The heart of the question is whether all Americans are to be afforded equal rights and equal op-

*portunities; whether we are going to treat our fellow
Americans as we want to be treated.*

*If an American, because his skin is dark, cannot eat
lunch in a restaurant open to the public; if he cannot
send his children to the best public schools available; if
he cannot vote for the public officials who represent him;
if, in short, he cannot enjoy the full and free life which
all of us want, then who among us would be content to
have the color of his skin changed and stand in his place?*

The onslaught of sit-ins and demonstrations transformed
the Legal Defense Fund. Requests for legal help poured into
the office in New York. The staff worked nights drawing up
legal papers, checking airline schedules for the latest flights
and connections to heretofore unheard-of towns like Albany,
Georgia, and Jackson, Mississippi. Looking back, lawyers compared the time to the Super Bowl, the adrenaline rushing through
their bodies as they geared up for battle with the obstructionist
South.

If Thurgood Marshall was the legal hero of the battle against
school desegregation that culminated in the *Brown* v. *Board
of Education* decision in 1954, Greenberg was the legal hero
of this next phase of the civil rights movement.

In the fall of 1961, as the civil rights protests were swelling,
Marshall called Greenberg into his office. President Kennedy,
he said, had decided to nominate Marshall to the Second Cir-
cuit of the U.S. Court of Appeals. Marshall wanted Greenberg
to succeed him. He was a fine lawyer and a fine administrator,
the best man to carry on the Legal Defense Fund's work.

To the people inside the Legal Defense Fund, Greenberg's
appointment marked the end of a long rivalry between him
and Bob Carter. Carter was disappointed. He wanted the job,
of course, but he believed that if he didn't get it, another black
lawyer should. The Greenberg appointment rankled. For the
first time, the question of Greenberg's religion was breached.

"Would a Jewish group appoint a black to head the American Jewish Congress?" Carter asked himself and others.

Carter and others muted their criticism for fear of dividing the civil rights movement. But outside the Legal Defense Fund, the appointment stirred controversy as well. *The Amsterdam News*, the largest black newspaper in Harlem, criticized the Greenberg appointment, saying a black should have gotten the job. At a conference of New York chapters of the NAACP, delegates tried to pass a resolution opposing Greenberg's appointment. They were stymied when told that the Legal Defense Fund was legally separate from the NAACP even though they shared the same initials—and that it would be wrong for one civil rights organization to criticize another.

Greenberg dismissed these criticisms in the integrationist spirit of the day. King had cast the issue in stark moral terms. Would blacks continue to be second-class citizens? Should they be deprived of their basic constitutional rights because of their color? This was not a black-white question, but an American one, a human one. "After all," Greenberg told black journalist Louis Lomax, "civil rights is not a Negro cause; it is a human cause, a serious problem in world society. True, our organization is designed primarily to aid Negroes in the push for equality, but the cause is human, not Negro." By 1963 Greenberg had increased the budget of the Legal Defense Fund to $1.5 million; in its earliest days the fund had gotten by on $10,000 a year. He filled its ranks with Ivy League–educated attorneys, many with prestigious law review credentials sparkling on their résumés. Working with 102 cooperating lawyers throughout the South, the Legal Defense Fund in 1963 defended 10,487 civil rights demonstrators, fought 168 groups of legal action in 15 states, and brought 30 cases to the Supreme Court. Other lawyers, many of them Jewish as well, enlisted in the movement in the South and won important, path-breaking cases, but for consistency in civil rights work and the changes he wrought in the law, none could match Greenberg or the Legal Defense Fund. His pursuit of top legal talent to enlist in the cause of civil rights was relentless. One Texas-born lawyer—enjoying the sun of a summer on Cape Cod—wrote of the efforts of Greenberg and his deputy, James Nabrit, in doggerel:

Each summer while the sun has burned
To Greenberg's bondage I've returned,

And Nabrit, overseer-in-chief,
Has made me slave on writ and brief.

But now, to put the matter clinically,
My epidermis as actinically

So altered been upon this shore,
That I'm an ASP, a WASP no more,

And Chief Bull Connor, were he here,
Would seat me in the bus's rear.

So now the NAACP
Has got to start advancing me!

Greenberg's goal was twofold: first, to protect the protesters from cruel and inhuman treatment on the part of southern police and southern courts; second, to embed in the law the changes that the protesters were winning by throwing their bodies on the line. Along with Martin Luther King, Greenberg believed that the courts were essential to the long-term success of the civil rights movement. Greenberg's arguments placed the civil rights movement squarely in the constitutional mainstream. When whites asked him whether the sit-in protesters and protest marchers flooding the South should obey the law just like everyone else, he responded: "Yes, they should, and with few exceptions they do. . . . But violation of state segregation laws or rules that stifle free speech are not violations of the law as determined by the United States Constitution. . . . Dr. King calls these laws 'unjust.' A lawyer would call them unconstitutional . . . [King's] philosophical position means disobedience of unjust laws such as Hitler's Nuremburg laws, even though they were perfectly legal within the Nazi system. Most Americans ought to agree with him. In Germany, there was no redress. Here the contrary is true."

This was not a revolutionary movement. Blacks were demanding rights that the Supreme Court had granted them. Gradually, the Supreme Court was coming around to agreeing with Greenberg. In the spring of 1963, the Supreme Court overruled the South Carolina conviction of 187 demonstrators who had marched peacefully on the grounds of the South Carolina statehouse to protest discrimination. The protest, the Supreme Court ruled, was an exercise of free speech in its "most pristine form." Greenberg's style was that of a low-key, scholarly appellate lawyer. He refused to turn trials into media-oriented indictments of the prevailing system of justice, like William Kunstler. He didn't want to put the Alabama courts or the courts of Mississippi "on trial."

Greenberg saw himself as a lawyer, a legal strategist. The pace of litigation called him from city to city. The Legal Defense Fund was in charge of bailing out the thousands of protesters being arrested across the South. Contributions were coming in so fast that Greenberg set up a separate account for the money and wrote checks on it himself. He occasionally joked with friends that if he ever died, opponents of civil rights would pounce on news of his "slush fund." He attended meetings of civil rights leaders and gave advice. It was up to others whether they took it.

But this belied the power and influence Greenberg was building up. It also belied what those who had to work with him—and fight with him—saw as the arrogance of intellect, the belief that Greenberg knew the best legal strategies and approaches. By 1963, Greenberg and the Legal Defense Fund had become the principal legal adviser to King and the SCLC. With King, it was clear who was in charge. Greenberg gave advice. King sometimes ignored it. Deciding in 1965 whether to march in Selma, King ignored a federal court injunction. And he was not above showing his impatience with Greenberg and the Legal Defense Fund's legal tactics. "Let him know that we don't feel that they are moving fast enough," King told Andrew Young at the time of the Selma march.

With other black activists, and their white supporters, tensions had begun to surface in 1964, especially those connected with SNCC, by then the most radical civil rights group. In the months leading up to Freedom Summer in 1964, Greenberg fought against using lawyers affiliated with the National Lawyers' Guild to defend southern demonstrators. He threatened to cancel plans to provide legal assistance to the volunteers if he had to work with the Lawyers' Guild lawyers. Officially, Greenberg claimed that these lawyers would not be able to give the time necessary to the cases. But many believed that Greenberg was in fact leery of the Guild's longtime association with communists and left-wing groups, that he wanted to keep the civil rights movement mainstream American. James Forman, the head of SNCC, accused Greenberg of "red baiting." Under a compromise, students heading south and volunteers working in the South were allowed to choose their lawyers— either from the National Lawyers' Guild or from the Legal Defense Fund. But the bad taste created by Greenberg's demands lingered. Many in SNCC, white and black, resented Greenberg's influence and what they saw as his establishment role.

Here and elsewhere, the question of who controlled the civil rights movement was bubbling up. As he had in 1961, Greenberg dismissed it. There were white kids coming south for Freedom Summer and there were black kids. There were all kinds of people. That he was white seemed irrelevant. To the extent that a small minority of the country could control anything, blacks controlled the civil rights movement. He worked with many different people. Many of the members of the board of directors of the Legal Defense Fund were black. The leadership of the movement itself was black. Many of the cooperating attorneys that Greenberg worked with in the South were black.

When Greenberg thought about the large presence of Jews in the movement—which he did not do very often—he ascribed it to the heritage of labor Zionism and socialism among Jews, like himself, active in public affairs in the 1940s, 1950s, and 1960s, and to the fact that many of the changes benefiting blacks benefited Jews. There were elements of truth to that analysis. But it was also becoming clear, as the early battles of the late 1950s and early 1960s against "American apartheid" passed into the tougher battles of the mid-1960s for economic equality, that the glue that had held Jews together in the civil rights movement was flaking away. As early as December 1964, he sensed the country was about to engage in new battles: "Nationally, all of us consumed with race relations will become increasingly occupied with those most difficult economic and social issues which transcend racial status but are completely bound up with it. Both kinds of questions, however, will stimulate the same kinds of approaches that have been called for in the past. Legal pressure must continue; demonstrations will be provoked by delay in advancing the southern-oriented quest for legal status and the northern-oriented quest for economic and social achievement. Newfound political strengths will be brought into active service whenever possible."

"Liberal" was a generous term in the early and mid-1960s; it took in people who fifteen years later would be bitter enemies. Greenberg parsed supporters of the civil rights movement this way: Within the civil rights coalition there were those—Jews and other whites—who opposed the legal barriers of segregation. But they did not believe government should be in the business of guaranteeing equality. Give people equal opportunity, they agreed, but no one can guarantee equal results. Others, like Greenberg, saw segregation as only part of a greater oppression of blacks imposed from without. Desegregating schools didn't just mean declaring laws unconstitutional; sometimes it meant busing children from one neighborhood to another. Ending discrimination in employment didn't just mean winning a court case; it also meant affirmative action and careful monitoring. Looking back on this time, Greenberg invoked the image of an onion. The coalition for civil rights looked solid, but peeling away the skin, no one knew how many divisions and layers lay underneath.

It was among Jewish intellectuals that the liberal consensus for civil rights first cracked.

Many of the earliest demands for blacks had been articulated by Jews or in Jewish-sponsored forums, like *Commentary*, the official publication of the American Jewish Committee and an increasingly influential magazine. James Baldwin had published several articles in *Commentary*; his first, in 1948, warned about black-Jewish tensions in Harlem. Kenneth Clark had written on similar issues two years before. Throughout the 1950s and 1960s, Jewish authors in *Commentary* and in more general-interest magazines and newspapers were at the forefront in forging the liberal consensus that argued for America to set right its historic debt to blacks. It was Jewish intellectuals, as well as lawyers and fund-raisers, who made the greatest contributions to the civil rights movement.

In February 1963, following an angry discussion with James Baldwin, who had promised a piece to *Commentary* but sold it to *The New Yorker* instead, *Commentary*'s editor Norman Podhoretz published an article entitled "My Negro Problem —and Ours." It began:

> Two ideas puzzled me deeply as a child growing up in Brooklyn during the 1930s in what today would be called an integrated neighborhood. One of them was that all Jews were rich; the other was that all Negroes were persecuted. These ideas had appeared in print; therefore they must be true. My own experience and the evidence of my senses told me they were not true, but that only confirmed what a day-dreaming boy in the provinces . . . discovers very early: His experience is unreal and the evidence of his senses is not to be trusted. Yet even a boy with a head full of fantasies incongruously synthesized out of Hollywood movies and English novels cannot altogether deny the reality of his own experience —especially where there is so much deprivation in that experience. Nor can he altogether gainsay the evidence of his own senses—especially such evidence of the senses as comes from being repeatedly beaten up, robbed, and in general hated, terrorized, and humiliated.
>
> And so for a long time I was puzzled to think that Jews were supposed to be rich when the only Jews I knew were poor, and that Negroes were supposed to be persecuted when it was the Negroes who were doing the only persecuting I knew about—and doing it, moreover, to me. . . . A city boy's world is contained within three or four square blocks, and in my world it was the

whites, the Italians and Jews, who feared the Negroes, not the other way around. The Negroes were tougher than we were, more ruthless, and on the whole, they were better athletes. What could it mean, then, to say that they were badly off and that we were more fortunate? . . .

The term *schwartze*—Yiddish for "black"—had not originated in the South among rednecks but in the ghettos of New York's Lower East Side and in the working-class Jewish neighborhoods of Brooklyn and Chicago. Podhoretz exposed the disparity between what many Jews had experienced and what they wanted to believe—that there was a natural alliance, born in common suffering, that linked blacks and Jews together. In fact, many Jews had felt toward blacks as they felt toward other immigrant groups. Their encounters with blacks had often been patronizing—blacks as maids or employees in stores. Jews had been taught it was prejudiced to feel fear in front of blacks, but in fact many did. That fear was growing as neighborhoods across the country began changing from Jewish to black and Jews began to feel unsafe walking down their own streets to their own temples and stores. Confirmation of that fear came dramatically in the summer of 1964. While FBI agents combed the Mississippi woods for Schwerner, Chaney, and Goodman, riots erupted in New York and a handful of other cities, with Jewish-owned stores the targets of burning and looting.

A few months after the 1964 summer riots, Nathan Glazer, a Jewish sociologist, took to the pages of *Commentary* to argue that a sea change was occurring in the civil rights movement. "As the Negro masses have become more active and more militant in their own interests, their feelings have forced themselves to the surface; and Jewish leaders—of unions, of defense and civil rights organizations—as well as businessmen, housewives, and homeowners, have been confronted for the first time with demands from Negro organizations that, they find, cannot serve as the basis of a common effort." Glazer turned out to be prophetic, not only for Jews, but for many whites as well. The goals of the civil rights movement were shifting—from demands for political and legal equality to de-

mands for economic equality, from demands for equal opportunity to demands for equal results. Up until now, the price
of racial change had been taken out of the hide of the South.
Northerners, including northern Jews, did not have to deal
with consequences directly.

At the same time these Jews were moving away from the
civil rights movement to the right, other Jews remained firmly
on the left. For those on the Jewish left there was the restless
desire to be on the edge of change, to find the latest social
movement and become a part of it. Many of the Jews most
active in the movement—the organizers who lived down South,
the staff members of the various civil rights organizations—
came from left-wing backgrounds, from families that had either embraced socialism or flirted with or joined the communists in the 1930s. Andrew Goodman's family had been
sympathetic to the Communist Party during the 1950s and
held fund-raising parties in their large Manhattan apartment
for professors under attack for their Communist Party ties.
One of Carolyn Goodman's early memories of Andy was of
him crying when one friend of the Goodmans left their apartment to go to jail during the era of Senator Joseph McCarthy.
It was the man's birthday. "Why does he have to go to jail on
his birthday?" young Andy asked.

If Greenberg was heir to the socialist-turned-liberal tradition
of middle-class parents with middle-class aspirations for their
son, families like the Goodmans were heirs to the tradition
of Jewish radicalism. Jews from this tradition often made the
strongest impression on blacks in the South. They stayed the
longest and became more fully involved in the struggle than
students visiting for a summer or fund-raisers dashing off a
check or attending a fund-raising party in New York.

Howard Zinn, for example, had moved to Atlanta in 1956,
with his street-coarsened New York accent, his radical political ideas, and a newly minted degree in political science from
Columbia. The poor son of working-class parents, he began
adult life as a shipyard worker with copies of books by Marx
and Engels in his back pocket. Soon he was trying to organize
the workers in the shipyards. After bombing Nazis from an

air force plane during World War II, Zinn entered college at twenty-seven under the GI Bill. He decided to become an academic and in his last year the president of Spelman College—a small, black women's school in Atlanta, part of a group of colleges known as the Atlanta University Center—offered him a job as chairman of the Department of Political Science. Zinn's political radicalism would have impelled him to action on the "Negro question" no matter where he was. In Atlanta he didn't have to look far. "What can we do that is useful in this putrid, segregated city?" he asked his students soon after arriving.

The answer was sit in and integrate. Three years before students in North Carolina made their widely publicized sit-ins at Woolworth's in Greensboro, Zinn led a group of students—including Julian Bond, who would later become a key civil rights leader—to the state legislature, where they defiantly sat in the whites-only part of the gallery. Two years later, in 1959, Zinn sent black and white students and faculty to the main branch of the segregated Atlanta Library. They politely asked the librarians for copies of "An Essay on Human Understanding" by John Locke and for books on liberty. "We want to get the librarians by guilt," he told students. The "request-in" succeeded. Later that year Zinn—joined by another white professor and two black professors—signed up for full library privileges, inaugurating the desegregation of Atlanta's libraries.

Like Greenberg, Zinn was not a religious man; his ties to Judaism consisted of occasional December forays to local stores for Hanukkah candles. The political lessons he took from Judaism mattered more to him than the religious ones. His alliance with black protesters in the South was a natural marriage. Through his contacts with Bond and other students, Zinn was asked to serve on the executive board of SNCC and to serve as one of its advisers and unofficial historian. As the civil rights movement picked up momentum, Zinn knew there were Jews he could count on among the liberal whites fighting segregationists in Atlanta. But Jews also owned stores that were targets of civil rights activity. Rich's department store, the largest in Atlanta, was owned by a Jewish family and was the scene of a lengthy and bitter sit-in campaign. Occasionally, Zinn used his Jewishness to try to stir feelings of remorse in his Jewish opponents. One Passover, Zinn, together with a Jewish student and two black students, sat in at a local Jewish delicatessen known for its pastrami and corned beef. An hour passed. Waiters refused to serve them. A black busboy surreptitiously passed them four glasses of water. The owner rushed by and swept the glasses away. After another hour the group looked longingly at a dish of pickles resting on a table nearby. They debated switching tables so that, even if they were not served, they could munch on pickles to stem their hunger. They rejected the tactic as "opportunistic." Finally, Zinn called over the owner and said, plaintively, "It's Passover." But the owner would not yield. It took months of picketing before blacks could eat pastrami in Atlanta.

Like Zinn, Dotty Miller came from a left-wing family. She had graduated from Queens College in New York and headed south after reading about the first sit-ins in *The New York Times*. Coming from a radical background, she saw the sit-ins in political terms. These protesters were actually doing what everybody else was only talking about. They were making their lives useful in a political way. They didn't think about going to court. They just sat in. Miller became one of the first whites to join SNCC and soon was busy recruiting students from northern campuses. "If you can make a contribution by getting your whole hometown upset" by heading south and getting arrested, Miller told potential northern recruits, "good, that is a contribution."

For Jews like Miller and Zinn, for left-wing lawyers like Morton Stavis, Arthur Kinoy, and William Kunstler, who worked closely with SNCC, Greenberg represented the establishment trying to put the brakes on the activists in the civil rights movement. They believed he was too cautious, preferring the courts, while they were on the front lines.

There was a double edge to the presence of so many liberal, activist Jews at the center of the civil rights movement. It contributed enormously to the success of the movement. But it also left blacks with a false impression of the depth of the Jewish commitment to the black struggle. Greenberg, Zinn, Miller, Schwerner, Goodman—all may have represented the best of American Jews. But they did not represent all American Jews. By the late 1960s, they did not reflect the growing unease of Jews up North with calls for Black Power or the growing importance of Israel as a focus for Jewish life and politics. They did not reflect the group of Jewish intellectuals growing up around *Commentary* who were developing a powerful critique of Great Society liberalism, especially the changing demands of blacks. They certainly did not reflect the fear of lower- and middle-class Jews who were taking the brunt of change as neighborhoods in city after city shifted from Jewish to black and blacks in New York demanded control over schools with Jewish teachers in their neighborhoods.

And yet, as the polarization between blacks and whites grew—as Black Power began to rise, as the ghetto riots exploded, as SNCC unleashed its attacks on Israel—Greenberg kept to his liberal, integrationist beliefs.

In the midst of the controversy over community control in New York's public schools, a battle that was tearing New York apart over whether black neighborhoods should have control over their own schools, a supporter of black demands for community control traveled uptown to Greenberg's apartment on New York's Upper West Side to see if she could enlist Greenberg and the Legal Defense Fund on the side of the black parents. Greenberg demurred. He told her he could not support what was in effect a black separatist movement. He agreed to help with a lawsuit challenging civil service exams in New York that were racially biased and prevented blacks in the school system from getting promotions, but integrated schools and an integrated society remained his goal. "Some support the all-black school, controlled by the black community and dedicated to attaining racial pride, identity and dignity," he wrote in an article in the *Saturday Review* in 1968. This was not the solution. Writing six months after the riots that tore apart American cities in the summer of 1967, Greenberg declared: "The Urban Coalition of industrial, political and social leaders . . . should see that the ghetto school is the prime perpetuator of the ghetto, without which there would have been no riots. . . . The fundamental question transcends education. We face the question of whether America will develop into a single nation or two nations, one black and the other white."

But amidst the growing demands for Black Power, many blacks felt that question had already been answered. America was already two nations. The only remaining question was how to build up the power and influence of the black nation. In 1947 Jackie Robinson had been the symbol of one version of the American dream—the underdog breaking into an all-white sport, defeating prejudice by excelling. Now that image was replaced by a far different one, a far more militant one, even in sports.

An article in Time *magazine, October 25, 1968, reporting on the Olympic Games in Mexico City*

[Tommie] Smith had just won the 200-meter dash in a record-breaking 19.8 seconds. [John] Carlos, his bearded teammate from San Jose State College, had finished third. Together they turned up for the awards ceremony shoeless, wearing knee-length black stockings and a black glove on one hand. . . . Along with Australia's Peter Norman, the second place finisher, they mounted the victory pedestal to receive their medals. Then, as the U.S. flag was raised and the band struck up "The Star Spangled Banner," the two black athletes bowed their heads and raised their gloved hands in a clenched-fist salute. . . .

At a press conference later, the two men explained that the black stockings represented poverty; the black fists meant black power and black unity. Said Smith: "We are black and proud to be black. White America will say 'an American won,' not 'a black American won.'

If it had been something bad, they would have said 'a Negro.' "

Throughout the late 1960s, the Legal Defense Fund was an island of calm in stormy seas. It retained its interracial staff —and retained Greenberg as its head—even as whites were being expelled from civil rights organizations like SNCC and CORE, and their role was being reduced even in such organizations as the NAACP. The Legal Defense Fund was not the kind of place where militants might stage a palace coup. It was more insulated than other civil rights groups; Greenberg was responsible only to its board of directors, which respected and admired his work. He didn't have to cope with out-of-control membership conventions. Greenberg was also successful. He had won and continued to win landmark cases. Perhaps most important of all, the Legal Defense Fund operated within a legal culture of civility and clear rules. This wasn't the street, where a hothead could get a crowd by shouting "Black Power!" It was a law firm filled with graduates, black and white, of Harvard and Yale law schools.

Greenberg's brother Dan, who was living overseas during much of this time, would occasionally come into New York to have lunch with him. Jack struck Dan as one of the few whites who was truly color-blind. Dan would join his brother and other Legal Defense Fund lawyers for lunch. They struck him all as buddies in the army, all united in a common cause.

There were controversies at the Legal Defense Fund. In 1971, the fund staff split badly over whether it should represent Angela Davis, then held in a New York jail. Margaret Burnham, a young black lawyer, wanted to take the case, but Greenberg vetoed it, arguing Davis was able to get good legal advice elsewhere. Burnham felt Greenberg didn't understand how important it was for her, as a black woman, to defend a black woman who had become the symbol of resistance to white oppression. This was to some extent a generational issue. The younger lawyers on the Legal Defense Fund staff, white and black, by and large backed Burnham, while James Nabrit, who was black and a longtime colleague of Greenberg's, joined Greenberg in saying the Legal Defense Fund should not take on Angela Davis's case. So deep was the split that the fight eventually went to the Legal Defense Fund's board of directors which, not surprisingly, backed Greenberg. Burnham left the Fund to defend Davis and win her acquittal.

The battle over whether to defend Angela Davis was one sign of the change in perception the Legal Defense Fund was undergoing in the black community. Greenberg's tenacious commitment to integration had placed him at the forefront of the civil rights movement in the 1950s and early 1960s. But what had once seemed a radical notion now, in a different political climate, seemed more conservative. For a segment of the black leadership, integration was chimera. Blacks had to fight far more important battles for self-determination and control of their own lives. Greenberg began shifting the energies of the Legal Defense Fund into new areas. He established a poverty law project designed to help poor people fight for their rights under government programs. And the Legal Defense Fund launched an ultimately successful campaign against the death penalty, which Greenberg argued was clearly discriminatory since four times as many blacks as whites were executed for crimes. But as the 1970s began, some white and Jewish lawyers at the Legal Defense Fund who had joined during the heroic days of the civil rights struggle began to leave, believing it was time black lawyers took control of their own struggle. Some black lawyers in and out of the Legal Defense Fund believed Greenberg was concentrating too much of the Legal Defense Fund's efforts and energy on the South, pressing for continued school desegregation, instead of focusing on the problems of housing discrimination and ghettos in the North that were corroding the lives of millions of blacks. Fighting the death penalty was a good thing. It wasn't that Greenberg was not a good lawyer. He was brilliant, and dedicated to the cause. But the Legal Defense Fund was the only legal group in the country whose sole job was to defend the interests of blacks. Would the Legal Defense Fund be following the same agenda, many black lawyers asked themselves, if a black were in charge? Greenberg was still perceived as stubborn and aloof. He skirmished regularly with the leadership of the NAACP over fund-raising—skirmishes which in 1982 culminated in a lawsuit in which the NAACP tried to stop the NAACP Legal Defense Fund from using its initials. The Legal Defense Fund won the case. The fight reinforced the image of Greenberg and the Legal Defense Fund as a fiefdom determined to set its own course.

If Greenberg was becoming too conservative for the taste of some blacks, he was becoming too liberal for some Jews. As legal cases involving affirmative action began to appear in the courts in the early 1970s, the Legal Defense Fund began filing lawsuits and legal briefs in support of blacks struggling to open up jobs. One of the first cases involved a challenge to the New York prison system, which had never promoted a black correction officer above the entry level. It was, Greenberg felt, a case of rampant racism and discrimination. The Legal Defense Fund sued successfully, forcing the city to hire and promote equal numbers of black and white officers. When the case was appealed, Greenberg was stunned to discover that the Anti-Defamation League had filed a brief opposing the affirmative action plan. Greenberg could not believe it. He did not know officials at the ADL well. But he had met them at various civil rights banquets and called several of them up. "This is a mistake," he told them. The ADL's position bothered him not only on its merits—they were clearly wrong—but for what it portended for the future of black-Jewish relations. The longer the battle over affirmative action raged in the 1970s—with black groups on one side and Jewish groups like the ADL, the American Jewish Committee, and the American Jewish Congress on the other—the more Greenberg believed he was right. The Jewish groups were handling this issue terribly, he thought. Virtually every black who had achieved success, Greenberg believed, had achieved success because of affirmative action or because of pressures stirred by the demand for affirmative action. Jewish groups opposing affirmative action were attacking the most successful, the best placed, the most articulate, the most influential, the most powerful segments of the black community. These blacks would be crazy not to fight back. The fallout would be—and was—devastating for black-Jewish cooperation.

There was no love lost between any of the organized Jewish groups and Greenberg. The Jewish organizations found him cold and hard to work with. Greenberg felt some officials of the ADL, the most vociferous opponents of affirmative action, had become "haters." The bitterness seeped through into personal encounters. It showed how affirmative action and the changing nature of civil rights had opened deep divisions within the Jewish community as well as between blacks and Jews.

A letter from the Third World Coalition of Harvard Law School to the Harvard Law School Community, May 1982

The Third World Coalition of Harvard Law School feels strongly that the course created and taught by former Harvard Law School Professor Derrick Bell, Constitutional Law and Minority Issues, *should continue to be instructed by a Third World professor. This course is concerned with the legal system and Third World people in the United States and, therefore, it is extremely important that it be taught by an instructor who can identify with and empathize with the social, cultural, economic, and political experiences of the Third World community.*

The Law School community would greatly benefit if Third World professors were brought to the School. . . . The lack of Third World professors at Harvard Law School is not due to a vacuum of qualified Third World legal professionals, but rather to the institution's inadequate search methods and the biased criteria it uses to judge prospective Third World faculty candidates. . . .

The Third World Coalition will urge the members of its constituent organizations to boycott Constitutional

Law and Minority Issues *for the following reasons: (1) the extremely low number of Third World professors at the Law School, (2) the appropriateness of a Third World instructor to teach the* Constitutional Law and Minority Issues *course, (3) the availability of qualified Third World legal professionals to teach this course in particular and at the Law School in general, and (4) the inadequate efforts of Harvard Law School to find these professionals and the biased criteria it uses to judge prospective Third World faculty candidates.*

Greenberg had clashed with blacks in Mississippi in the summer of 1964 over his role in the civil rights movement, and there had been grumblings among some black lawyers about his stewardship of the Legal Defense Fund in the 1970s. But to see most clearly the clash between the philosophy Greenberg represented and the changing nature of black demands, it is necessary to jump ahead to Harvard Law School in the spring and fall of 1982, and the winter of 1983.

For several years in the late 1970s, Harvard Law School had offered a course on race and the law taught by its first tenured black law professor. When that professor, Derrick Bell, left to become dean of the law school at the University of Oregon, the course lapsed. Black students became increasingly angry at the absence of the course and the even more glaring paucity of black professors at the country's top law school. Of sixty-five faculty members at Harvard Law School in 1982, two were black. Only one had tenure.

In an effort to expand Harvard's course offerings on race and law, the dean of Harvard Law School, James Vorenberg, an old friend of Greenberg's, invited Julius Chambers to teach an intensive course as part of the school's intensive winter term—compressing a semester's worth of work into a month. Chambers was a well-known black lawyer from Charlotte and president of the board of directors that oversaw the Legal Defense Fund. Chambers demurred, saying he could not take off that much time, but suggested that he and Greenberg split the course. The prospect thrilled many people on the law school faculty where, as one black professor wrote at the time, "Many of us were excited at the prospect of a core course covering four areas that these two towering figures have been absolutely central in shaping: school desegregation, voting rights, capital punishment, and employment rights."

But a group of black students objected. In an open letter to Harvard students, a group called the Third World Coalition called for a boycott of the course, declaring, "This course is concerned with the legal system and Third World people in the United States and, therefore, it is extremely important that it be taught by an instructor who can identify and empathize with the social, cultural, economic, and political experiences of the Third World community."

The driving force behind the boycott was Muhammed Kenyatta, a thirty-eight-year-old law student with a long history in the civil rights movement and black nationalist movements during the 1960s and 1970s. Despite his name, Kenyatta was a Baptist, not a Black Muslim. He had changed his name in 1968 to show sympathy with the emerging black nationalist movement. Articulate and forceful, with a charisma that impressed several professors, Kenyatta believed the appointment of Greenberg and Chambers was a chance to rally students and bring pressure on Harvard to hire more black faculty. But as a veteran of SNCC who had worked on the Mississippi Freedom Summer project, he also bore a grudge against Greenberg for Greenberg's opposition to the use of National Lawyers' Guild lawyers during the 1964 protests. More than any of the other students—most of whom were too young to be familiar with the dynamics of black-white and black-Jewish cooperation in the civil rights movement—Kenyatta understood the subtext of the challenge to Greenberg. He insisted that the main issue at stake was affirmative action at Harvard. But the protest soon began to stand for much more.

All at once, Greenberg's presence at Harvard became a magnet for issues that had simmered beneath the surface of black-Jewish relations for years: affirmative action, the role of whites in the civil rights movement, Jewish feelings of betrayal, and black resentment of paternalism. Kenyatta's Muslim name inserted into the dispute the aura of black nationalism and Islamic hostility to Jews and to Israel. Once, Greenberg's arrival on the scene of a civil rights crisis meant resolution, legal victory, and bail money. Now he was on the opposite side.

For liberals, black and white, the call for a boycott marked a repudiation of the integrationist ethic and insulted one of the great champions of civil rights law—because of his color. "W. E. B. Du Bois, the great black leader and a graduate of Harvard, once wrote that the problem of the 20th century 'is the problem of the color line,' " began an article in *The New York Times.* "He probably did not envision that black students at his alma mater would someday help make his words ring true. But black law students at Harvard are calling for a boycott of a course in race and legal issues because one of its teachers, Jack Greenberg, is white." Black columnist Carl Rowan wrote, "Bad times make for bad moods and bad actions" and denounced the boycott as "racist, anti-intellectual and anti-civil rights."

Black students used the boycott to highlight the lack of black faculty at Harvard and to criticize Greenberg's tenure as head of the Legal Defense Fund. In literature and discussions on campus, they brought up Greenberg's refusal to work with radical lawyers during Freedom Summer, his ongoing fight with the NAACP over fund-raising, and the fact that he, a white man and a Jew, was heading the country's premier black legal organization. Through it all the students and their supporters emphasized that there was something special about being black and that someone black would bring special insights to a course on civil rights and the law.

Greenberg seemed more annoyed than hurt by the boycott. He had agreed to teach the course as a favor. During the negotiations, Greenberg and Chambers met with the black students. Privately, several black students came up to him and said they didn't agree with what Kenyatta was doing. Greenberg asked them: Why don't you take the course? Why don't you audit it instead of taking it for credit? The students responded that they were afraid to suffer the consequences of breaking ranks. He could not summon much sympathy for them. What they feared were the strictures of peer pressure. It did not take much courage to take a course. In thirty-three years Greenberg had seen a great deal of courage. The plight of a few black students at Harvard afraid of being ostracized by some of their friends moved him very little. Greenberg felt anger and contempt for Kenyatta, the leader of the protest. But for most of the black students he just felt sorry—sorry for people who couldn't stand up and take a course they believed in.

The dispute between Greenberg and the black law students at Harvard ended in a stalemate. Greenberg and Chambers went ahead and taught their course anyway. Outside the classroom building, black students and their supporters marched in a picket line. The faculty was divided. Derrick Bell, the black law professor whose departure had left Harvard bereft of a civil rights course, and who had once worked for Greenberg at the Legal Defense Fund, sympathized with the students. Randall Kennedy, another black teacher at Harvard, saw in the attack on Greenberg a resurfacing of the debate over the role of whites in the struggle for civil rights. Kennedy acknowledged that Greenberg's conduct over the years and his refusal to step down and turn over his post to a black had bred resentment among many blacks. But, he declared, "in criticizing white liberals, it is . . . necessary to distinguish between liberal hypocrites and liberal heroes—those whites who have dedicated themselves to the struggle against racial oppression. From Wendell Phillips and Thaddeus Stevens to Andrew Goodman and Michael Schwerner to Thomas I. Emerson and Arthur Kinoy, there have been whites who have seized every opportunity to enlarge the scope of freedom for blacks. Jack Greenberg belongs in this category."

Julius Chambers, who taught with Greenberg, described the dispute in terms that approached the classic definition of tragedy. Both sides were right, Chambers felt. Greenberg was right because he was, of course, qualified to teach the course. Greenberg had hired Chambers in 1963 as the Legal Defense Fund's first black intern. Now Chambers was president of the Legal Defense Fund Board. In a few years, he would be chosen by Greenberg to succeed him as the fund's director-counsel. No one could doubt Greenberg's commitment to civil rights law and his immense contributions. But the students were also right in their anger at Harvard, Chambers felt. They were right to demand that Harvard recruit more black faculty. For Chambers, the boycott at Harvard illustrated the chasm that had opened between what the law could accomplish—the law that men like he and Greenberg had devoted their lives to changing—and what the students wanted. All the laws passed and all the work Greenberg had done had still not brought more black professors to Harvard Law School. The students were still frustrated.

So much had changed. In another era, Greenberg might have been the lawyer to bring a case charging Harvard with discrimination or consulted with students on how to pressure Harvard to hire more black professors. How powerful Greenberg's voice would have been if it had been added to the students' demands. How appropriate it would have been for the students to acknowledge their debt to Greenberg, whose work had paved the way for many of them to come to a place like Harvard. But such cooperation was not to be. Greenberg was far from a tragic figure. After retiring from the Legal Defense Fund he joined the faculty of Columbia Law School, his alma mater, as a professor. He continued to speak out and write vigorously on civil rights, broadening his concerns to human rights in South Africa and the Soviet Union, mounting challenges to discrimination in private clubs in New York. The tragedy was that the liberalism that had linked blacks and Jews, and blacks and liberal whites, had collapsed. The possibility for coalitions—buffeted and strained by the rising militancy of the 1960s and the disputes over affirmative action in the 1970s, now so vividly under attack on the Cambridge campus of Harvard—had ended. People could no longer work together.

CONFRONTATION

4

Into the Cauldron: Rhody McCoy

The riot in the Watts neighborhood of Los Angeles had been going on for several days and nights when Martin Luther King arrived with his aides. King had debated for several days whether or not to go but finally decided he had no choice. The Selma-to-Montgomery march had ended with a great victory, the signing of the Voting Rights Act in August 1965. Now, just a week later, mobs were roaming the streets of Watts, setting block after block on fire, looting, hurling Molotov cocktails through store windows. King flew to Los Angeles from San Juan, where he had gone for a vacation, and with Bayard Rustin, one of his top advisers, met with the publisher of the *Los Angeles Times* and with California's governor. Then King and Rustin walked the streets of Watts, trying to calm the rioters down. A group of black teenagers turned on them and began shouting at King.

"What are you middle-class niggers doing coming here?" they yelled. "Do you have a job? Do you have a home? We don't!"

The teenagers wouldn't listen to King. King was shaken. That night he and Rustin talked. In nine years of demonstrations in the South, from Montgomery to Selma, battling George

Wallace and Sheriff Jim Clark and "Bull" Connor, there had never been any major rioting by blacks. The civil rights revolution had changed the lives of blacks in the South. But here, in Watts, King faced a different reality. The civil rights movement had not changed the lives of blacks in the North or West much at all.

From the Autobiography of LeRoi Jones/Amiri Baraka

The Supremes' "Where Did Our Love Go?" and Mary Welles's "My Guy" reached me in 1964. And Dionne Warwick's "Walk on By." These tunes seemed to carry word from the black to me. Monterey, the downtown streets of the forming Black Arts core, the dazzle that black women presented to me now. Marvin Gaye's "Stubborn Kind of Fellow" was playing when we got up town. "Keep on Pushing," which poet David Henderson made into a great poem, was one of our themes, and all of us would try for Curtis Mayfield's keening falsetto with the Impressions. Plus their "We're a Winner" also moved us and spoke, it seemed, directly to our national desire.

It was as if I had a new ear for black music at that point in the middle 60's. I was a jazz freak, though we rhythm-and-bluesed to Ray Charles, "I Got a Woman" and "Drown in My Own Tears" at our downtown loft sets. But now the rhythm and blues took on special significance and meaning. Those artists, too, were reflecting the rising tide of the people's struggles. Martha and the Vandellas' "Dancing in the Streets" was like our national anthem. Their "Heatwave" had signaled earlier, downtown, that the shit was on the rise. But "Dancing in the Streets," which spoke to us of Harlem and other places, then Watts and later Newark and Detroit, seemed

to say it all out. "Summer's here and time is near/ for
dancing in the streets!"

Paul Parks and Rhody McCoy liked to have long talks over
the phone between McCoy's office in Brooklyn and Parks's
office in Boston. They were both large men, light-skinned and
soft-spoken, almost avuncular in manner. It became a running
joke that people often mistook Parks for McCoy and McCoy
for Parks at civil rights meetings. But their backgrounds and
outlooks could not have been more different. In the fall of
1967, when the two men began talking, Parks was still a committed integrationist—a negotiator and a healer willing to
play the deft middleman's role to integrate restrooms in the
South and schools in the North. Parks had begun to reap some
of the benefits of the civil rights movement. He had joined
the administration of Boston's new reform mayor Kevin White,
running anti-poverty programs that had become part of Lyndon Johnson's burgeoning Great Society.

McCoy, by contrast, was an angry and determined man who
had distrusted whites as long as he could recall. A New York
City teacher who had risen to become acting principal of a
school for violent teenagers, McCoy believed whites had sold
integration to blacks as a bill of goods. While Parks was traveling to the South and to the March on Washington to hold
hands with whites and sing "We Shall Overcome," McCoy
was taking the subway from West End Avenue and Eighty-
third Street, where he was a teacher, to Harlem's Mosque
Number 7 to hear Malcolm X speak about the Devil White
Man and about the need for blacks to seize control of their
own neighborhoods, stores, and lives. McCoy believed Malcolm spoke the truth when he said blacks had to control their
own destiny and their own future.

In many ways, McCoy and Parks represented the two strains
emerging from the civil rights movement in the wake of the
Watts riot. Parks came from a southern and midwestern tra-

dition, steeped in the church. Blacks in the South rarely came into contact with Jews and, when they did, Jews often contrasted favorably with other whites. McCoy was part of a new generation of frustrated, angry urban blacks, stymied by whites and often dealing with Jews in ghettos and in the civil service who were in positions of power. McCoy had long felt that Jews controlled the public school system in New York. He felt stymied as time and again Jewish teachers with less talent and fewer qualifications than he won important promotions and better assignments. For blacks like Parks, Martin Luther King embodied hope and change; for blacks like McCoy, change lay in ringing rhetoric and piercing analysis of Malcolm X.

In the fall of 1967, after eighteen years in New York's school system, McCoy was finally being given his chance. He had been named the first black head of a school district. It was a temporary, experimental district known as Ocean Hill–Brownsville, 75 percent black, 25 percent Hispanic, just about all poor or close to it, created as part of a plan to "decentralize" New York's schools, uncoupling them from the overweening central bureaucracy so that parents could have more of a say—and develop more of a stake—in the education of their children. For the first time, McCoy believed, blacks were going to have a say in who taught their children and what they were taught.

Parks had read in the newspapers about McCoy's bold new experimental school district in New York. Education was one of Parks's areas of interest. He began calling up McCoy to give advice. Their telephone friendship blossomed. While Parks admired the concept of a black-run, black-controlled school district, he didn't believe it would work.

"You can't separate us out to one place," he told McCoy. "Separate us out to one place and we'll be isolated in that place."

But McCoy was long past believing that whites would voluntarily give up any control, especially the white power structure that controlled politics and education in New York City. Parks could believe that integration might work in Boston and

Indianapolis, or in Magnolia, Mississippi. McCoy liked Parks and appreciated his interest. But in the end, he believed Parks was naive. Parks often hung up the phone with McCoy's words ringing in his ears:

"It's better to be free without any power than to be a slave and have it all."

The rioting in Watts had signaled a new phase in the civil rights movement. The years following the deaths of Schwerner, Chaney, and Goodman in 1964 were increasingly bitter for blacks, especially in the North. Over and over again, the millenarian expectations raised by the March on Washington and the passage of the Civil Rights Act of 1964 crashed into the ceiling of de facto segregation in the North, the intractability of ghetto poverty, and the wiliness of big-city politicians. The crisis of blacks in the North was quieter than the crisis blacks had faced in the South. It lacked the dramatic markers of lynchings, "Bull" Connor, and police dogs. Blacks jammed into the South Side of Chicago could vote, but nearly half were not making enough money to support their families. They could go to restrooms with whites and eat at lunch counters with them in the Loop, but the unemployment rate among blacks in Chicago—and in Los Angeles, New York, Detroit, and across the United States—was twice that of whites. Police patrolling the ghettos harassed and beat black residents; in ways large and small, they treated blacks like second- and third-class citizens. "There are few things under heaven more unnerving than the silent accumulating contempt and hatred of a people," wrote James Baldwin. "[The policeman] moves through Harlem, therefore, like an occupying soldier in a bitterly hostile country; which is precisely what and where he is."

It was Malcolm X who symbolized and gave voice to the frustrations and despair of northern ghettos. When the first riots broke out in Harlem in 1964 and Malcolm X was in Cairo, Egypt, at a conference, black teenagers roamed the streets shouting at police, "Malcolm! We want Malcolm! Wait till Malcolm comes."

McCoy had begun traveling uptown to Mosque Number 7

to hear Malcolm X speak in the early 1960s. McCoy's years in New York up until then had been years of frustration. He had grown up in Washington, D.C., and had watched as his mother, who worked as a cook for a white family, had to walk fourteen or fifteen miles in the winter snow when the buses weren't running. The whites who ran Washington simply cut off the bus service to the black neighborhoods whenever it snowed. McCoy had gone to all-black Howard University, the leading black school in the country. He was the first member of his family to go to college. His parents wanted him to be a professional man, a doctor perhaps. His own dream was to return to Howard and become its president, or at least its dean.

McCoy had come to New York to take graduate courses at New York University. But when he arrived in 1949, with his wife and fourteen dollars in savings, he soon realized he would have to get a job. He visited the city employment agency, walked up to the window labeled "professionals," and was given the address of a "600" school, a public school for teenagers considered too violent for regular classes.

The principal escorted him into a classroom, walked out, and shut the door. McCoy looked around. All the students were black. It was the meanest class, the class with the most incorrigible students. McCoy took off his jacket and draped it over the chair behind the teacher's desk.

"I'm here to stay," he announced. "You're going to do what I tell you to do. Every morning when I come in, I'm going to hang my jacket on the chair. That is my symbol that I am the boss. So if any of you decide that you want to be the boss, you're going to have to take my jacket off and suffer the consequences."

He had found a career. There were only a handful of black teachers in New York, and McCoy found it easy to move from "600" school to "600" school as a teacher. But he never rose as high as he wanted. Advancing in the New York City school system meant passing through a maze of standardized tests. The tests, the courts would rule later, often had little to do with teaching and administrative ability and often served to keep out black and Puerto Rican candidates. Nevertheless, for a teacher with dreams of advancing like McCoy, the road lay through those tests, and through cram courses run by other teachers, principals, and administrators—most of them Jewish. Just about all the teachers, principals, and supervisors McCoy came in contact with were Jewish. Friends of McCoy encouraged him to swallow his pride and take the cram courses. McCoy himself believed that if you signed up for a course, the administrators would make sure you passed the test. The fix was in. He wouldn't do it. For years he was classified only as a substitute teacher because he refused to take the tests. He would not play their game.

Malcolm X had a powerful impact on McCoy. Soon McCoy was visiting Malcolm in his home on Long Island. McCoy found the private Malcolm quiet and passive, a thinker, friendly. But beneath that quiet lay a vibrant man, full of conviction. You could hear it in his voice. Malcolm wouldn't knuckle under to the system. McCoy would travel to Malcolm's house with several friends—Herman Ferguson and Sonny Carson, both of whom would become key figures in New York's Black Power movement—and talk about educating black young people. McCoy believed Malcolm X had a network of thinkers, lawyers, and fund-raisers that he could draw on. He wasn't as isolated on the fringe as many in the white community liked to think. It would scare whites, McCoy thought, if they could see just how organized Malcolm X and the Black Muslims were.

In those conversations on Long Island, McCoy crystallized his thinking about education. He wanted black kids to understand the things he had come to understand: the way whites controlled the system, the way blacks had to take control of their own lives. Like Paul Parks, McCoy had grown up in a neighborhood where the local store was owned by Jews. The lesson for him was not, as it had been for Parks, that the Jewish merchant sometimes helped you out. Nor was the lesson, as it was for many in Harlem, that the Jewish storeowner overcharged or sneaked a few cents out of every welfare check he cashed. The question of overcharging or not overcharging was irrelevant to McCoy. His question was: Why didn't blacks support their own mom-and-pop store, run by black people for black people? McCoy wanted to change people's attitudes, and that meant reaching young people and freeing up their minds. This was McCoy's goal: to free up the minds of black young people. "You may have to clean floors," he would tell them, "but that ain't got nothing to do with how you think."

Ossie Davis, describing why he gave a eulogy at Malcolm X's funeral in 1965 after Malcolm X was gunned down by assassins

---

. . . Whatever else he was or was not—Malcolm was a man!

White folks do not need anybody to remind them that they are men. We do! This was his one incontrovertible benefit to his people.

Protocol and common sense require that Negroes stand back and let the white man speak up for us, defend us, and lead us from behind the scene in our fight. This is the essence of Negro politics. But Malcolm said the hell with that! Get up off your knees and fight your own battles. That's the way to make the white man respect you. And if he won't let you live like a man, he certainly can't keep you from dying like one!

Malcolm, as you can see, was refreshing excitement; he scared hell out of the rest of us, bred as we are to caution, to hypocrisy in the presence of white folks, to the smile that never fades. Malcolm knew that every white man in America profits directly or indirectly from his position vis-à-vis Negroes, profits from racism even though he does not practice it or believe in it.

. . . Now we all knew these things as well as Malcolm did, but we also knew what happened to people who stick their necks out and say them. And if all the lies we tell ourselves by way of extenuation were put into print, it would constitute one of the greatest chapters in

the history of man's justifiable cowardice in the face of other men.

But Malcolm kept snatching our lies away. He kept shouting the painful truth we whites and blacks did not want to hear from all the housetops. And he wouldn't stop for love nor money.

Malcolm X was assassinated in 1965, but his influence grew in the years after his death. McCoy and Malcolm X had never talked directly about Jews in their conversations. Their focus was on education. But the growing militancy among blacks transformed the way many blacks looked at Jews. Whereas the civil rights movement up through the mid-1960s had operated with the assumption of Jews as friends, this increasingly nationalist movement began with the assumption of Jews as the enemy.

For Malcolm X and the Muslims, part of this was religious and stemmed from their ideology: "The Jews, with the help of Christians in America and Europe, drove our Muslim brothers out of their homeland, where they had been settled for centuries, and took over the land for themselves," said Malcolm X. "This every Muslim resents. . . . In America, the Jews sap the very life-blood of the so-called Negroes to maintain the state of Israel, its armies, and its continued aggression against our brothers in the East. This every Black Man resents."

For some black intellectuals, the history of Jewish involvement in black scholarship, black entertainment, civil rights organizations, and, especially, left-wing politics symbolized a colonization of black thought and creativity. These views received their most explicit airing in Harold Cruse's 1967 book, *The Crisis of the Negro Intellectual.* Cruse argued that Jews in the Communist Party, with their rigid position on the "Negro question," had stifled the intellectual development of the black community, preventing black intellectuals from coming

up with black solutions to black problems. The pattern was
repeated, Cruse charged, in unions with Jewish leadership, in
the film and publishing industry with Jewish editors and pro-
moters, in civil rights organizations like the NAACP with
Jewish contributors and Jews on the boards of directors. "There
are far too many Jews from Jewish organizations into whose
privy councils Negroes are not admitted, who nevertheless are
involved in every civil rights and American-African organization, creating policy and otherwise analyzing the Negro from
all possible angles," Cruse wrote. "No matter what motivates
such activity, the Negro in America will never achieve any
kind of equality until more Negro intellectuals are equipped
with the latest research and propaganda techniques to move
into control and guidance of every branch of the Negro movement."

A sour mood had descended on many blacks in the civil
rights movement—especially younger blacks—disappointed
and disillusioned with the Jewish response to Black Power,
especially the decision by organizations like SNCC and CORE
to expel white members and become exclusively black-led and
black-controlled. By the time McCoy and Parks began talking
in the fall of 1967, riots had ripped apart Newark and Detroit.
In 1966 they had broken out on Chicago's West Side, despite
strong efforts by King—who had moved into a slum apartment
on the West Side to symbolize his concern for the black
poor—to stop them. The "beloved community" of King had
become the ravaged ghetto. The songs of the Freedom Rides
had been replaced by the smoke of the riots.

The arrival of the civil rights movement in the North also
meant reopening festering hostility and distrust toward Jews
who worked and owned property in black ghettos. In the South,
the enemy had been clear: white racists, southern sheriffs, the
Klan. Jews had little power. King had focused attention on the
national struggle, on changing the attitudes of government
and of whites. But in Harlem, on the West Side of Chicago,
in Watts, in Los Angeles, or in Roxbury in Boston, the world
view often extended only as far as the neighborhood. And the
people in the neighborhood with power, with the most im-

mediate impact on black life, were often Jews. On the eve of the worst rioting, according to the Kerner Commission, Jews owned about 30 percent of the stores in black neighborhoods like Harlem and Watts; many of the largest stores that blacks frequented were owned by Jews or carried Jewish-sounding names: Blumstein's in Harlem, for example. A popular saying in the 1960s went: Of the five people that a black meets in the course of the day—his landlord, the storeowner, the social worker, the teacher, the cop—one, the cop, is Irish. The other four are Jews. There was nothing new in this economic tension between blacks and Jews; James Baldwin had written about it in 1948 and Kenneth Clark several years before that. But while the struggle was in the South, no one paid much attention and anger was buried. As the civil rights struggle moved north, the tensions were primed to break the surface.

These growing tensions between blacks and Jews existed in cities across the country. But nowhere were they—in no place could they be—as focused as in New York.

New York was the capital of black America, home to many of its most influential intellectuals and thinkers. A camera sweeping across New York in 1967 would have found a cauldron of black nationalist feelings: in Greenwich Village, the poet and playwright LeRoi Jones demanded "Black Art"; up in Harlem, followers of Malcolm X plowed the streets for converts, and even those uninterested in becoming Muslims were captivated by his *Autobiography*; in Brooklyn, the local CORE chapter, far more radical than the national CORE, preached a combination of militancy and Marxism that showed less and less of a commitment to nonviolence.

New York was also the capital of Jewish America, home to most Jewish intellectuals and leaders, to the major Jewish "defense" organizations like the Anti-Defamation League, the American Jewish Congress, and the American Jewish Committee. It was home as well to the largest concentration of middle-class and working-class Jews in the country. Many had found jobs and security teaching in the public schools. Up through the 1940s, New York's school bureaucracy and classrooms had been run mostly by Irish teachers and supervisors.

Following the Second World War, however, Jews graduating from the public city colleges had poured into the system, valuing its job security and good benefits. By 1967 approximately two-thirds of New York's teachers, supervisors, and principals were Jewish.

Just as conditions and attitudes had changed dramatically for blacks between 1964 and 1967, so had they for Jews. Jews were unhappy with the rising militancy and anti-white sentiment emanating from the more militant parts of the civil rights movement. Frightened by the run-up to the 1967 war, when Israel seemed imperiled, and now basking in the glory of the victory of the Six-Day War, they were more attuned than ever to threats to their interests and more confident in their ability to beat those threats back. Most Jews in New York still considered themselves liberals, but like Italians in Canarsie and working-class whites in Queens, they were becoming scared. Crime had skyrocketed in the 1960s, rising faster than at any time since the 1930s. In 1960, narcotics were blamed for 200 deaths in New York, the most ever recorded. By 1967, narcotics were killing 700 New Yorkers a year, and robberies and muggings tied to drugs had also increased. In 1966, Mayor Lindsay proposed establishing a civilian review board to consider complaints of police brutality. With the eruption of the slogan "Black Power," the forthcoming election quickly became a referendum on "law and order" and the fear of crime. Most liberal unions and reform groups, and the major Jewish organizations, backed the proposal. Conservatives and the police opposed it. When November came, the civilian review board was defeated. Polls showed that a majority of Jews had voted against it. The heaviest Jewish opposition was in Brooklyn and Queens, where working- and middle-class Jews lived.

The rising black militancy was demanding power, real power. To many Jews, these demands for economic equality threatened them. Tensions were roiling in ghettos, in civil rights organizations, in black and Jewish neighborhoods across the city.

Into this cauldron stepped Rhody McCoy.

* * *

The Rev. C. Herbert Oliver was becoming increasingly concerned with the marks on his son's report card in the fall of 1966. A carefully groomed man whose politeness belied the toughness that had led him to stays in several southern jails while protesting segregation, Oliver had moved from Birmingham, Alabama, to Brooklyn with his family in 1965. After six years as head of the Inter-Citizens Committee of Birmingham, documenting civil rights violations, Oliver had seized the chance to return to the ministry by taking over a church in the Ocean Hill–Brownsville section of Brooklyn. Ocean Hill–Brownsville was a yoked-together neighborhood that linked the working-class Ocean Hill with desperately poor Brownsville. Ocean Hill took its name from its hilly streets; people said that from the top of the brownstones you could see Coney Island and the ocean just beyond. But by the time Oliver arrived, the land below was a land of desperation. There were some blocks of pleasant, owner-occupied homes, but most families lived in deteriorating rooming houses and tenements. Less than one-third of the adults in Ocean Hill–Brownsville had finished high school. One half of the households subsisted on less than $5,000 a year.

In Birmingham, Oliver's son had been reading a year ahead of grade level. After a year in his new school, the boy was bringing home failing grades from his seventh-grade class. It was time to speak to the principal.

Oliver walked over to the school and headed for the principal's office. A man who was clearly not the principal gruffly asked him what he wanted. Oliver told him.

"The principal is not here," the man said.

"I'll wait," said Oliver, and took a seat. A half-hour later the principal came in and Oliver told him that his son had been reading above grade level in Birmingham but that here in Brooklyn he was failing courses and wasn't bringing home any homework.

The principal sent Oliver to the boy's teacher. The teacher said Oliver's son was doing fine.

"But he's bringing home failing grades," Oliver said.

"He's doing fine," the teacher said.

This was not the way things were done in Birmingham. Back in Birmingham, the teachers and principals who taught Oliver's children lived in the neighborhood; some went to his church. If Oliver was worried about his son's performance, he could go right up to the principal and find out what was wrong. Here in Brooklyn there were only a handful of black teachers and no black principals at all. No one seemed to care about his son. It looked to Oliver as if the young black students were being used as a training ground for white teachers to get experience before moving on.

Oliver hadn't planned to get involved in civil rights up North; he had come to Brooklyn to get involved in the ministry. Any thoughts he had of taking on discrimination and racism in the North had been quenched that summer as he watched his colleague Martin Luther King frustrated again and again in his battles with Mayor Richard Daley of Chicago. Southern boys were better on their home turf, Oliver had concluded. But the treatment of his son angered him. When a group of parents and teachers in Brownsville, upset with the same issues that troubled Oliver, asked him to join in their fight for greater control over the schools in Ocean Hill–Brownsville, he agreed. In later years, as his son dropped out of school and turned to drugs, he would blame the troubles that started in the seventh grade in Brownsville.

It was schools in the South that blacks felt had imposed the system of segregation from the time a child was five or six; it was schools in the North, many blacks felt, that walled children inside the hopelessness and poverty of the ghetto. Back in 1954, a few weeks after the Supreme Court outlawed school segregation, Kenneth Clark, the NAACP Legal Defense Fund's star witness, had charged that New York's schools were segregated, with all-black schools having fewer experienced teachers and crammed into older, poorly maintained buildings. Over the next ten years, city officials proposed plan after plan to integrate the schools. Conditions for black students just got worse. By 1966, standardized reading tests showed black twelve-year-olds reading two years behind white twelve-year-olds. In a city where over half the students were black or Hispanic, the school teaching staffs and administration were overwhelmingly white and Jewish. Only 8 percent of the teachers were black. There were no black high school principals, and only a handful of black school administrators. By contrast, 90 percent of the teachers in Washington, D.C., and 30 percent of the teachers in Philadelphia were black. There were good teachers, but there were many teachers who were paternalistic, culturally insensitive, and unable to respond to the needs of poor black children. They considered themselves good liberals, but they did not understand the growing demands of blacks, and would never understand them.

This anger over the state of the schools coalesced over the opening of Intermediate School 201, a school for grades four through eight that opened in Harlem in 1966. Parents demanded that the Board of Education appoint a black principal. The Board of Education refused. In New York, as McCoy had learned, teachers were hired and principals were promoted by means of an exam system that churned out lists of candidates ranked by test scores and seniority. When it came time to name a principal for I.S. 201, the Board of Education pulled out its principal list and appointed Stanley Lisser, a well-regarded Jewish principal who headed another school in Harlem. Parents boycotted the school in protest, but eventually classes resumed and Lisser was the principal.

John Lindsay had been elected in 1965 as a liberal mayor and had made his reputation by keeping the streets cool as riots broke out in other parts of the country. Nelson Rockefeller was New York's liberal Republican governor planning a run for President in 1968. McGeorge Bundy, a protégé of John F. Kennedy's, had recently left Washington for New York to take over the Ford Foundation, one of the richest in the country. In the wake of growing demands for black control and the fury and publicity surrounding the appointment of a principal at I.S. 201, all three agreed that something had to be done to help the schools and meet growing discontent among black parents. Lindsay appointed Bundy to head up a panel to study the school system. In 1967 the "Bundy report," writ-

ten by Ford Foundation official Mario Fantini, proposed decentralization—breaking up the school system into smaller
neighborhood districts and electing community boards to run
the schools close to their homes. This would give parents more
of a stake in their children's schools and make the school
system more accountable, its supporters believed. It was agreed
that three school districts would be created to test decentralization in practice.

Ocean Hill–Brownsville was a natural candidate. Parents
had been organizing there for over a year together with concerned white teachers, led by Sandra Feldman, a Jewish representative with the teachers' union, the United Federation
of Teachers, and former member of CORE. With the help of
a grant from the Ford Foundation, the Ocean Hill–Brownsville
parents organized themselves into a school governing board
in the summer of 1967. The board included teachers, parents,
and community representatives from the neighborhood. Reverend Oliver was named the chairman. Like the parents at I.S.
201, the Brooklyn parents insisted that the head of their new
experimental district be black. Edith Gaines, a black junior
high school principal in Manhattan, recommended that the
parents interview McCoy, then an acting principal at a "600"
school in Manhattan.

McCoy's great strength was that he had credentials that
could satisfy everyone. He was black, and an advocate of black
control. He had solid educational credentials after eighteen
years with the school system. He did not object to whites
teaching or even being principals in the schools. He just wanted
to make sure that the black parents could choose the people
doing the teaching and oversee what was being taught. That
was important.

The national mood of black militancy—which wanted to
sever connections with whites altogether—had its local
expressions. There was Brooklyn CORE, headed by Robert
Carson, known as Sonny Carson, whom McCoy knew from
his days talking with Malcolm X. Carson always traveled with
"bodyguards," large, tough-looking men who intimidated whites
and scared many white teachers. There was also the Afro-

American Teachers' Association, formed in 1964 and centered in Brooklyn's schools. Several of the group's leaders, including Les Campbell, who was being transferred into the Ocean Hill district, were openly anti-Semitic. The group's official publication included articles like this: "We are witnessing today in New York City a phenomenon that spells death for the minds and souls of our black children. It is the systematic coming of age of the Jews who dominate and control the educational bureaucracy of the New York public school system, and their power-starved imitators, the black Anglo-Saxons. . . . In short our children are being mentally poisoned by a group of educators who are actively and persistently bringing a certain self-fulfilling prophecy to its logical conclusion." From the day he came into Ocean Hill–Brownsville, McCoy would have to keep a wary eye on this militant left flank.

McCoy understood the value of playing different roles for different audiences. At one moment, he could puff on his pipe and be the educational philosopher, delivering talks at Harvard on the future of educational change. The next moment he could slip comfortably into "street talk" with double negatives and slang expressions. McCoy could be a compromiser, persuading militants to go along with "the system" if the alternative was defeat. Or he could stir people to stiffen their resolve. He kept his own anger buried. Even twenty years after the Ocean Hill–Brownsville experiment, whites who had worked closely with him did not know of his admiration for and early dealings with Malcolm X.

Oliver and the parents liked the fact that McCoy had worked with troubled kids in the "600" schools. They believed he would not be thrown by coming into Ocean Hill–Brownsville with its high poverty rate. The teachers on the community board, while they would have preferred the selection of Jack Bloomfeld, a popular Jewish principal in the district, were impressed with McCoy's pipe-smoking thoughtfulness. The Ford Foundation's Mario Fantini thought that of all the people he had met, McCoy had the best grasp of the task at hand: making the public schools accountable to the people they served.

Oliver and the Ocean Hill–Brownsville Board had summoned McCoy to be interviewed for a job as director of summer programs or perhaps a principal's job at one of the
neighborhood schools. But he soon was being offered the district's top job, administrator of the entire experimental district.

What should have been clear from the start was that McCoy,
Oliver, and the parents of Ocean Hill–Brownsville had vastly
different expectations of what the experiment meant than did
the New York Board of Education, the Ford Foundation, or the
teachers and administrators in the schools.

The difference was evident in the way people referred to the
program. The Board of Education and the teachers called it
"decentralization"—chopping away at the bureaucracy so that
each district could get more resources. The teachers hoped
that Ocean Hill–Brownsville would be able to lobby for more
funds, for smaller classes and better equipment. Fantini and
the Ford Foundation talked about creating a coalition of neighborhood parents and teachers that would battle against the
system on behalf of the children. Teachers and parents would
work together for the education of the kids.

But McCoy and the Ocean Hill–Brownsville parents spoke
of "community control"—the right of the black community,
at last, to control who educated their children and what their
children were taught; to provide black and Puerto Rican role
models for their children; to make the teachers accountable,
just as the teachers in Reverend Oliver's church in Birmingham were accountable when he would go up to them to discuss
the progress of his son. Many blacks in Ocean Hill–Brownsville were not interested in coalitions. What the city and Board
of Education saw as a fresh start for education, many in Ocean
Hill–Brownsville saw as the system's last chance. "Men are
capable of putting an end to what they find intolerable without
recourse to politics," the Ocean Hill–Brownsville board said
in a statement in the summer of 1967 announcing its goals
for the school year. "The ending of oppression and the beginning of a new day has often become a reality only after people
have resorted to violent means. . . . The following plan . . . is

acknowledged to be the last threads of the community's faith in the school system's purposes and abilities."

The educational revolution began in a storefront. The Board of Education put McCoy in a small, unheated triangular office, while they tried to find a larger office for him to use. Throughout most of the fall, McCoy worked there, without heat, trying to put his and the community board's plans into action.

The first obstacle he faced was a citywide school strike. Several issues had led the teachers to walk out: demands for more funding, smaller classes, and the power to expel "disruptive" children. The disruptive-child issue was fraught with racial overtones—most of the children being expelled would be black, most of the teachers doing the expelling would be white. But no matter what the issues, the newly empowered people of Ocean Hill were not going to start their experiment by closing the schools. On the eve of the strike Albert Shanker, the union president, came to McCoy and the board and reminded them that the union had backed the Ocean Hill–Brownsville experiment. He asked for their support in the strike.

Shanker was the son of Jewish immigrant parents and had grown up at a time when Father Coughlin spewed his anti-Semitic statements from the radio. As a student at the University of Illinois, he had participated in the earliest CORE sit-ins in the late 1940s, and as a graduate student in New York had joined a picket line in front of Palisades Amusement Park when the amusement park would not allow blacks in. Shanker's creed was simple: Anybody who hated Jews hated blacks; anybody who hated blacks hated Jews. After becoming president of the teachers' union, in 1964, Shanker had kept the union in the mainstream of civil rights protests. He had raised money for Freedom Summer and had flown to Alabama in 1965 to join King on the march from Selma to Montgomery.

Now, however, Shanker was speaking as a union leader. Over the previous year he had become disillusioned with the tack the civil rights movement was taking. When black parents objected to the appointment of a Jewish principal at I.S. 201 in Harlem, Shanker called up Bayard Rustin and asked him to ask King to lead a protest march in Harlem. Here was a perfect way to show the civil rights movement wasn't just for blacks, Shanker argued. Come out and support a man being discriminated against by black racists because he is white. After meeting with black leaders, Rustin said such a march wouldn't be possible. Shanker felt betrayed. Here he and other white liberals had marched for blacks, but blacks would not march for whites.

McCoy listened quietly to Shanker's presentation in support of a strike. After Shanker left, he exploded. "Fine," he told the board members. "I don't want to give you a choice and waste my goddamn time. I'm going back to Manhattan to get my old school ready. I mean it's that simple. Because if you're not going to operate, you've already acknowledged the fact that somebody else controls you. That's the game. These are our schools. We decide what the hell we're gonna do."

Ocean Hill kept its schools open, hiring 500 substitute teachers, mostly newly minted college graduates seeking draft deferments to avoid going to Vietnam.

As the city negotiated with the teachers' union, McCoy prepared to put his educational plans into action. The grand plan, drawn from those conversations years earlier with Malcolm X, was to create an all-black part of the school system, with elementary and junior high schools in Ocean Hill tied into a high school and a college. McCoy set his sights on Boys' High in Brooklyn, which he hoped might be turned over to black control, and newly opened Medgar Evers Community College. Community control, decentralization—he didn't care what they called it. McCoy wanted blacks to take that segment of the educational system where the black kids were and control it.

In Ocean Hill–Brownsville his top priority was naming new principals to fill several vacancies. The exam system that McCoy detested required that he select principals from a civil service list, but the list included only a handful of black candidates. So McCoy and the community board received permission to modify the requirements, allowing McCoy to appoint a Hispanic principal and two black principals—one of them

Herman Ferguson, his friend from his days in Malcolm X's living room.

The Ferguson appointment created a blaze of controversy. Ferguson had joined an extremist organization and two months earlier had been indicted for conspiring to kill Roy Wilkins, the executive director of the NAACP, and Whitney Young, head of the National Urban League. McCoy thought the charges were trumped up; so did Oliver. It wouldn't be the first time an outspoken black was railroaded into prison. Both men believed that Ferguson, at the least, deserved his day in court, and was innocent until proven guilty.

For the teachers, the Ferguson appointment confirmed their worst fears about black militants taking over the schools. Ocean Hill–Brownsville was a typical school district in that most of its teachers and principals were Jews. Many had taught in the schools for years, and they believed they were doing the best for the kids. Most, the men especially, worked two jobs, often teaching in after-school programs to supplement their salaries. The annual teacher's salary of between $8,000 and $16,000 a year was not enough to support a family. Politically, most of the teachers considered themselves civil rights liberals. In the fall of 1967, the first fall of decentralization, the head of the local union chapter in Ocean Hill–Brownsville was Fred Nauman, a Jewish refugee from Nazi Germany who held a membership in the NAACP.

Nauman considered himself more liberal than many of his colleagues. He had backed the civilian review board and winced when some of the more conservative teachers talked ominously about the WASP elite, headed by Lindsay, joining forces with black militants to strip them of their jobs. Nauman had been troubled in the months leading up to McCoy's appointment. The teachers, he believed, had been promised a full voice in the decentralization plan and in the selection of a district administrator. That hadn't happened. The teachers who spoke at the community board meetings were often ignored or insulted. There were secret meetings of black and Puerto Rican members of the community board. On the fringes stood militants like Sonny Carson. Still, Nauman was ready to give McCoy the benefit of the doubt. But to work for a man like Ferguson was inconceivable.

Under pressure from the teachers and in a storm of bad publicity, the Ferguson appointment was blocked. The city-wide school strike was settled, but in Ocean Hill–Brownsville relations between the teachers and McCoy and the community board continued to deteriorate. Barely a few weeks into the school year, the teachers pulled their representatives from the community board and decided to join in a lawsuit demanding the ouster of the new Ocean Hill–Brownsville principals. In February 1968, Jack Bloomfeld, the popular principal of Nauman's school, Junior High School 271, transferred out of the district—along with thirty teachers, representing a quarter of the teaching staff, and five of six secretaries. More and more teachers at the school began calling in sick. There were days when the school didn't have enough teachers to watch the children. From Junior High School 271 and other schools in the district, McCoy received reports that many teachers, including Nauman, were openly criticizing and ridiculing his plans.

McCoy plowed ahead. He went into Ocean Hill's schools to shake them out of what he saw as their lethargy in educating children. He visited with a group of social studies teachers and told them: "I don't want you reading the book to these kids. I don't want these kids reading the books. I want you to take them down to the courts, to the [state] assembly, take them where they can see, then you come back, you dissect it and talk about it." He hired 500 parents and community people to work as aides in the schools. Many had never stepped inside a school before.

The decision by McCoy and the Ocean Hill–Brownsville board to keep schools open during the teachers' strike had soured relations between the new district and many of the teachers. By the spring, teachers had another concern: rising militancy in the district, especially at Junior High School 271.

At the center of concern stood Les Campbell, one of the leaders of the Afro-American Teachers' Association. At J.H.S.

271, Campbell had formed an African-American Student Association. Nauman and several other white teachers believed it attracted the toughest kids in the school, those with the worst behavioral problems. Campbell used the association bulletin board to post Black Power broadsides, many of them anti-Semitic. When Nauman would protest to the principal that they be taken down, they would reappear on another bulletin board.

Tension built steadily throughout the year. It exploded the first day school opened after the assassination of Martin Luther King in April 1968.

Nauman walked into school that morning and found the walls plastered with signs: "They've killed him." "Whitey has killed our King." A leaflet taped to the school wall signed by the African-American Student Association read: "Wake up, black people ... Martin Luther King, a nonviolent man, a Nobel Peace Prize winner, has been savagely shot down by a vicious *white* man. Wake up! Please wake up before it's too late. As a black individual *prepare*!!! As a member of the black race *unite*!!!" The halls were in turmoil. Students were running everywhere. Nauman and many of the teachers were still in shock themselves from the news of King's death. They corraled the students they could and took them into classrooms. At 11:00 A.M. the principal called all classes down to the auditorium for an assembly to discuss the assassination.

Nauman led his classes downstairs and listened as several members of the Ocean Hill–Brownsville governing board spoke. Then the new black principal of J.H.S. 271 rose to say that the white teachers in the audience might want to leave before Campbell got up to speak. Nauman looked at several of the other white teachers and decided to walk out. But several whites stayed, and brought out notes of Campbell's speech. The notes chilled Nauman: "If whitey taps you on the shoulder," the notes read, "send him to the graveyard." "Don't steal from a brother. Don't steal a comb. Steal what you can use."

Pandemonium followed the meeting. Bands of students roamed the hallway. Three white teachers were caught alone in the hallway and attacked. One was hospitalized with a concussion. That night, more than fifty teachers called Nauman at home, saying they would never go back to J.H.S. 271. Nauman wondered whether he could ever go back either.

In the meantime, McCoy was feeling increasingly frustrated. The new black and Hispanic principals he had appointed were operating under a cloud, the validity of their appointments being challenged in court. Many of the teachers were rebelling against McCoy's directives; others were incompetent to teach the children. The Board of Education refused to give McCoy and the community board the power to fire disruptive teachers, hire good black teachers, and place parent aides in every class. Salary checks arrived late, requests for supplies were lost. From the neighborhood, McCoy was under pressure from militants like Carson, Ferguson, and Campbell to assert his power and force a confrontation with the city and the teachers.

McCoy believed he could keep control of the situation by transferring out some of the most disruptive teachers and fiercest opponents of community control. Many parents on the community board wanted to go further. They wanted to fire the teachers outright. Crucial to the dream of a community-controlled school system was the ability to hire and fire teachers. Why not confront the issue squarely?

McCoy persuaded them to compromise and try the transfer approach first. He and the community board assembled a list of the teachers and supervisors they believed were most hostile to the experiment. There were thirteen teachers, including Nauman, five assistant principals, and the one remaining principal not appointed by the community board. On Friday, May 8, McCoy sent the nineteen letters, saying the community board had voted to "terminate their employment" in Ocean Hill–Brownsville. The dismissed teachers and supervisors were to report to Board of Education headquarters the following Monday for reassignment.

No one on the community board took much notice that almost all the dismissed teachers and supervisors were Jewish.

Jason Epstein writing in The New York Review of Books, *March 1969*

By a grotesque accident of history the drama of decentralization has begun to play itself out in New York as a conflict between Jews and blacks for the simple (and pathetic) reason that one of New York's most malignant and vulnerable bureaucracies happens to be its school system, which is controlled not by Stalinist bureaucrats or Cromwellian Ulstermen or complacent Gaullist deputies, but by Jewish liberals, whose antagonists turn out to be, of all people, the very ghetto residents whom these liberals had typically been proud to feel themselves the special benefactors. . . .

For no matter how decadent the school system may be, the teachers who have given their lives to it are human beings, vulnerable to the usual fears and delusions that affect people when the normal conditions of their lives are threatened with change. Nor is it simply a matter of fears and delusions, for there is also the question of self-esteem and the honest conviction on the part of many that they have, after all, given their best efforts, that they should therefore be protected from the animosity of parents who feel that these efforts have been insufficient.

McCoy guessed wrong. Although McCoy and the community board claimed they had simply transferred uncooperative employees, the teachers' union argued successfully that the teachers had, in fact, been dismissed and were, therefore, entitled to a hearing. Over the summer, a black arbitrator heard the charges against the ten teachers, including Nauman, who said they wanted to go back to Ocean Hill–Brownsville (the others either agreed to be transferred out or were removed from the community board's list). All the teachers were Jewish. The arbitrator found against McCoy in every case and ordered the district to take the teachers back. The 350 other teachers in Ocean Hill–Brownsville had already announced in May that they would not go back to work until the teachers were reinstated. Shanker now said he would take all 57,000 teachers out on strike and close down the city's school system.

McCoy and the community board refused to knuckle under. The Board of Education, the union, the so-called arbitrator— all were ganging up on Ocean Hill–Brownsville. They were concerned with "due process," and "academic freedom," but they didn't care about incompetent teachers who believed poor black children were "uneducable." For McCoy and the community board the issue was independence, the right to control the destiny of their children. The question of community control of the schools symbolized the struggle for self-determination, the battle of blacks against those who oppressed them. The NAACP and civil rights leaders like Bayard Rustin attacked McCoy for not being "moderate." What had moderation gotten black people, he responded? What had 100 years of "integration" in the North gotten them? Over the summer McCoy and the board used the refusal of union teachers to work in Ocean Hill–Brownsville to hire 350 replacement teachers—again, mostly recent college graduates, drawn to the drama of a black community trying to assert control over its own children and by the hope of doing good in a slum neighborhood.

Every teacher was interviewed by a group of parents. McCoy was struck by how simple the questions that the parents asked were:

"Are you afraid of black kids?"

"Can you come to my house?"

"Have you ever seen roaches on the floor?"

For all the talk of Black Power and fear of anti-Semitism, 70 percent of the teachers the community board chose were white. Half were Jewish. The important thing, McCoy emphasized over and over again, was that the neighborhood parents had selected them.

The teachers' union went out on strike. Within two days,

the Board of Education agreed to guarantee that the ten teachers plus all remaining union teachers who wanted to go back would be reinstated in Ocean Hill–Brownsville. McCoy refused to go along. The press descended on Ocean Hill–Brownsville to find out the "story." But the real story, McCoy believed, lay in the twenty years and more of neglect that had left parents in Ocean Hill–Brownsville at the end of their rope.

The day the teachers returned to Ocean Hill–Brownsville, McCoy summoned them to a meeting in the auditorium of the district's largest school. Supporters of the community board lined the walls. McCoy told the teachers that they were not wanted here and would not get class assignments. Outside, pickets yelled taunts at the teachers. Inside the auditorium, people chanted and jeered. McCoy told the teachers to go home. They walked out in single file, through a gauntlet of angry blacks.

Then the city snapped. For months, Shanker had been concerned by the persistent reports of anti-Semitism and intimidation in Ocean Hill–Brownsville. Shanker distrusted McCoy. He always seemed to be smoking his pipe and standing by quietly while militants like Ferguson and Sonny Carson ran around. If McCoy could dismiss teachers at his whim, then no teacher's job could be safe, especially—judging by the tenor of things in Ocean Hill–Brownsville—in a school system that was more than 50 percent minority and the teachers overwhelmingly white and Jewish. Shanker had to protect his people. As the second strike began in mid-September, Shanker received copies of leaflets that teachers said had been put in their mailboxes in the Ocean Hill–Brownsville schools. Shanker ordered 500,000 copies printed, to be distributed throughout the city. People should see, he said, what his teachers were up against.

One handout quoted an anonymous leaflet placed in teachers' mailboxes in Junior High School 271:

> If African American History and Culture is to be taught to our Black Children it Must be Done By African Americans who Identify With And Who Understand The Problem.

It Is Impossible For The Middle East Murderers of Colored People to Possibly Bring To This Important Task The Insight, The Concern, The Exposing Of The Truth That is a *Must* If The Years Of Brainwashing And Self-Hatred That Has Been Taught To Our Black Children By Those Bloodsucking Exploiters and Murderers Is To Be OverCome. The Idea Behind This Program Is Beautiful, But When The Money Changers Heard About It, They Took Over, As Is Their Custom In The Black Community, If African American History And Culture Is Important To Our Children To Raise Their Esteem Of Themselves, They Are The Only Persons Who Can Do The Job Are African-American Brothers And Sisters, And Not the So-Called Liberal Jewish Friend. We Know From His Tricky, Deceitful Maneuvers That He is Really Our Enemy and *He* is Responsible For The Serious Educational Retardation Of Our Black Children. We Call On All Concerned Black Teachers, Parents, And Friends to Write To The Board of Education, To the Mayor, To The State Commissioner of Education To Protest The Take Over Of This Crucial Program By People Who Are Unfit By Tradition And By Inclination To Do Even An Adequate Job.

Other union handouts reprinted statements by Les Campbell and anti-Semitic slurs that had circulated around the fringes of the Ocean Hill–Brownsville dispute.

As a device to win the strike, Shanker's decision to print the handouts was a brilliant tactical move. Overnight it changed the debate from one over community control and decentralization—over which many in the city, including Jews, were divided—into a debate over anti-Semitism in the black community. Are these the kind of things, Shanker asked, that you want said in your schools? Are these the kind of people you want running the schools and teaching children? In fact, as reporter Fred Feretti later reported, several of the union handouts were inaccurate, quoting statements out of context. None of the anti-Semitic leaflets represented official Ocean Hill–Brownsville policy. Both Sandra Feldman, who was Shanker's personal representative at Ocean Hill–Brownsville, and Nauman, who was the local chapter chairman, felt that reprinting the leaflets was a mistake. They believed the dispute was anti-white, not anti-Semitic. But they were not consulted.

In the forces it unleashed in New York, however, Shanker's decision to reprint the anti-Semitic leaflets and focus on the question of black anti-Semitism was devastating. The leaflets uncorked the fears and uneasiness among Jews that had been building up in recent years—the fear of anti-Semitism in civil rights organizations, the rise in black crime, the fear that blacks intended to take away Jewish jobs, the fear of violence. Stories filled the newspapers of threats and intimidations against teachers in Ocean Hill–Brownsville and other black communities. They vied for space with reports of student takeovers and violence at Columbia University and with stories of a plan to adopt "open admissions" at the City University of New York, alma mater to a generation of Jewish New Yorkers. "Open admissions" were necessary, it was said, to increase the number of blacks and Puerto Ricans enrolled. For middle- and upper-middle-class Jews, the debate over Ocean Hill–Brownsville in the context of such upheaval and change posed a painful dilemma. Was this what liberalism led to? Was anti-Semitism part of the black experience? The old rules no longer seemed to apply. For poor and working-class Jews, the plight of the teachers resonated directly. Every morning he woke up after receiving his letter of transfer from McCoy, Fred Nauman worried that the union might lose the fight, that he would be considered unemployable as a teacher, that he would have to change careers. His oldest child was only in elementary school. Working-class Jews and Jews not far removed from working class could identify with that. Jewish teachers were being asked to make way for blacks. Where were they supposed to go? And who would be next?

McCoy believed—and many Jews supporting him agreed—that the charges of black anti-Semitism were a smoke screen designed to rally support for the strike. Shanker was on the ropes. He would do anything to win the strike. The union was predominantly Jewish; black anti-Semitism was the perfect issue with which to strike back, to keep the teachers in line and to rally support in the Jewish community. McCoy himself had never seen the anti-Semitic leaflets the teachers said were being put in their mailboxes. He had been told the teachers were putting them in themselves. Jewish organizations kept demanding that he denounce the leaflets, that he make statements. He refused. That would be playing Shanker's game, playing on Jewish fears, rather than confronting the real issues which were community power and control.

As the reprints of anti-Semitic handbills appeared in more and more neighborhoods and the charges of black anti-Semitism in Ocean Hill–Brownsville grew stronger, McCoy met with a group of 100 rabbis. They demanded he make a statement denouncing anti-Semitism in Ocean Hill–Brownsville. He responded: "Go on TV with me and say you are 100 percent opposed to anti-black statements and I'll say I'm 100 percent opposed to anti-Semitism." The rabbis declined. McCoy refused to do it alone.

McCoy was convinced that he was not anti-Semitic. Half the 350 substitute teachers he and the community board had hired to replace the striking union teachers were Jewish. They had even taken out an advertisement in *The New York Times* to denounce the charges of anti-Semitism. One of his closest friends during the strike was Alan Colvin, a reading specialist that McCoy brought into the district, a man so dedicated to Israel that in later years he would serve volunteer stints in the Israeli army. McCoy's lawyer was Morton Stavis, the Jewish civil rights activist who had helped mount the challenge to the Mississippi Democratic Party in 1964.

Oliver couldn't understand the charges of anti-Semitism either. Every day on his way to church he would pass a Jewish Yeshiva school, a remnant of the days when Brownsville had been a Jewish neighborhood. Every day he watched as the Yeshiva boys walked into the school, or gathered outside talking. No one ever shouted anything at them. No one paid them much mind at all. How could Ocean Hill–Brownsville be riven with anti-Semitism, he asked himself?

Both men believed that the real issue here was power, and on that issue they would not compromise. Even if McCoy was inclined to compromise, the more militant members of Ocean Hill–Brownsville would not let him. "I can't in a public meeting put down somebody," McCoy told Mario Fantini at one point during the strike. "You have to understand—for me to maintain my credibility, I have to work with both worlds." As the strike dragged on, McCoy felt the entire power structure of New York—not just the union—turning against him. McCoy and the community board would not take back the dismissed teachers and they would not give up control over their schools. The only way the Board of Education could force them to give up would be to kick them out of office.

Which in the end is what the city did. On November 17, after two months of strikes, the Board of Education suspended the Ocean Hill–Brownsville community board and placed the district under the supervision of a state-appointed trustee. The union teachers who still wanted to work in Ocean Hill–Brownsville returned to their jobs. The principals the Ocean Hill–Brownsville Board had appointed were removed from their schools. McCoy's conversation with Parks had turned prophetic. He would not be a slave with everything. He would rather be a free man with nothing at all.

Rabbi Meier Kahane, founder of the Jewish Defense League, speaking in 1969. The JDL was formed in Brooklyn in September 1968

This city is polarized almost beyond hope—there's anger, hate, frustration. . . . The Jew is the weakest link in the white chain, and the black militant knows that few non-Jews are concerned with the Jew's plight. The Jew has always been more liberal than other white ethnic groups. So now most Jewish neighborhoods are integrated, and the militant blacks there practice terror, extortion and violence. The establishment Jew is scandalized by us, but our support comes from the grass-root. . . . [Criticism of the JDL] almost always comes from a rich Jew who lives in Scarsdale or some other rich suburb. How can a rich Jew or non-Jew criticize an organization

*of lower- and middle-class Jews who daily live in terror
because of the breakdown of government?*

The bitterness in Ocean Hill–Brownsville, and throughout
the city, lingered. In the fall of 1968, Julius Lester, a black
writer who ran a weekly radio show on WBAI, decided to visit
Ocean Hill–Brownsville to investigate stories he had heard of
Jewish teachers calling black children "nigger." There had
been much talk of black anti-Semitism during the strike; Lester believed there was Jewish racism as well. A musician as
well as a writer, endowed with a rich singing voice, Lester had
joined the movement in New York in the early 1960s as a
singer at SNCC fund-raisers. In 1964, during Freedom Summer, he headed south to sing at the Freedom Schools run by
white and black students from the North. He became more
and more involved with SNCC as it entered its radical phase,
culminating in the replacement of John Lewis with Stokely
Carmichael.

The Jewish response to the rising black nationalism and
Black Power had angered Lester. Black nationalism was a form
of Zionism, Lester believed. If anyone should understand the
importance of running your own organization, controlling your
fate, it should be the Jews. Yet here they were lecturing blacks
and warning them. Jews had always put themselves forward
in the civil rights movement as people who understood suffering because they had suffered. With the creation of Israel,
Jews now had a home of their own. Why, Lester asked, couldn't
Jews understand that blacks wanted an organization of their
own? By 1967, when he moved back to New York, Lester felt
that Stokely Carmichael was right when he told whites—and
Jews—to go organize in their own communities, examine racism in their own hearts and actions.

When Lester went out to Ocean Hill–Brownsville, he was
surprised to find that more than 50 percent of the teachers
hired by the community board were Jewish. He interviewed
several of the teachers and taped a class taught by Les Camp-

bell. Campbell struck him as a very good teacher and Lester invited him to appear on the live, call-in portion of his show on Thursday night, December 26. Too often, Lester felt, black people were only allowed on the air in an adversary environment. Lester wanted a relaxed environment where Campbell and others could say what was on their minds.

Campbell came to the show and brought with him several poems written by his students. Lester picked out one, written by a fifteen-year-old and dedicated to Albert Shanker, and said, "I want you to read this on the air."

"You got to be crazy," Campbell said.

"I want you to read this on the air so people know what feelings the strike has produced in one black child," Lester told him.

Campbell started reading:

Hey, Jew boy, with that yarmulke on your head
You pale-faced Jew boy—I wish you were dead
I can see you, Jew boy—no you can't hide
I got a scoop on you—yeh, you gonna die
I'm sick of your stuff
Every time I turn 'round—you pushin' my head into the ground
I'm sick of hearing about your suffering in Germany
I'm sick about your escape from tyranny
I'm sick of seeing in everything I do
About the murder of 6 million Jews
Hitler's reign lasted for only fifteen years
For that period of time you shed crocodile tears
My suffering lasted for over 400 years, Jew boy
And the white man only let me play with his toys
Jew boy, you took my religion and adopted it for you
But you know black people were the original Hebrews
When the U.N. made Israel a free independent State
Little four- and five-year-old boys threw hand grenades
They hated the black Arabs with all their might
And you, Jew boy, said it was all right
Then you came to America, land of the free
And took over the school system to perpetuate white
    supremacy
Guess you know, Jew boy, there's only one reason you made it

You had a clean white face, colorless, and faded
I hated you, Jew boy, because your hangup was the Torah
And my only hangup was my color.

Over the next few hours, listeners called in, many objecting
to the poem. "That was a very ugly poem," one listener said.
"What was it about the poem that made you feel we should
have heard it? It aroused anger in me."

"People should listen to what a young black woman is ex-
pressing," Lester replied. "I hope that will properly cause people to do some self-examination and react as you have reacted.
An ugly poem, yes, but not one-half as ugly as what happened
in school strikes, not one one-hundredth as what some teachers said to some of those black children. I would hope that
you would not have the automatic reaction, but raise a few
questions inside yourself. I had it read over the air because I
felt what she said was valid for a lot of black people, and I
think it's time that people stop being afraid of it and stop
being hysterical about it."

Listeners continued to call in about the poem the following
Thursday. The Thursday after that, when Lester played a tape
of the poem again, no one called in. Lester felt the controversy
had run its course. He had done what he intended: given blacks
an uncensored forum to vent some of their feelings.

The following Monday, January 15, Shanker and the United
Federation of Teachers filed a complaint with the FCC about
the Lester programs. "WBAI-FM is being used to spread anti-
Semitic propaganda in general and attacks against New York
teachers in particular," the complaint charged. The complaint
made the front page of *The New York Times*. "This city is
going to have to decide whether its teachers are going to teach
anti-Semitism or understanding and brotherhood," Shanker
declared.

From that day on, Lester found himself labeled an anti-
Semite. The Anti-Defamation League and the New York Board
of Rabbis joined the teachers' union in their criticism of WBAI.
On the West Side of Manhattan, near his home, Lester was
handed a leaflet that carried his picture surrounded by swas-

tikas. His answering service recorded threats against his life. Robert Goodman, father of Andrew Goodman and president of the board of directors of WBAI, called a press conference to defend Lester, whom he had known for several years. Two months after the complaint was filed, the FCC dismissed it, saying comments made on Lester's show were protected by the First Amendment. They cited comments made by Lester on the show in late January in which Lester had explained the context of his airing the poem:

> In Germany, the Jews are the minority surrounded by a majority which carried out against them rather heinous crimes. In America, it is we who are the Jews. It is we who are surrounded by a hostile majority. It is we who are constantly under attack. There is no need for black people to wear yellow Stars of David on their sleeves; that Star of David is all over us. In the city of New York a situation exists where black people, being powerless, are seeking to gain a degree of power over their lives and in the institutions which affect their lives. It so happens that in many of those institutions, the people who hold the power are Jews. Now in the attempt to gain power, if there is resistance by Jews to that, then of course blacks are going to respond.

The FCC went on to quote Lester saying on air that he felt "confident that those who have listened to this program more than once know that I have an intense reverence for life; and likewise, an intense love of people."

But "the Jew-boy poem" and Lester's name remained linked. Almost twenty years after it had aired, many years after he had left New York, Lester said he was angry still. He would never be able to forgive Shanker for attacking him and calling him an anti-Semite.

McCoy stayed on in Ocean Hill–Brownsville for another year after the strike, largely a figurehead. He left to obtain a doctorate at the University of Massachusetts. There he wrote a bitter dissertation that dissected the strike and the events leading up to it. "There exists a predetermined script, established by racist, capitalist America, which makes the education of black, poor white, and Third World children in this country impossible," he wrote. "A violent revolution is necessary to have America's public institutions serve all of its people. . . . White Americans not only refuse to have their children educated with black children, but they refuse to have black children [educated] at all. . . . Because . . . education can be translated into socioeconomic power, no white community is about to educate its black population." After taking a series of jobs at the University of Massachusetts, and then at the University of the District of Columbia in Washington, D.C., McCoy settled in San Francisco, where his friends learned never to ask him about the events in New York in 1968 and 1969 and his feelings about education. He no longer wanted to talk about them.

A few months after the strike ended, Mario Fantini, the official at the Ford Foundation who had drawn up the original plan for decentralization, was invited to speak at a synagogue. As he had watched controversy engulf the city, Fantini had become convinced that he was watching a preview of the next fifteen years. McCoy had confounded the liberals. Instead of backing desegregation and integration, McCoy had demanded black control over black lives. Even more, he wanted control over white lives as well: the right to replace white principals with black principals, the right to hire, and fire, white teachers as well as black teachers. He wanted to scuttle an examination system that teachers and supervisors had based their careers on—but which had prevented blacks in any significant numbers from becoming schoolteachers. These issues, in the form of affirmative action and quotas, in challenges to civil service rules and fights with unions, in debates over seniority rules versus discrimination, would dominate the 1970s and 1980s. Jews, who had been at the cutting edge of black demands for freedom in the 1950s and 1960s, were now at the cutting edge of the next phase of black demands. Only this time it was they who were being cut.

Ocean Hill–Brownsville and the bitterness it created was part and preview of clashes that would recur between blacks and northern whites. In the early 1960s, northern liberals had watched with horror the twisted faces of southerners and the brutal assaults upon blacks during the days of desegregation and sit-ins. Here in Ocean Hill–Brownsville they came face to face with their own ambivalent, and sometimes ugly, feelings. They would confront it again when school busing began in Irish and Italian neighborhoods in Boston. They confronted it when Martin Luther King decided to march for integration in ethnic neighborhoods in Chicago.

But unlike other groups, blacks and Jews had once been joined in an alliance, and that is what made the fight over Ocean Hill–Brownsville so bitter and painful. Blacks did not expect much from southern whites. It was an uphill battle for King to convince them that they had to love the person who hated them. They did not expect much from northern working-class, ethnic groups either. But the Jews were different. They had supported the black freedom struggle and provided much of the money, legal advice, and press coverage. They proudly stood side by side with blacks. Now, in the North, when blacks looked to see who was marching beside them, the Jews were gone. Many were now on the other side.

Jews had never expected much from other whites either. Generations of anti-Semitism had conditioned them to look for anti-Semitism from the right, from the moneyed interests and WASP elites that kept them out of certain businesses and certain clubs. Now they heard anti-Semitism coming from the left, from a black movement they had supported and cheered on. What had happened to "black and white together"? What had happened to "Let my people go"?

The sound heard in New York in 1968 and 1969 was the sound of a coalition ripping itself apart.

Much of this analysis was still in the future when Fantini walked into the synagogue to speak in 1969. As he stepped to the podium, the congregation rippled with hostility. He gave his speech and asked for questions. One Jewish congregant asked why the Ford Foundation was deliberately fanning anti-Semitism among blacks as a continuation of the anti-Semitic ravings of Henry Ford. Another wanted to know what Fantini was doing to stop blacks from being anti-Semitic. The rabbi of the synagogue intervened, saying he believed that Shanker and the union had deliberately fanned fears of anti-Semitism. The congregation erupted. Fantini was shouted off the stage.

As he left the synagogue, he thought back to the role Jews and Jewish groups had played in the reform movement in New York. For decades, Jews had been the vital core of every liberal movement: school reform, civil rights, political change. When Fantini drew up the Bundy report that proposed school decentralization, he made the rounds of the major Jewish organizations: the American Jewish Congress, the Anti-Defamation League, the American Jewish Committee. All were very supportive. Now, with the angry shouts of the Jews inside the temple still ringing in his ears, Fantini knew that things had changed. Jews were no longer automatic members of the liberal and reform movements. The vital core was gone.

5

The Last White Liberals: Bernie and Roz Ebstein

Mario Fantini was right. The vital, almost reflex-like liberalism that had powered Jews into civil rights and other reform movements was being dissipated. By the end of the teachers' strike, polls in New York showed that 59 percent of Jews in the city believed blacks were moving "too fast" in their demands. Nationally, Jews remained loyal to the New Deal dreams of the Democratic Party. In the 1968 presidential election, they gave 81 percent of their vote to Hubert Humphrey, backing him against Richard Nixon. But the Jewish vote for Humphrey masked deep fissures below the surface; it represented more an affirmation of what had been than what was about to be. In local elections that raised the troublesome issues of crime, race, and "law and order," the Jewish vote was being siphoned off by more conservative candidates. In the 1969 race for mayor of New York City, Lindsay squeaked into office with only 42 percent of the vote, with Jews among the major defectors. In Los Angeles, the contrast was even more striking. In 1968, Jews backed Humphrey over Nixon by 86 percent to 13 percent. A year later, they voted for Tom

Bradley, a black ex-policeman, over conservative Sam Yorty, but only narrowly, by 51 percent to 49 percent. By 1972, conservative candidates, especially conservative Democrats, would be openly vying to pry Jews away from liberalism and the civil rights coalition, relying on growing distaste with the excesses of the 1960s and concern over crime and lawlessness.

They might succeed. But if they did, it was going to be without the help of Bernie and Roz Ebstein.

The Ebsteins had the kind of background that persuaded people that Jews were allergic to injustice. Bernie had been a child in Germany, nine years old, when the Nazis, in an anti-Semitic orgy, smashed the windows of Jewish-owned stores and desecrated synagogues and Jewish schools during Kristallnacht. Two days later, Bernie's father just missed being taken away by the Gestapo. His family fled to America. They settled in a small town in southern Illinois where, in Bernie's mind, the daily teachings of the wonders of American democracy clashed with the reality that it was dangerous for a black to be caught in town after sunset. During the Korean War, Bernie ran afoul of McCarthyism when his commanding officer at Fort Monmouth in New Jersey ordered him transferred to Anchorage, Alaska, because he had gone to a "pink" university, the University of Chicago. In the 1950s, Bernie joined the American Jewish Congress, the most liberal of the established Jewish groups and one that put civil rights high on its agenda. He had helped set up its chapter on the South Side of Chicago and enjoyed occasional forays into community activism and Chicago reform politics. A lean, almost ascetic-looking man, Bernie burned with a passion for civil rights that surprised people who thought of him as a mild-mannered engineer with a love for classical music.

Roz Ebstein was her husband's physical and emotional opposite. Large, talkative, and outgoing, she had grown up on Chicago's Jewish West Side. When she was eleven, her mother had taken her to a demonstration protesting the treatment of Jews in Europe. By the time she was fifteen she was going to protests on her own, demonstrating in front of the British Embassy for the creation of the state of Israel. She'd kept a picture of herself at that demonstration and would take it out to show to her children. Growing up, Roz had been a Labor Zionist, believing in the creation of a socialist Israel that would treat workers with dignity and respect. On domestic politics, she was a staunch Democrat. She first met Bernie when both were at the University of Chicago; the two wore their affiliation with the University of Chicago as a badge of respect and intellectual rigor. Roz felt it set them a little bit apart from everyone else, just as their Judaism set them apart. For Roz, fighting for civil rights for blacks was a religious imperative. Her favorite part of the Passover Seder, the ceremony that commemorates the liberation of the Jews from Egypt, came about halfway through the reading of the Haggadah when everyone gathered around the table declared, "In every generation, each Jew must look upon himself as though he, personally, was among those who went forth from Egypt." That made it clear to Roz where her loyalties lay, and she was the kind of person who fought for what she believed in.

In the summer of 1966—at a time when many liberal Jews were beginning to become disenchanted with the civil rights movement—the Ebsteins were putting on their walking shoes and getting ready to march in downtown Chicago with Martin Luther King. King had arrived in Chicago in January, determined to bring the civil rights movement north. He moved into a slum apartment in the Lawndale ghetto to symbolize his concern for poor blacks and to focus his demands on better housing, better jobs, and better education. Winter and spring had been full of frustrations and crisis. Mayor Richard Daley was obstinate in insisting that Chicago was solving its slum problems with urban renewal. He deftly deflected King's attempts to call the city to account.

On June 6, James Meredith was shot and wounded as he tried to walk across Mississippi. King flew down South to join a march led by Stokely Carmichael, the newly elected chairman of SNCC, and others to protest the shooting. It was during this march that Carmichael turned to a crowd in Greenwood, Mississippi, raised a clenched fist, and shouted: "The only way we gonna stop them white men from whuppin' us is to

take over. We been saying freedom for six years and we ain't
got nothin'. What we gonna start saying now is Black Power!"
King tried to get Carmichael to stop using those words, but
the phrase caught on like a grass fire. Soon it was not only on
the lips of most blacks—especially young urban blacks, like
those in Chicago—but Carmichael was defending it in articles
in *The New York Review of Books* and on television. King's
Chicago march, called for Sunday, July 10—"Freedom
Sunday!"—was an attempt to reinvigorate the Chicago campaign and regain control of a civil rights movement that was
starting to slip from King's influence.

The Ebsteins lived in a small wood-and-brick duplex house
on Ninety-seventh Street and Crandon in a small neighborhood known as Merionette Manor, on Chicago's Far South
Side—a white, middle-class neighborhood of bungalow tract
homes about 40 percent Catholic, 40 percent Jewish, and 20
percent Protestant. They could walk to their temple and to
the Jewish Community Center on Ninety-first Street. They
had lived there for seven years. The year before the King march,
in 1965, the first black family had moved in to Merionette
Manor. The Ebsteins had watched with distaste as an all-white
neighborhood bordering theirs—Trumbull Park—and even
Mayor Richard Daley's own neighborhood of Bridgeport had
greeted the attempt of blacks to move in with stonings, threats,
and fire bombings. Merionette Manor would be different. The
Ebsteins were determined their neighborhood was going to be
a model for integration.

It was wretchedly hot that July 10. The temperature soared
to ninety-eight degrees. More than a half million people jammed
the beaches. King's organizers had hoped for 100,000 marchers; only 30,000 turned out. Some of their friends thought the
Ebsteins were crazy. A few days before the march, Bernie, as
head of his local American Jewish Congress chapter, had attended an organizational meeting to plan the march and had
been seated just across from King. Bernie didn't say anything
during the meeting, but he swelled with pride that he had
been in the same room as Martin Luther King. As the march
moved slowly down State Street, Bernie and Roz carried a

banner that declared "American Jewish Congress." As they walked, Bernie noticed how the chants echoed off the buildings. They filed into Soldier Field, alongside Lake Michigan, and that day heard King speak demanding an end to police brutality, an end to job discrimination, and an end to the real estate discrimination practices that made Chicago the most residentially segregated city north of the Mason-Dixon line.

Rabbi Abraham Joshua Heschel, January 1963

The plight of the Negro must become our most important concern. Seen in the light of our religious tradition, the Negro problem is God's gift to America, the test of our integrity, a magnificent spiritual opportunity. . . .

It is not enough for us to exhort the Government. What we must do is set an example, not merely to acknowledge the Negro but to welcome him, not grudgingly, but joyously, to take delight in enabling him to enjoy what is due him. We are all Pharaohs or slaves of Pharaohs. It is sad to be a slave of a Pharaoh. It is horrible to be a Pharaoh.

Daily we should take account and ask: What have I done today to alleviate the anguish, to mitigate the evil, to prevent humiliation?

Let there be a grain of prophet in every man!

Chicago's segregation was obvious to anyone—black or white—who lived in the city or looked at a map. Blacks were crammed into two areas: the gradually expanding "Black Belt" that began just south of the downtown Loop, detoured briefly around the University of Chicago, and ran several miles southward; and the newer West Side ghetto where King had taken an apartment to symbolize his concern for the plight of poor people. Between the five-day Chicago riot of 1919—in which thirty-eight people were killed following the drowning of a black boy who swam into a whites-only bathing area—and

King's arrival in 1966, the black population of Chicago increased eightfold, from 109,458 to well over 800,000. Unlike the South, which segregated blacks by law, Chicago segregated them by a combination of private artifice, political maneuvering, and violence.

Up until 1948, blacks were kept out of middle-class white areas through use of racial covenants inserted into deeds that prevented a white homeowner from selling his home to a black. When the Supreme Court declared these covenants unconstitutional, real estate agents simply refused to sell homes to blacks in all-white blocks. A survey of 241 white savings and loan associations in Chicago in 1959 found that only one would lend money to a black family buying a home in an all-white area. City Hall contributed to segregation by its own housing policies and through adroit use of street signs and one-way streets. The Chicago Housing Authority built subsidized housing for blacks only in neighborhoods that were already 75 percent black. A strict quota limited the number of black families allowed to move into white housing projects. Years of observation had also taught Chicago's city planners that people tended to move out of their neighborhood along main arteries—that if they lived on South State Street, for example, and wanted to move, they tended to follow South State Street down and look for housing in those neighborhoods. Thus, main streets in black neighborhoods were suddenly cut off, or turned into a maze of one-way streets that subtly discouraged the notion that there was an easy way to move out.

Reinforcing these bureaucratic and financial barriers to open housing was steady violence that echoed like a drumbeat through Chicago's tight-knit ethnic neighborhoods whenever blacks had the audacity to move in. In the closing years of World War II, as black soldiers fought for democracy against Germany and Japan, there was more than a firebombing a month on the fringes of the South Side Black Belt as blacks tried to move into all-white communities. In the summer of 1951, a mob of 2,000 whites in the white, working-class suburb of Cicero, bordering Chicago's western edge, stormed an apartment building that had a black family living inside. In 1957, 6,000 whites attacked black picnickers in Calumet Park on the Southeast Side. Throughout the late 1950s, vigilantes threatened and firebombed a small group of black families living in the Trumbull Park Homes, a public housing development that had become "accidentally" integrated when a light-skinned black family moved in.

Still, the burgeoning size of the black population meant blacks had to move somewhere. Hemmed in by violence and homeowners who refused to sell to them, they followed the path of least resistance. That path was Chicago's Jewish neighborhoods.

Unlike the Italians and Slavs of Trumbull Park, the Irish of Mayor Daley's Bridgeport neighborhood, or the Italians of "Little Hell" on the Near North Side, Chicago's Jews did not fire bomb houses or chase blacks down the street when they moved into "their" previously all-white neighborhood. Nor did Jews in Chicago have the clout at City Hall to turn streets around or guarantee that public housing would not be put in their neighborhood.

When blacks moved into Jewish areas, the Jews simply moved out. Often this was made easier by the fact that the Jewish areas were relatively poor and the more successful immigrants wanted to move anyway. But it was also true that, all things being equal, many Jews would have preferred not to have moved. Their ties to the old neighborhood remained strong. Along Maxwell Street on the West Side, Jews continued to own stores and buildings long after most Jews had left. The other side of black complaints about Jewish landlords and storeowners was that the Jews had been in the neighborhood first and had been unwilling—or, as the area deteriorated, unable—to sell all their property. Between 1940 and 1960, the number of blacks living in the North Lawndale section of the West Side, Roz Ebstein's old neighborhood, increased from 380 to 113,827. The white, largely Jewish, population dwindled from 102,048 to barely 10,000. Soon after, blacks began moving into the Jewish neighborhoods of the South Shore. In all that time— the same time whites in Trumbull Park were rioting because one light-skinned black family had moved into their neighborhood and whites in Calumet Park were rioting because blacks tried to eat at a picnic table—there were only a handful of racial attacks on the South Shore or the West Side.

The large-scale movement of blacks into once-Jewish neighborhoods was a phenomenon repeated across the country, and accounted for the fact that so many black churches in Brooklyn, Hartford, and Cleveland hung painted signs reading "Mt. Hope Baptist Church" or "Mt. Zion A. M. E. Church" over the entrances of former synagogues. The signs covered the stone carvings of the Ten Commandments, the Eternal Light, and the Jewish stars that decorated the entrances of buildings which, ten years before, had been neighborhood temples.

One writer coined a term for the Jewish response: *broygez*. "In our distaste for violence we differ hardly at all from our grandparents," wrote Milton Himmelfarb in *Commentary* in 1966. "When they were displeased they did not hit, they acted *broygez* [Yiddish: 'offended' or 'sulky'; from Hebrew: *berogez*, 'in wrath']: they did not speak to the person who had offended them, they avoided his—often her—company. (In his wife's presence, a man would say to his child, 'Tell your mother the soup is cold.') The characteristic response of Jews to an unpleasant situation is still avoidance, flight not fight. If a Jew does not like Negroes moving into his neighborhood, he moves out."

The Ebsteins were not *broygez*. They believed in civil rights and integration, and they believed in them as committed Jews. Roz believed Bernie's passion for civil rights stemmed from growing up under the Nazis in Germany. But Bernie always went back to the Bible, to the Old Testament prophets who railed against injustice. Roz loved the part of the Passover Seder where each participant had to recall as if he personally were freed from slavery; Bernie loved to quote the prophet Micah: "What doth the Lord require of thee, but to do justly, and to love mercy, and to walk humbly with thy God?" When he was a student at the University of Chicago, Bernie's parents had joined Temple KAM and he had joined the choir while a student at the university. The surrounding Hyde Park neighborhood was in the throes of integration and Bernie remembered the rabbi's sermons on social justice and the reasons why Jews, of all others, should support integration. Roz agreed with Bernie that support for civil rights was part of Jewish tradition, but she also had pragmatic reasons. She had no illusions about how accepted Jews were in America. The Holocaust, and the world's silence in the face of it, had shown that the world believed that Jews were expendable. It was important to defend blacks, Roz believed, because after whites had attacked the blacks, the Jews were going to be next. The working-class whites of Trumbull Park and Bridgeport hated the "niggers," Roz believed. They hated the "Jewboys" just a little bit less.

Steven Ebstein was in second grade when he first noticed a black kid in his class; his older brother, David, was in third grade. Some of the Ebsteins' friends, including some Jewish friends, had decided in the early 1960s to put their children in private schools or Jewish parochial schools. The education was better in private schools, and many sensed that a change in the neighborhood was coming. But Roz and Bernie remained committed to public education. They believed the community determined the quality of the school and that if there were plenty of Jewish kids enrolled, the schools would be better. Roz had been a teacher before Steven and David were born and she still taught Sunday school and weekday Hebrew classes at Temple Rodfei Sholom. When the Head Start program began she joined it eagerly and worked for several months training paraprofessionals to assist teachers in the public schools.

In the months leading up to and just after the King march, as a trickle of blacks bought homes in Merionette Manor, Steven and David seemed to fulfill their parents' hopes that they would grow up in an integrated neighborhood. The boys liked several of the black kids who moved into Merionette Manor. They became friends with them. Several blacks joined the Jewish Community Center basketball team and in talking with them, David was starting to get a sense of what life was like for them.

It contrasted so sharply with the violence breaking out in other parts of the city. A week after the Ebsteins marched to Soldier Field, a riot erupted in Roz's old neighborhood, the West Side, now a black ghetto. With temperatures topping 100 degrees—the heat wave that had stunted the turnout for Freedom Sunday had continued without letup—police cars with sirens wailing had descended on the West Side to shut off the fire hydrants children were using to cool down. Angry crowds surrounded the police and the confrontation spiraled. Two days later, two people lay dead, fifty-six injured, and 282 arrested, despite frantic efforts by King and his lieutenants to keep the ghetto calm. Three weeks later, King announced that he would broach the question of segregated housing directly. He would lead a march of blacks and whites supporting open housing through Marquette Park, on Chicago's southwest side, an all-white, heavily ethnic neighborhood. The reaction to the march stunned King. A thousand whites surrounded the 600 marchers, waved Confederate flags and Nazi banners, chanted "Nigger go home!" and let loose a fusillade of rocks, bottles, and bricks. One brick struck King on the head and knocked him to the ground. "I've never seen anything like it," King said. "I've been in many demonstrations all across the South, but I can say that I have never seen—even in Mississippi and Alabama—mobs as hostile and as hate-filled as I've seen in Chicago." King had come up against the fierce resistance of the North to civil rights and integration.

Following the Marquette Park march, civil rights groups announced other marches in all-white neighborhoods. Bernie decided to join a march planned for the Bogan neighborhood, another white ethnic enclave on Chicago's Southwest Side, and another march on the East Side, adjacent to Merionette Manor. Roz urged him not to go. She was frightened. But Bernie insisted.

For the East Side march, the marchers assembled in a park where Bernie joined a circle including Andrew Young and Jesse Jackson playing drop-the-handkerchief, and chasing each other around to defuse the tension. Then they assembled to march, and as they entered the Bogan neighborhood, Bernie stiffened. As in Marquette Park, an angry mob surrounded the marchers, straining against the solid wedges of police that surrounded the demonstrators. Some of the mob spit on the marchers. Then they turned on the whites like Bernie, and Bernie became scared.

"Nigger lover!"

"Dirty Jew!"

"Nigger lover!"

If it hadn't been for the police lines, Bernie told Roz when he came home, the marchers all would have been assaulted.

The jeers against Jews on the East Side confirmed for Bernie that he was dealing with people who hated all outsiders. By marching for blacks, Bernie knew, he was marching against intolerance.

The reaction in Bogan and in Marquette Park was extreme, but it reflected a broader shift in white attitudes. Whites were becoming fed up with the demands of the civil rights movement. Shock at the treatment of blacks in the South and admiration for the protesters in Birmingham and Selma, Alabama, had culminated in the passage of the Civil Rights Act of 1964 and the Voting Rights Act of 1965. But the rioting in Watts in 1965 and in Chicago and forty-two other cities during the summer of 1966 alienated whites by droves. It was one thing to demand civil rights, as King did, wrapped in the Constitution and the Judeo-Christian tradition. It was quite another to present demands with a Molotov cocktail and an upraised fist. The more Carmichael used the phrase "Black Power," the more blacks responded. And the more many whites became frightened. In Illinois, 1966 was the year of the white backlash vote. Republicans dented the famous Daley Democratic machine, electing the president of the Cook County Board and the sheriff, and turning out of office Senator Paul Douglas, replacing him with industrialist Charles Percy. Nationally, polls showed that widespread support for the civil rights movement had begun to evaporate. Eighty-five percent of whites believed that blacks were asking for too much; 88

percent objected to interracial dating. And 50 percent said they did not want a black family living next door to them in their neighborhood.

In the school in Merionette Manor, the black girls had begun to frighten David. They were bigger and more aggressive than the boys. David had learned to hold his own with the boys. In seventh grade, he had been the only white to go out for the elementary school basketball team. Everyone laughed at him but he made it.

But these girls were something else. They scared him. Suddenly there were a lot more fights after school. It became a big thing to stand up and fight when someone insulted you. David was tall and skinny. He'd fight when pushed, but he usually lost. David had inherited his parents' open-mindedness, but he also knew that violence at the school was increasing.

Steven, a year behind David, was feeling much the same way. These blacks his parents had talked about were not his natural allies. They were very different. Their values and their standards were different.

The Ebsteins had fought for good schools, but Steven's fifth-grade teacher was the worst in the school. She was so bad, that the family joked about her at home.

Rabbi Gerald Zelermyer, a rabbi in the Mattapan neighborhood of Boston, speaking in 1970. Between 1968 and 1972, the Jewish population of Mattapan fell from 10,000 to 2,500 as thousands of blacks moved in. Zelermyer finally left Mattapan himself after two blacks came to the door of his house and threw acid in his face, leaving him temporarily blind in one eye

---

Fear is the order of the day. . . . I was told it was a dying [Jewish] community but nobody anticipated it would go that fast. We heard that people would be afraid to venture out to go to the synagogue for the High Holy Day services. We met with the police who mapped out the routes which the worshippers would most likely be using

*and placed [police] details carrying walkie-talkies. Our
outdoor bulletin boards were broken repeatedly; glass in
the building had to be replaced almost daily. Once some
youths came into the chapel during prayer. They taunted
us and called us derogatory names. We called police and
they left. . . . Near the end, last fall, I shuddered to think
of what I might find on arrival at services every Saturday
morning. . . . Some time ago a proprietor told me of an
old woman so scared to venture forth from her Wood-
lawn Avenue tenement more than once a week. She received donations from local merchants to purchase her
meager necessities. She spoke only Yiddish and, with no
one to call her own, was alone in the world.*

The telephone calls started soon after the first black family
moved in. A man identifying himself as a real estate agent
would say, "I've just sold several houses in your neighborhood
and I wonder if I could help you sell yours." Roz always hung
up on the callers. They were panic buyers, she knew, trying
to get the white families to sell their homes at distress prices,
triggering a stampede from the neighborhood.

Broygez. Across the country, real estate agents, banks, and
insurance companies were feeding the collapse of neighborhoods, accelerating the fear that accompanied the arrival of
blacks into all-white neighborhoods. The temptations to real
estate agents were great. As black families moved into a once
all-white neighborhood, many homeowners would become
frightened, fearing the value of their homes would go down.
At the same time, the black families were often willing to pay
a premium for a house—any house—since their black neighborhoods were so overcrowded. An unscrupulous realtor could
buy a house worth $25,000 for $20,000 from a white family
and sell it for $28,000 to a black family. The potential profits
were enormous.

As neighborhoods underwent change, insurance companies
became reluctant to write policies and banks reluctant to write

loans. Many black families ended up buying their homes "on contract," paying them off month by month like a car loan, without ever building equity in them. Miss one payment, and the house would be repossessed by the realtor. Rising insurance premiums fed the fear that the neighborhood was becoming more dangerous and less stable. White homeowners feared the value of their homes would soon plummet. There was no incentive to stay, every incentive to leave.

Ever since moving to Merionette Manor the Ebsteins had been members of Rodfei Sholom, a conservative synagogue a few blocks from their house with a congregation of 500 families and a thriving after-school Hebrew school. Bernie had become a vice president of the temple. When the panic calls began he went to the temple and drew up an oversized testimonial parchment that declared, "We the undersigned are determined to stay." He went door to door with it along the streets of Merionette Manor, trying to get other members of the temple to sign. Some signed the declaration, but others refused. Roz and Bernie were both becoming struck by the anger with which some of their friends now talked about blacks. It made Roz cringe. Civil rights, which was so much a part of the Ebsteins' definition of what it meant to be Jewish and to be liberal, no longer meant the same thing to some of their friends. Some detested the notion that blacks were moving into Merionette Manor; others couldn't be bothered. As he scrambled to create a foundation of Jews who would agree to stay in Merionette Manor, Bernie contacted a close friend, an orthodox rabbi. The rabbi's congregation was in South Shore, a little farther north. They operated a Jewish day school. They had an investment in the community. But when Bernie tried to enlist the rabbi in his struggle, his friend was reluctant. He was so busy being Jewish, so busy keeping up the facilities an orthodox Jewish community needed and making sure the butcher shop abided by kosher rules, that he had little time for secular activities. Bernie and Roz could not understand that. They shook their heads in disappointment that a man who could have been a liberal ally was so concerned with his religious duties that he could not spare time to make sure integration succeeded and that people would live together in harmony.

Whenever his friends would warn him that it was time to move out, that the neighborhood was heading downhill, Bernie would reassure himself with a conversation he had heard in a friend's living room. There, a white man had told a black neighbor of the Ebsteins', Tearched Scott, that he was worried about what would happen to the neighborhood, the schools, as more blacks moved in. Scott reassured him. "If those things go down, you'll move to the suburbs," Scott said. "And I'll be right behind you. I don't want that either."

Fifth grade was a wasted year for Steven; sixth grade promised to be better. The teacher was good, one of the best in the school. David had been in her class the year before and liked her. Then, four weeks into the school year, the teacher asked Roz to come to school for a meeting.

"Take Steven out of this school," she said. "There is nothing I can do for him here. It kills me to say this, but there is no one for him to interact with."

There had been boys in the first five grades that Steven was friendly with. By summer, after the fifth grade, the last of their families had moved away. Sixth grade now threatened to be a repeat of fifth grade, a wasted year. The teacher's advice was blunt: "Take him out of here."

The Ebsteins had been considering putting Steven in private school; now they did. They enrolled him in Akiba, a Jewish day school a half-hour's drive away.

But David remained. The bulk of his friends were still in his class, but he was angry when Steven was transferred. He was scared at school, too, yet his brother was being taken out. No one understood what he was going through. He felt more and more isolated.

It was around this time, in 1967, that the Ebsteins' daughter, Ellen, was born. From her very first days, almost all of Ellen's playmates came from the neighborhood, and almost all of them were black. The infants played easily with each other, and continued to play easily as they became toddlers and pre-schoolers.

Bernie had always enjoyed politics. In 1964 he had canvassed door-to-door for Lyndon Johnson, believing it was critical to keep Barry Goldwater out of the White House. He and Roz had also worked for the election of a local Congressman, Abner Mikva, and for some reform city aldermen.

Nineteen sixty-eight was harder. For months, many of their liberal friends had been pounding away at Johnson and the war in Vietnam. There were discussions and arguments. Bernie wanted to believe that Johnson knew what he was doing in Vietnam, but he was concerned enough to sympathize with Minnesota senator Eugene McCarthy when McCarthy challenged Johnson for the presidency. As time wore on, though, Bernie became disillusioned with McCarthy. He didn't like Robert F. Kennedy either. Whatever his ambivalent feelings about the war, Bernie didn't like the antics of the students who were protesting it and who were promising to descend on Chicago for that summer's Democratic Convention. At the root of his lack of involvement, Bernie realized, was the feeling that the Vietnam War was not that big an issue for him. Civil rights was.

But the battle for civil rights that was consuming the Ebsteins had, by 1968, ceased consuming the rest of the country. Vietnam had replaced civil rights as the issue of conscience for American liberals. Between 1960 and 1965, polls had consistently shown that civil rights ranked at the top or among the top issues that people cared about. The top issue now was the war. Many of the prominent Jewish leaders of the Vietnam protests were veterans of civil rights struggles: Allard Lowenstein now headed the Dump Johnson movement, and civil rights financial backer Martin Peretz was now among the largest donors to the anti-war movement. Many black activists resented the country's preoccupation with the Vietnam War. It seemed to them that contributors, most of them Jewish, had become bored with civil rights, and turned their attention to the peace movement. But for others the issues of American racism at home had become tied up with the war abroad— King believed it was impossible to separate the two. He had begun opposing the Vietnam War in 1965. By 1967—frustrated by what he saw as the immorality of the war and by what many of his supporters saw as his inability to hold sway over the increasingly militant civil rights movement—he had become one of its most vociferous critics, joining Benjamin Spock. Some talked of a Peace Ticket in 1968 that would team King as a presidential candidate with Spock as Vice President. In 1965 President Johnson had declared "We shall overcome" and pushed Congress to pass the Voting Rights Act. After that, however, his attention was increasingly consumed by Vietnam and by the attacks of his critics.

The summer of 1968, Roz was working as the music director of Camp Chi, a camp run by the Jewish Community Centers in the Wisconsin Dells, about a three-and-a-half-hour ride from Merionette Manor. Bernie spent just about every weekend up there as well as some of his vacation. The week of the Democratic Convention, Bernie and Roz flipped on the television set to watch the proceedings. They were sickened by what they saw: police attacking demonstrators with mass clubbings, shoving demonstrators through broken restaurant windows. Intercut with pictures of the beatings stood Senator Abraham Ribicoff of Connecticut, a supporter of Senator George McGovern, who had entered the race after the assassination of Robert F. Kennedy, saying, "If we had McGovern we wouldn't have the gestapo in the streets of Chicago." If the Ebsteins needed to be radicalized by what the war was doing to the country, it happened that night.

But a far more troubling revelation had come to Bernie four months before, when Martin Luther King was assassinated. When Bernie heard the news he was devastated. King stood for everything he believed in.

Bernie was working at the IIT Research Institute, affiliated with the Illinois Institute of Technology and located on Thirty-fifth Street on the South Side, right in the heart of the South Side black belt and across the street from a large black housing

project. The night of King's assassination on April 4, riots
erupted on the West Side. The South Side was tense as people
wondered whether riots would break out there as well. For
the next several weeks, it was a tense time for a white man
to be driving into the heart of a black area. The tensions passed;
the South Side never rioted. Those weeks, Bernie did a lot of
rationalizing to himself. This was a reality he was reluctant
to face: that blacks could be so angry that they might turn on
him, just because he was white.

Martin Luther King, Jr., writing in April 1968.
The article was published in Look magazine on
April 16, 1968, twelve days after his
assassination

---

*The fact is inescapable that the tactic of nonviolence,
which [a few years ago] had dominated the thinking of
the civil rights movement, has in the last two years not
been playing its transforming role. . . . Today, the northern cities have taken on the conditions we faced in the
South. Police, National Guard, and other armed bodies
are feverishly preparing for repression. They can be curbed
not by unorganized resort to force by desperate Negroes
but only by a massive wave of militant nonviolence.
Nonviolence was never more relevant as an effective tactic than today for the North. It also may be the instrument of our national salvation. . . . But I'm frank enough
to admit that if our nonviolent campaign doesn't gen-
erate some progress, people are just going to engage in
more violent activity, and the discussion of guerilla warfare will be more extensive. . . .*

For almost a year David had practiced for his bar mitzvah,
the Jewish ceremony when a boy, on his thirteenth birthday,
first reads from the Torah and is considered a man in the eyes
of the Jewish community. Relatives and friends often shower

the birthday boy with gifts. An old borscht-belt joke had the typical bar mitzvah boy standing in front of the congregation and announcing solemnly, "Today I am a fountain pen." True to tradition, David had received a Cross pen-and-pencil set for his bar mitzvah. He loved the feel of the sleek silver pen and carried it carefully to school. One day one of the black girls in his class, the one he feared the most, grabbed his pen. David had had enough. He asked for it back. When she refused, David went to the teacher and reported her. He got back the pen. As he walked back to his seat, the girl leaned over and whispered, "Your ass is mine after school." For the next week, David made sure he went home early every day, so he wouldn't have to face the girl outside.

Soon after David's bar mitzvah the Ebsteins' house was broken into and many of David's presents were stolen. Roz was furious. If there was anything that was keeping her in Merionette Manor it was her liberal Jewish commitment. And here her oldest kid's bar mitzvah presents had been stolen because of the change in the neighborhood. It didn't help matters when the police caught the person who did it: a black kid. The police recovered some of the presents and the night they went down to the police station to identify their property, Roz and Bernie saw the kid sitting there on a bench with his mother.

By 1969 the Jewish population of Merionette Manor had fallen by more than half. It was hard to get exact numbers; few people would admit they were leaving. Merionette Manor was an extraordinarily close-knit community. Marshall Rosman, Roz's brother, had moved to the neighborhood the year before to run the teen program at the local Jewish Community Center on Ninety-first Street. Despite the departure of many whites, the center was still a thriving, cacophonous place. There were basketball tournaments, swim teams, theater groups, and other programs. On a Wednesday night there might be 800 people packed into the sprawling, ranch house–style structure. Rosman thought of the center as the neighborhood's rumpus room.

Rosman and his sister had grown up in a Jewish community on the West Side, but that was a group of people who happened to live in the same area. This part of the South Side was different. It was a true neighborhood. One Wednesday night, word came suddenly that the father of one of the boys in the teen program had died. As soon as the call came, the community center evacuated. Everyone went to the boy's home to give the family support.

But now, in 1969, Rosman would see moving vans pulling in front of people's homes at night. They would be moving, but too embarrassed to tell anyone. The Jewish Community Center began holding forums to discuss the changes in the neighborhood. They always seemed to break down into angry shouting matches.

"We need to advertise for more white families to move in," someone would say.

"That's racist," someone would shout back.

Rosman stayed out of the discussions; privately he sympathized with both sides. He, too, had marched with King in 1966 and was committed to living in an integrated neighborhood. It was healthier for his children, he believed. But here in Merionette Manor people's values were being challenged directly. Not only Roz and Bernie, but so many people he knew were struggling over whether to stay or leave. It wasn't a question of racism. There was a great deal of pain, and a great deal of judging of people's motives. If we all believed in integration—as Rosman and others did—why was this happening?

The trend, though, was clear. The Jewish Community Center was having trouble fielding teams for citywide competitions. The teenagers would sit around and reminisce about the "good old days"—three or four years earlier—when there were so many kids to play with. Rosman made some contact with the surrounding black community in the hope that an organization there might be willing to take over the center; the center even hosted a convention of Black Hebrews, a sect claiming to be descended from the lost tribes of Israel that was active in Chicago. But in the end negotiations with black organizations fell through, and in 1971 the center moved most of its activities to a new building in Hyde Park, in an integrated neighborhood near the University of Chicago. Rosman moved out of Merionette Manor to Hyde Park to become the center's new director.

Meanwhile, the Ebsteins' synagogue was facing the reality of declining membership as well. At its peak it had close to 800 families. By the late 1960s that was down to 500—smaller, but still vibrant. Between 1969 and 1970, however, membership began declining seriously. It was obvious to Bernie and the other temple officers that it was only a short time before there would not be enough people to support the congregation. The synagogue's leaders considered simply closing up shop but rejected the idea. They decided instead to merge with Rodfei Tzedek, a synagogue in Hyde Park. That way, Bernie and the others felt, Jews remaining in Merionette Manor would still be able to attend services and feel they had a spiritual home. The mechanics of the merger were hammered out over a period of months: Bernie's rabbi became an assistant rabbi at the new temple; the two boards of trustees merged. The members of Rodfei Sholom took the sacred objects from the sanctuary and gave them to other temples. The prayerbooks were donated to a poor congregation. One Torah scroll was given to a university Hillel, a college Jewish center; another was given to a Jewish camp. When the sanctuary was empty and negotiations for the merger complete, the synagogue was sold to the Chicago Board of Education for $60,000. The city turned it into a magnet school called the Black School, after a man named Black. The irony was not lost on Bernie.

A friend of the Ebsteins, Walter Roth, had seen it all before. He had watched as Jews fled the West Side when blacks moved in there, and fled the Hyde Park area around the University of Chicago. Only the intervention of the University of Chicago—its decision to buy up buildings and establish a middle-class integrated enclave amidst an all-black South Side—had prevented Hyde Park from becoming all black, too, Roth believed. Watching what was happening in Merionette Manor was like watching a cattle stampede. Roth was the first to admit that he didn't like muggings and people were very worried about the schools. But 98 percent of the people had no

incidents at all. When there were murders in the affluent suburb of Evanston, you didn't see people flying out of Evanston.
But Jews in the South Shore and Merionette Manor, Roth
believed, wanted an excuse to leave. The liberals like the Ebsteins would stay, but at times Roth wondered how long they
would stay, too. Roth had come to believe that Jews were
nomads, living in a neighborhood for five, maybe ten years,
then picking up and leaving. He had attended a meeting at
the South Side Temple, and had joined in when the rabbi led
everyone in a declaration that they would all stay in the neighborhood and not succumb to panic buying. Many of his fellow
congregants turned around and sold their homes anyway.

In a sense, the position of the Ebsteins had come to mirror
the position of their neighborhood. Merionette Manor, at the
southern tip of Chicago, was one of the last white neighborhoods in what would soon become an all-black South Side;
similarly, the Ebsteins were a final dim outpost of concern
over issues that fewer people, and fewer of their friends, cared
about.

Still the Ebsteins would not give in. They had always prided
themselves on being the intelligentsia, part of a charmed circle, a group of intellectuals from the University of Chicago
who were a cut above, who would not succumb to the passions
of the rabble. What some of their friends said made them
shiver. They prided themselves on their two sets of friends,
their Jewish friends and their secular political friends. Neither
group, it seemed, could ever understand why they hung out
with the other. The battle to keep Merionette Manor integrated had come to dominate their lives. Meetings spawned
meetings. Every evening, it seemed, they left the house to
attend a political meeting or a Southeast Community Organization meeting or a Manor Association meeting. At night,
exhausted, they would lie in bed and fear would nibble at the
edges of their consciences. They would ask each other: What
are we going to do?

The summer of 1969 Roz took Steven, David, and Ellen to
Camp Ramah, a Jewish summer camp in Wisconsin that com-

bined Hebrew school and Jewish studies with the usual camping, swimming, softball-playing, and arts and crafts. When they came back after eight weeks, half the homes on their street had been sold. David's best friend, Greg Levitan, had moved away. The two had made a pact: They would be in the same homeroom for eighth grade. When David found out the Levitans had moved away he was furious, not at the black families moving in but at all the whites who were leaving. Why did they have to go? Why Greg? But he was also beginning to resent his parents' insistence on staying in Merionette Manor. With the temple and Jewish Community Center now sold, he and Steven had to travel half an hour to go to temple and Hebrew classes in Hyde Park. Why were his parents staying? Why were they staying when he was sometimes afraid to go to school?

Looking back, had more whites decided to stay in Merionette Manor, had the real estate agents pushing panic buying been controlled, had the city taken a greater interest in bolstering the schools, the change in the neighborhood might have gone differently. But the Ebsteins and Merionette Manor were part of a sociological and demographic change over which neither they nor their neighbors had any control. Chicago's black population, especially families that could afford to buy their first house, was expanding. Violence and city policy kept them out of many poor and working-class white areas. Moving into Jewish areas like the South Shore, or partially Jewish areas like Merionette Manor, was their only option. Certainly no one in Chicago's City Hall gave much thought—or cared—about how to manage the transition of neighborhoods. After the stoning of King at Marquette Park, Chicago's business leaders and Mayor Daley had agreed to set up a "summit conference" that would push open housing throughout Chicago. Invited to attend one of the meetings in 1967, Rabbi Robert Marx, head of the Jewish Council on Urban Affairs, a liberal Jewish civil rights group, found that the business leaders—most of whom were neither black nor Jewish—had chosen five neighborhoods to start integration. Three of them were Jewish neighborhoods. The Jewish areas, one of the busi-

nessmen told Marx, would be "easier to integrate." Marx left
the meeting convinced that Jewish neighborhoods were being
sacrificed to protect other institutions, including the Catholic
Church, which had a great deal of property and schools in
Chicago's stubbornly white ethnic enclaves.

Most blacks didn't seem to mind the decision of Jews to
move out. To Vernon Jarrett, a black newspaper columnist
whose children had played with the Ebsteins' children one
summer at a resort on Lake Michigan during this period, the
reaction was typical. Blacks were used to whites moving away.
That Jews moved away didn't seem to make much difference.

But for Jews, the disruption was profound. Even more profound were the crime and violence that accompanied the change
from working-class and middle-class white neighborhood to
poor black neighborhood. By the late 1960s, the writings of
Jewish intellectuals distancing Jews from the civil rights
movement were being matched by an inchoate fear and anger
gripping the mass of rank-and-file Jews, an anger which per-
versely mirrored the widespread support the civil rights movement had enjoyed among Jews just ten years before.

Surveying all this, Rabbi Marx had developed a theory of
interstitiality. Taking a term from biology that literally means
"in the spaces between," he argued that Jews were the people
"caught in between," forced by society into a marginal role,
squeezed between a rock and a hard place.

The Ebsteins were interstitial. But what could they do? As
he entered eighth grade David was despondent. The violence
that had troubled him outside class, on his way to and from
school, at the hockey rink, had now burst inside. His regular
eighth-grade teacher was out for months at a time; the substitute teacher could not control the class and the class spun
out of control. Students would hit and slap one another. It
was hard for David to concentrate; he was afraid of what would
happen next. One day, he and Steven went down to a park on
110th Street to play tennis. They were jumped by an integrated
gang—white kids, black kids, and Hispanic kids. They wanted
David's watch. It was a cheap watch; he turned it over. One
of the black kids then surreptitiously stuffed it back in David's

pocket. David appreciated the kindness. Then the gang members started asking David and Steve: "Who are you? Where are you from?"

David knew what they wanted to hear. But he wouldn't say it. "What d'ya mean?"

"Who are you? What are you?"

David wasn't afraid of telling them who he was. "I'm Jewish."

Pow! They punched him in the face. David knew it wasn't just because he was Jewish, that it was because he was white, and had money, and there were a lot of them and only him and his brother. But it didn't make any difference anymore. He and Steven confronted his parents. "You believe this stuff about integration," David said, "but we're living it."

Saul Bellow writing in Mr. Sammler's Planet, published in 1970. Artur Sammler, an aging Jewish man, has been riding the bus on New York's Upper West Side and has spotted a black man working the crowded bus as a pickpocket. He gets off the bus and walks into the lobby of his apartment building. The pickpocket comes up behind him:

He was never to hear the Black man's voice. He no more spoke than a puma would. What he did was to force Sammler into a corner beside the long, Blackish carved table, a sort of Renaissance piece, a thing which added to the lobby melancholy, by the buckling canvas of the old wall, by the red-eyed lights of the brass double fixture. There the man held Sammler against the wall with his forearm. The umbrella fell to the floor with a sharp crack of the ferrule on the tile. It was ignored. The pickpocket unbuttoned himself. Sammler heard the zipper descend. Then the smoked glasses were removed from Sammler's face and dropped on the table. He was directed, silently, to look downward. The Black man had opened his fly and taken out his penis. It was displayed to Sammler with great oval testicles, a large tan and purple uncircumcised thing—a tube, a snake; metallic hairs bristled at the thick base and the tip curled beyond the supporting, demonstrating hand, suggesting the fleshy mobility of an elephant's trunk, though the skin was somewhat iridescent rather than thick or rough. Over the forearm and fist that held him, Sammler was required to gaze at this organ. No compulsion would have been necessary. He would in any case have looked.

It was Roz who decided they had to leave. Bernie wanted to stay. This was part of the long-standing difference in their personalities. Bernie was always slow to make decisions. In this case, he tenaciously held on to his idealism. He did not want to move until it was clear they had no other choice. But Roz believed things had gone too far. There were reports of knives at school; her sons were being mugged. David would be entering high school the next year. The house was too small. It was a natural time to move.

The discussions went on for nights as Bernie and Roz argued about what to do. Bernie advocated moving to Hyde Park, a safer neighborhood but still integrated. Failing that, he suggested Evanston, an affluent suburb but one with a large black population, ensuring that David and Steven would still be exposed to blacks in school.

But in both cases, the high schools were unsettled. There were reports of classes out of control. Roz did not want to go through that again, did not want to put David and Steven through that again. Many of David's and Steven's friends from Camp Ramah had settled in Highland Park, an affluent suburb north of Chicago, overwhelmingly white, like most of Chicago's suburbs, and with a substantial Jewish community. A synagogue they liked lay just down the road.

So they moved there. It was unreal, Roz knew that, but it was quiet and she didn't have to be scared. As she drove the streets of her new hometown in 1971, Roz felt a sense of serenity, but also of retreat. She and Bernie—the big social activists—felt no desire to get involved in town politics or in any other issues. They joined one synagogue and became co-music directors at a second. They became active in temple activities and spent more time with Steven and David. As far back as 1965, Roz had been involved in early childhood education in the black community. Now she had her chance to become a full-time teacher at Kennedy-King Community College, a largely black college on the South Side, teaching classes to students who planned to become teachers and day-care workers. Three times a week—then five times a week—she would drive the forty-five-minute to one-hour commute from her home in Highland Park to Kennedy-King, located about ten miles from Merionette Manor. She would reflect how that drive put her in two different worlds: a Jewish world at home, and a black world at work. Her marching days might be over, but Roz felt that by teaching black students she was having a direct effect on what happened in the black community, or at least on some black students. She might have had to give up where she lived, but she had not given up what she believed in. In her classes she was very honest about her Jewish identity. When she talked about teaching music she talked about her work as music director at the synagogue. There was an honesty between her and her students, and Roz was proud of that.

Bernie consoled himself by telling people that it had taken Merionette Manor five years to change from a white neighborhood to a black neighborhood. Most neighborhoods in Chicago had changed in just two years. That was a victory of sorts.

David and Steven did well in Highland Park. There were tensions there, too, this time between Italians and Jews, but both boys went on to college. After playing with the idea of being a social worker, David began studying to become a rabbi. Steven went to graduate school at Harvard and became a scientist.

Roz feared that she had turned her David and Steven into bigots. Had they grown up in the suburbs, she reasoned, they would have seen the troubles of the 1960s through rose-colored glasses. They would have said, "Oh, how bad those conditions are." Instead, she feared, their exposure to blacks had coarsened them, the exact opposite of what she and Bernie had dreamed when they first marched with King in 1966.

She was wrong. In high school, David read Charles Silberman's *Crisis in Black and White,* a landmark book that bluntly outlined the problems of American race relations and the aspirations of blacks. He was proud of his parents' involvement in civil rights. He remembered the times black friends of theirs would come over and debate politics with his mom and dad. Looking back, he was madder at the Jews and whites who left Merionette Manor than he was at his parents or, certainly, at blacks who were moving in. Talking to the black students at his school, David had gotten an acute sense of how much harder life was for them; how much more attractive Merionette Manor, the schools, the hockey rink, and the tennis courts nearby were than the neighborhoods they had left. But those years in Merionette Manor had left a scar on David. He tried to be intelligent about the whole business, but he was still careful whenever he saw someone on the street who looked suspicious, especially if the person was black.

Steven developed an outlook that would come to be known as neoconservative. He was no bigot. But he would not call himself a liberal either. Liberals, Steven felt, embraced the cause of the underdog. But he didn't feel like an underdog; he never had. Many of the liberals and radicals he saw in college seemed to embrace causes because it made them feel good, not because it would do any good. They wouldn't rally to improve schools in the inner city. Instead they would rally against divestment in South Africa.

Steven had not felt that blacks were his natural allies when he was growing up, and he did not feel that way in his twenties. There were traits in black culture that he did not like, a certain showiness and lack of responsibility. He had no time for leaders like Jesse Jackson who made statements he considered clearly anti-Semitic. He had fine antennae for statements he felt had any hint of anti-Israel bias. He agreed with more conservative Jews like Morris Abram that the goal of the civil rights movement had been to make the society color-blind.

So he was troubled by affirmative action. Yes, there had been a great historical wrong done to blacks. But you couldn't redress that through quotas and numbers.

Roz and Bernie Ebstein never went back to Merionette Manor. There was no reason to. Their new house was large, two stories, with a winding walkway that led through the front yard to the entrance. Just off to the right as you walked in was a big hall closet. When the Ebsteins moved in the summer of 1971, they filled it with boxes of odds and ends, including the American Jewish Congress banner they had carried along the streets leading to Soldier's Field in 1966. The banner rested in the front closet for years. Then one day when she was cleaning, Roz took it out of the closet and threw it out.

COMPETITION
AND CONFLICT

6

Choosing Comrades: Martin Peretz

In his most famous short story, I. L. Peretz, one of the nine-teenth-century's greatest Yiddish writers, describes how his character Bontsha the Silent stands before the bar of justice in heaven, listening—silently—as one of the angels speaks on his behalf before the heavenly judge.

The angel begins:

"His sufferings were unspeakable. Here, look upon a man who was more tormented than Job!"

Who? Bontsha wondered. Who is this man?

"Facts! Facts! Never mind the flowery business and stick to the facts, please!" the judge called out.

"When he was eight days old he was circumcised—"

"Such realistic details are unnecessary—"

"The knife slipped, and he did not even try to staunch the flow of blood—"

"—and distasteful. Simply give us the important facts."

"Even then, an infant, he was silent, he did not cry out his pain," Bontsha's defender continued. "He kept his silence, even when his mother died, and he was handed over, a boy of thirteen, to a snake, a viper—a stepmother!"

Hmm, Bontsha thought, could they mean me?

"She begrudged him every bite of food, even the moldy rotten bread and the gristle of meat that she threw at him, while she herself drank coffee with cream."

The angel goes on to catalogue Bontsha's sufferings: He never earns more than a few pennies; a rich man cheats him out of his wages; his wife deserts him; he dies in a hospital where nurses and doctors ignore him. Bontsha never complains. The heavenly judge is moved to awe by Bontsha's silent acceptance of suffering:

"There, in that other world, no one understood you. You never understood yourself. You never understood that you need not have been silent, that you could have cried out and that your outcries would have brought down the world itself and ended it. You never understood your sleeping strength. . . . But here in Paradise you will be rewarded. You, the judge can neither condemn nor pass sentence upon. For you there is not only one little portion of Paradise, one little share. No, for you there is everything! Whatever you want! Everything is yours!"

Now, for the first time, Bontsha lifts his eyes. He is blinded by light. The splendor of light lies everywhere—upon the walls, upon the vast ceiling, the angels blaze with light, the judge. He drops his weary eyes.

"Really?" he asks, doubtful, and a little embarrassed.

"Really!" the judge answers. "Really! I tell you, everything is yours. Everything in paradise is yours. Choose! Take! Whatever you want! You will only take what is yours!"

"Really?" Bontsha asks again, and now his voice is stronger, more assured.

And the judge and all the heavenly host answer, "Really! Really! Really!"

"Well, then"—and Bontsha smiles for the first time—"well then, what I would like, Your Excellency, is to have, every morning for breakfast, a hot roll with fresh butter."

At that point, writes Peretz, "a silence falls upon the great hall, and it is more terrible than Bontsha's has ever been, and slowly the judge and the angels bend their heads in shame at this unending meekness they have created on earth."

I. L. Peretz wrote that story as a black-humored parody of Jewish meekness. It was a repudiation of Jewish passivity in the face of their own suffering, of Jews who would not stand up for themselves or to those more powerful than they. Whatever people said about I. L. Peretz's great-grand-nephew Martin Peretz—and they would say many things in the 1970s and 1980s—they could never accuse him of being a Bontsha the Silent. As he fervently defended Israel and attacked its critics, criticized black leaders Jesse Jackson or Louis Farrakhan, questioned the liberal politics of the Democratic Party, Peretz refused to accept suffering, meekness, or guilt as his lot or as the lot of the Jews. He was part of a new generation of Jews and a new style of leadership. His combative style was a repudiation of the image of Jewish meekness. But it also contrasted with the conciliatory spirit of many Jews, and many white liberals, in the early days of the civil rights movement. His critics—even his wife—saw in Peretz some of the arrogance and lack of compassion about blacks and the black struggle that suffused discussions about the "black underclass" and black political power in the late 1970s and early 1980s. Peretz seemed puzzled by blacks and especially by black leadership, frustrated with them, angered by them. Yet there was also in Peretz a wistfulness for how the country had changed since the early 1960s, how many of the early dreams of the civil rights movement that he had shared had vanished.

At the center of many of these feelings, as at the center of the concerns of so many Jews in the 1960s, 1970s, and 1980s, was the fate of Israel.

Rabbi Arthur Hertzberg, writing in Commentary, *August 1967*

As soon as the Arab armies began to mass on the borders of Israel during the third week in May, 1967, the mood of the American Jewish community underwent an abrupt, radical and possibly permanent change. . . . The immediate reaction of American Jewry to the crisis was far more intense and widespread than anyone could have foreseen. Many Jews would never have believed that grave danger to Israel could dominate their thought and emotions to the exclusion of everything else; many were surprised by the depth of their anger at those of their friends who carried on as usual, untouched by fear for Israeli survival and the instinctive involvement they themselves felt. . . .

Two days after the war, there was a major gathering in New York of Jewish leaders from all over the country, many of whom, as I happened to be able to attest, remote from the synagogue. Yet when the meeting was concluded with a very simple recitation of the blessing in which we thank God for "having allowed us to live and be present to witness this day," almost everyone in the room cried.

Nothing since the Holocaust more transformed Jewish identity in America than the Six-Day War in June 1967.

The realization of the threat to Israel came quickly. On May 15, Egypt mobilized its army, signaling the possibility of an invasion of Israel. Two days later President Nasser ordered the United Nations to withdraw its troops from the Sinai and from the Strait of Tiran. On May 22, Nasser announced a blockade of the Gulf of Aqaba, cutting off the Israeli port of Eilat. One hundred thousand troops stood massed at Egypt's border with Israel. "As of today, there no longer exists an international emergency force to protect Israel," declared Cairo Radio. "We shall exercise patience no more. We shall not complain to the U.N. about Israel. The sole method we shall apply against Israel is a total war which will result in the extermination of Zionist existence." On May 30, Jordan signed a formal treaty placing its troops under Egyptian command. Iraq did the same. Syria mobilized its army on the Golan Heights overlooking Israel. By June 3, Israel was surrounded on three sides by Arab armies. Over its shoulder lay the Mediterranean Sea. "When the Arabs take Israel, the surviving Jews will be helped to return to their native countries," Ahmed

Shukairy, head of the Palestine Liberation Army, declared, "but I figure there will be very few survivors."

America's Jews seemed powerless to help. They gave astonishing amounts of money—between May 22 and June 10 the United Jewish Appeal took in $100 million—and many American Jews volunteered to go to Israel to take the jobs of Israelis who were being mobilized into the army. But none of this directly affected the fate of Israel. The United Nations accommodated Nasser's demand to withdraw peace-keeping troops. France cut off arms shipments to Israel. The United States refused to intervene, even though after the 1956 Arab-Israeli War it had signed a memorandum of understanding guaranteeing Israel's free passage through the Strait of Tiran. A catastrophe seemed imminent.

Then, on June 5, Israel attacked the surrounding Arab countries. Within a week, the war was over, Israel victorious. From the depths of despair Jews shot to the euphoria of victory. But the fear of those previous three weeks had etched a cicatrix in the American Jewish psyche. With a poignant stab, Jews realized—many for the first time—how vulnerable they had left Israel, and how vulnerable they themselves had felt during the perilous month of May. Had it not been for the Israelis themselves, Israel would have been destroyed.

For people like Roz Ebstein's parents or some of the people in Jack Greenberg's neighborhood—fervent Zionists who dreamed of a homeland in the Middle East—Israel had always been a symbol of Jewish survival. But in the wake of the 1967 war—the fear that preceded it, the relief and joy that followed—the importance of Israel mushroomed until it matched or exceeded many of the other touchstones of what it meant to be a Jew.

The Six-Day War, and the feelings that flowed from it, threw into sharp relief the changing status of American Jews in the United States. In 1967, most Jews over sixty-five had never graduated from high school, evidence of the working-class and immigrant origins of most Jewish families. But 87 percent of Jews in their twenties and thirties—the children and grandchildren of those immigrants—were college graduates; almost half had graduate degrees as well. Their incomes were rising rapidly. Gradually, Jews were exceeding, in accomplishments, education, and income, the mainstream groups that had long kept them excluded. At the same time, the political moorings of most Jews—support of the Democratic Party, civil rights, the New Deal liberalism symbolized by Franklin Roosevelt and John Kennedy—were being buffeted by the growing disorders of the 1960s. The rise of Black Power, the radical rhetoric of student protests, the convulsive change of neighborhoods, the soaring crime rate—all challenged the verities by which many Jews had guided themselves for two decades.

Changes in politics and attitudes probably would have flowed from these economic and social changes even without the Six-Day War. But the 1967 Arab-Israeli War forced a reexamination not only of American Jewish attitudes toward Israel but of American Jewish attitudes toward themselves. "In those days many of us felt that our own lives were in the balance and not only the [lives] of those who dwelt in the land; that indeed all of the Bible, all of Jewish history was at stake," wrote Rabbi Abraham Joshua Heschel, whose writings about civil rights had stirred Jews in the early 1960s. ". . . The world that was silent while six million died was silent again, save for individual friends. The anxiety was grueling, the isolation was dreadful. . . . I had not known how deeply Jewish I was." America's Jews would never be the same.

A response to Black Power presented by a group of Jewish students to a high school principal in Minneapolis, Minnesota, 1969

---

1. *Students shall be excused on all Jewish holidays. Mezuzot shall be affixed to every classroom door.*
2. *All school books shall be read from right to left.*
3. *All food dispensers shall issue only Kosher food. Separate dispensers shall be provided for meat and dairy dishes.*

4. *During recess only Jewish and Israeli music shall be heard in the halls.*
5. *In all grades, Jewish history and culture shall be taught.*
6. *All students shall study Hebrew.*
7. *All anti-Semitic teachers shall be expelled from the high school.*
8. *Additional Jewish teachers shall be employed, a Jewish Student Advisor and Vice Principal shall be engaged.*
9. *The Jewish Community of Minneapolis shall have the right to interview Jewish applicants for teaching positions. No assimilated Jews shall be hired.*
10. *A Jewish student organization bearing the name "Kosher Corner Club" shall be formed.*
11. *An employee of the school shall fulfill the function of "Yiddishe Mame."*

If these demands shall not be met, then the Jewish students will march seven times around the school building, sounding the Shofrot, until the walls will cave in, as they did at Jericho.

> *Curly hair is beautiful*
> *We are Jewish, therefore wonderful*
> *Being Jewish is beautiful*
> —Reprinted in Jewish Morning Journal,
> January 9, 1969

Zionism and support for Israel had always played a large role in Peretz's life. His parents had been middle class and fervent Zionists. In 1947, when he was eight, they took Peretz to Lake Success, New York, to hear the announcement of the Partition Plan that led to the creation of Israel six months later. That same year his mother took Peretz to a rally at the Polo Grounds, home of the New York Giants, where Albert Einstein and the black singer Paul Robeson both spoke in favor

of the creation of the state of Israel and the start of free immigration by Jews. The crowds cheered and chanted: "2—4—
6—8! Open up Palestine's gate!" Peretz moved in circles of
young people who grew up in left-wing homes. In 1948, as
Thomas Dewey and Harry Truman battled for the presidency,
Peretz was surprised to read in the newspapers that Dewey
was expected to win. Although he supported Truman, in his
straw poll at public school, the third-party candidate, leftist
Henry Wallace, had Truman in a dead heat.

Yet even back then, Peretz showed signs of backsliding.
Growing up in New York in the 1940s, Peretz rooted for the
New York Yankees. It was the Brooklyn Dodgers, not the
Yankees, who were the team of choice among young Jewish
baseball fans in the late 1940s and early 1950s. Some of his
friends considered him an apostate.

"How can you not be for the Dodgers with Jackie Robinson?" they asked. "How can you not root for the Dodgers after
what Branch Rickey did?"

For Peretz, that didn't matter. He was glad when Robinson
hit a home run or stole home. But Peretz checked his psyche
at the ballpark entrance. He came from the Bronx. He cheered
for the Bronx Bombers.

Peretz went to college at Brandeis, and there fell under the
spell of Max Lerner, Lewis Coser, Irving Howe, Philip Rahv,
and Marie Syrkin, several of whom would form the core of
the group of liberal, anti-communist intellectuals at *Dissent*
magazine. The Montgomery bus boycott had begun in Alabama, but at Brandeis, the two burning issues in 1956 as Peretz
entered his sophomore year were the Arab-Israeli War and the
Hungarian Revolution. The uprising in Hungary had nothing
to do with Jews at all; Soviet tanks crushed an indigenous
socialist uprising. There were debates across the Brandeis campus. Herbert Marcuse, one of the heroes of the New Left in
the late 1960s, defended the Soviet invasion. Peretz's room-
mate kept his alarm clock attached to a shortwave radio. One
morning Peretz woke up to the voice of the Hungarian foreign
minister, talking in English, weeping. The revolution was being
crushed. At seventeen, Peretz joined the Greater Boston Col-

legiate Committee for a Free Hungary and gave a speech at Boston's Faneuil Hall saying that America had let the Hungarians down, casting his lot firmly with the Hungarians and not the Russians. It was a feeling toward the Soviet Union he would carry for the rest of his life.

From its founding in 1948, Israel, and the existence of a Jewish state, were central to Peretz's intellectual makeup. Aside from the emotional feelings of pride and safety that it stirred, Israel, Peretz felt, normalized the Jewish people. It gave them independence, the right to make their own decisions, even the wrong decisions. While the fate of Israel was important to Peretz—and to other Jews—in the 1940s and 1950s, it assumed nowhere near the importance it did after the 1967 Six-Day War.

In the fall of 1957 and the winter of 1958—just a year after the 1956 Arab-Israeli War—a sociologist interviewed Jews in Highland Park, the suburb north of Chicago that Bernie and Roz Ebstein would move to fifteen years later. The sociologist asked the Jewish residents to rank beliefs and feelings they felt were essential to being a "good Jew." Their answers revealed how modest a place Israel held in their political universe. Only 21 percent said it was "essential" to support Israel in order to be a good Jew. Forty-seven percent thought supporting Israel was desirable; 32 percent thought it made no difference. Far more important to these upwardly mobile Jews of 1957—far more intrinsic to their notion of being a "good Jew"—was supporting humanitarian causes, leading an ethical and moral life, promoting civil betterment and virtue, and accepting being a Jew and not trying to hide it. In Highland Park in the 1950s, only one in five Jews thought being a good Jew meant it was essential to support Israel. Twice as many believed it essential to support the struggle for the Negro in America. Jewish dreams were, essentially, American dreams. Insofar as there was a "Jewish agenda" it mirrored the agenda of a liberal, tolerant society. A planning guide published for Jewish agencies in local communities in 1955—seven years after the creation of the state of Israel—mentioned Israel only in passing. It focused instead on pressing social issues of the day: the desegregation of public schools, the passage of local civil rights laws.

Civil rights first pushed itself into Peretz's consciousness when he was a graduate student at Harvard. In February 1960, Peretz read reports in *The New York Times* of the sit-ins in Greensboro, North Carolina. Patriotism and liberalism impelled him to do something about the sit-ins. Many of the blacks he had known or heard about as a child, people like Paul Robeson, had been philo-Semitic; they seemed empathetic to Jewish goals and aspirations. Robeson sang Yiddish folk songs and songs of the Jewish struggle, including songs from the uprising of the Warsaw ghetto. The few blacks Peretz had met at Brandeis and Harvard were extremely impressive, more talented than many of the whites. To get that far at that time, they had to be.

Peretz did not feel personally threatened by northern or southern racism. He was an academic, soon to become an instructor at Harvard, living in a comfortable home in Cambridge. He was drawn by the injustice of segregation. This was an injustice that had to be righted. Peretz called together a number of his friends from his Brandeis days, including Michael Walzer, later to become a political philosopher, and formed EPIC, the Emergency Public Integration Committee. Peretz liked the sound of the name. It recalled the campaign of the crusading progressive Upton Sinclair for governor in California, with its slogan "End Poverty in California." And it signaled that the emerging civil rights movement was to be an epochal struggle. Peretz and Walzer organized picket lines in front of Woolworth's, on Tremont Street in downtown Boston, and soon were raising funds from many of their friends and contacts.

Over the next seven years, Peretz gave and raised hundreds of thousands of dollars for the civil rights movement. In the early 1960s, Peretz had married the daughter of the well-to-do owner of a fruit business. That marriage ended within two years and Peretz began to see—first as a friend, later romantically—Anne Labouisse Farnsworth, heiress to part of the Singer Sewing Machine fortune, whom he eventually married. The two gave large sums of money to the SCLC and SNCC. Farnsworth would regularly give between $10,000 and $50,0000 to King, often when SCLC most needed the money. Anne and Marty Peretz quickly emerged as two of the biggest "angels" in the civil rights movement.

Parallel to his involvement in civil rights, Peretz had become committed to the peace movement, pouring into it a great deal of time and energy. Support for the anti-war movement began to crystallize after 1965, and in the summer of 1966 Peretz convened a meeting at his summer house on Cape Cod to discuss bringing peace activists and civil rights activists together to influence and perhaps make inroads into the Democratic Party. The civil rights movement had years of experience organizing demonstrations and registering voters; the peace movement had an emotional issue that could unite the country. It was the "political" people in both camps, the liberal pragmatists, who attracted Peretz's interest. He didn't have time for the more radical activists in both groups—groups like Students for a Democratic Society, black nationalists, and various Marxist groups, even though he had been close to many of the students who founded SDS. Either their analysis was so radical it had nothing to do with the facts, Peretz felt, or their solutions were so radical they were worse than the problem. The people he was attracted to were fellow academics, together with peace activists with "establishment" credentials, like Dr. Benjamin Spock, author of the standard book on child care; William Sloane Coffin, chaplain at Yale; and mainstream civil rights leaders like Andrew Young and King. Peretz envisioned a multi-racial, multi-issue coalition that could harness the energy of the peace movement and the strategies of the civil rights movement to transform the Democratic Party and American politics. It might even nominate, or threaten to nominate, a third-party ticket in 1968 of Martin Luther King and Benjamin Spock. A convention was set for the fall of 1967.

Yet even as Peretz pursued his dream of a multi-racial coalition, the tensions between blacks and Jews were breaking the surface. One night in the summer of 1967, during a planning meeting for the New Politics convention held at Peretz's Cape Cod home, after most of the people had been dispersed to local motels and homes of friends, Peretz was awakened by the sound of people singing down in his living room. As he listened, Peretz realized they were singing an anti-Semitic song, about being overcharged by Jewish landlords. He tumbled downstairs and confronted the group, a mixture of blacks and whites, and threw them out of the house. He found himself increasingly enveloped in conversations with James Forman of SNCC on Jewish issues. Forman believed that the Jews of Harlem owed black residents reparations. "You know, you're picking on puny victimizers," Peretz told him. But Forman believed the merchants were the most direct victimizers and so should pay reparations. Peretz believed the strategy silly and futile. "So let's say you have an adversary relationship with the Jew who owns the hardware store on 125th Street in Harlem," Peretz said to Forman. "Let's say you beat him. What do you have?"

The SNCC leaflet denouncing Israel after the 1967 war sickened Peretz. The week of the Six-Day War had begun in terror, the month of May fraught with anxiety as the Arabs massed for their attack; it ended in a romp, with Israel triumphant. If the creation of Israel had meant the normalization of the Jewish people, the Six-Day War, Peretz believed, meant the return of power to the Jewish people. The world had wanted Israel to be a "pathetic Samson," a "heroic weakling." Israel's decisive victory had forced the world to accept the reality of Jewish power. But the suddenness of Israel's victory remained tinged with the fear that had preceded it. Peretz later compared the feeling to a man leaping over an abyss—and making it. And there, on the other side, stood the leaders of SNCC churning out their cartoon of Moshe Dayan with dollar signs on his epaulets. Peretz first saw the leaflet at his Cape Cod home. It reminded him of the Nazi propaganda of Julius Streicher.

Peretz confronted some of his Jewish friends—all staunch liberals and longtime supporters of the civil rights movement—with the leaflets. They waffled. "You have to understand," one said to him. "The movement is young. The movement is feeling its oats." It was a typical response, Peretz felt, of people unwilling to recognize what was happening. They wanted him to understand. But he did not want to "understand" so much that it would seem to pardon this garbage.

By the time the National Convention on New Politics met in the Palmer House over the 1967 Labor Day weekend, Peretz had a feeling something bad was about to happen. Instead of staying at the Palmer House, he checked into a hotel a few blocks away from the convention site. Over at the Palmer House, radicals gathered in the carpeted and chandeliered ballrooms. They ate in the hotel restaurants, charging steak dinners to the organizers.

Peretz soon found himself caught up in the vortex of Black Power and increasingly radical politics. Martin Luther King came to give the keynote address and was heckled by black teenagers who jeered and shouted threats. He left the next morning. Julian Bond, co-chairman of the convention and the person in SNCC whom Peretz liked best, left as well. A group calling itself the Black Caucus seceded from the convention and began to draw up demands. Militant blacks prowled the convention floor, whispering that Rap Brown might be coming. Andrew Young, who had worked with Peretz on the planning of the convention, left shaking his head at the black militants. "These cats don't know the country has taken a swing to the right," he told a white lawyer. "I wish the violence and riots had political significance, but they don't."

The number of caucuses and factions in the Palmer House multiplied. In addition to the Black Caucus, there was a White Radical Caucus, a Whites-in-support-of-the-Black-Caucus Caucus, a White Revolutionary Caucus, a Radical Alternatives Caucus, a Poor People's Caucus, a Women Strike for Peace Caucus, a Labor Caucus, and an Anti–King-Spock Caucus. The Black Caucus demanded that it be given 50 percent of the votes at the convention, and that the convention agree to adopt all its demands, sight unseen, as a measure of good faith.

Peretz, who was picking up the largest chunk of the bill for the convention, kept shouting at conference participants and threatening to walk out. The organization of the conference disintegrated. Committees began voting resolutions to send congratulatory telegrams to Ho Chi Minh on the occasion of the twenty-second anniversary of Vietnamese independence. On Sunday afternoon Peretz watched as Forman, whom he had known for years, entered surrounded by men wearing dashikis. He seized the microphone at the front of the convention hall and declared himself "dictator." "We in SNCC have been the victims of the liberal-labor circle lies, their false propaganda, their attempts to destroy our organization, their misleading of the masses of people in this country, and we say NO," Forman declared. He went on:

> No longer can we allow young black militants to assemble in the presence of these double-crossing, liberal-labor coalition exponents, both Negro and white, without raising our voice in protest and without telling those who have not experienced what we have experienced the truth about some of the activities of this syndrome, the liberal-labor leadership circle.

Peretz walked out. The convention then agreed to give the Black Caucus 50 percent of the vote—in effect turning over the control of the convention. Then, by a three-to-one margin, the remaining delegates voted to approve all the Black Caucus's resolutions, including one that condemned the "imperialistic Zionist war"—Israel's victory in the Six-Day War.

The Black Caucus later rescinded the resolution on Israel, but the damage was done. The New Politics Convention, one reporter observed at the time, had been neither new nor politic. Called as a way of forming new coalitions, it ended up pitting black against white, radicals against liberals, blacks against Jews. It ignored the truly pressing problems of poverty, opposition to the war, and continuing racism and discrimination. Peretz believed it had been a tragicomic opera, a witches' sabbath with every participant dancing a mass St. Vitus' dance. He was haunted by the sight of a Jewish radical screaming at one of the caucuses, "After 400 years of slavery it is right that whites should be castrated!" It was as if, Peretz felt, in one fell swoop the suffering of black people was to be avenged.

Renata Adler, writing a few weeks later in *The New Yorker*, saw the New Politics Convention marking the death throes of radical politics and the end of serious efforts by the left to address the country's problems. "A radical movement born out of a corruption of the vocabulary of civil rights—preempting the terms that belonged to a truly oppressed minority and applying them to the situation of some bored children committed to choosing what intellectual morsels they liked from the buffet of life at a middle-class educational institution in California—now luxuriated in the cool political vocabulary, while the urban civil rights movement, having nearly abandoned its access to the power structure, thrashed about in local paroxysms of self-destruction."

The New Politics Convention left Peretz profoundly disillusioned with radical politics. The pressure to submerge all differences, to agree to resolutions without seeing them, reminded him of the worst excesses of the communist popular fronts. The descent into anti-Semitism unnerved him. As Jim Forman marched in, Peretz had an epiphany: This is madness. From his Brandeis days he carried deep suspicions of the radical left, especially communists, whom he felt were alert to the opportunity to seize any popular movement and set people against one another for their own reasons. He felt he saw the hands of the communists in the tumult that surrounded the convention in Chicago and saw the opportunity for them again in the burgeoning anti-war movement.

Peretz marched in only one anti-war demonstration after the convention, the October 1969 Moratorium. In meetings at his house in Cambridge he became more and more convinced the peace movement was falling under the influence of people he considered communists and fellow travelers. He had never allowed himself to be allied with such people, and would not now. At the October 1969 march he believed more strongly than ever that many of the people marching genuinely wanted the Viet Cong to win and were hoping for a communist victory in Indochina. His thoughts kept returning to an essay by Ignazio Silone he had read in *Dissent* in 1955. In the essay, Silone, a one-time member of the Italian Communist Party, told how a generation of idealistic young people had decided to join the Communist Party following the First World War and later became disillusioned. What stayed with Peretz was not so much the substance of the essay, but its title, "A Choice of Comrades," and Silone's observation that "a choice once made, the rest, as experience shows, follows automatically." As he saw the anti-war movement being taken over by people he considered radicals, revolutionaries, and millenarians, he came to a conclusion: These people were not his comrades.

The late 1960s and early 1970s were a time of growing black studies and growing black involvement on campuses. Universities established Afro-American studies departments and special courses on black literature. One day in 1970 Peretz had lunch with a colleague at Harvard, a writer and essayist who was Jewish.

"You know, one of the things I've been thinking about is I teach a course on black fiction and on the Abbey Theater," his friend said. "There's something wrong with that, because I've never read a story by Sholom Aleichem."

That struck Peretz as ripe with the contradictions of the involvement of many Jews with the civil rights movement. Here many Jews had been involved in the struggle of blacks for self-determination. Yet they knew very little about their own history. Peretz was not an observant Jew; his wife, Anne, was not Jewish. But he considered himself a well-educated Jew. He was steeped in Jewish culture and read widely in Yiddish literature and Jewish history. He knew the writings of Jewish thinkers and novelists. These things were important and he intended to pass them on to his children. So many Jews that he knew, intimately familiar with the black struggle and black fiction, could not recognize the names of well-known Jewish writers. He recalled an argument in a short story by Arthur Schnitzler between a Zionist and an assimilationist. The metaphor the two use in arguing is roots versus wings. In that argument, Peretz chose roots.

There was an irony here, of course. The civil rights movement, by raising issues of Black Power and Black Consciousness, stimulated others to examine their own backgrounds. Jewish studies, together with women's studies and other ethnic fields, boomed in the 1970s. Following the end of World War II, there were only two full-time professors of Jewish history and thought at American universities; by 1985, 300 American colleges and universities were offering courses in Judaic studies and twenty-seven offered graduate programs. By the 1980s, polls found, American Jews in their twenties were more likely to attend a Seder than those in their sixties.

Yet the more others explored their own backgrounds—women in feminist studies, Jews in Jewish studies—the more the energy of these groups became wrapped up in their own concerns. Civil rights no longer commanded the sole attention of liberals and idealistic young people. The growth of Black Power and Black Consciousness had made it legitimate to examine one's own ethic roots. Yet at the same time it helped fracture some of the forces that had spurred whites to join the civil rights movement.

The early 1970s were a time of political transition for Jews. As far back as 1963 and 1964, Norman Podhoretz and Nathan Glazer had expressed concern, both personal and political, over growing demands by blacks for economic equality to supplement the legal equality won by demonstrations in the South. The outbreak of riots in Newark, Watts, and elsewhere, the rise of student protests first at Berkeley and then around the country—all added urgency to their concerns. For a time in the late 1960s many wondered if civil war might break out. Coupled with this was an assault by blacks and white radicals on the most cherished institution of intellectuals, the university. In April 1969, Harvard students seized the university's main administration building and the resulting protests shut down the campus for a week. Later that month, black students seized a campus building at Cornell. When they emerged several days later they were carrying rifles and shotguns.

By the early 1970s, discontent with—and fear of—what *Commentary* called "revolutionism" had blossomed into a full-blown movement that argued that the United States had entered a period of decline, that stability was a prerequisite for social justice, and that the country needed to return to a time of political and cultural moderation. The leaders of the movement became known as neoconservatives. Many of the most prominent figures in the neoconservative movement were not Jewish: Daniel Patrick Moynihan, for example. And many Jews in the neoconservative movement, especially university professors under siege from radical students, had sound reasons for being neoconservatives without being Jewish. But the neoconservative movement had a very Jewish strain to it. Jews like Podhoretz, Glazer, and Irving Kristol were among its most articulate and forceful exponents, and *Commentary*, published by the American Jewish Committee, became the neoconservative flagship. The neoconservatives made a special appeal to other Jews, believing they, most of all, were imperiled by the rise of the radical left. At the heart of their argument was the fear that anti-Semitism, which many had always thought could come only from the right, could now come from the left. "Whatever the case may have been yesterday, and whatever the case may be tomorrow, the case today is that the most active enemies of the Jews are located not in the precincts of the ideological Right but in the precincts of the Radical Left," Norman Podhoretz told an annual meeting of the American Jewish Committee in the spring of 1971.

The demands of blacks and of leftists, the neoconservatives argued, were not liberal at all, but illiberal. The civil rights movement had preached and embraced tolerance; the New Left and Black Power movement were intolerant. There was a special Jewish interest in stability rather than social upheaval, the neoconservatives argued. "Jewish interests are clearly tied up with the fate of liberalism, of tolerance of nonviolence," Nathan Glazer wrote in 1971. The demands of the Black Power movement and the New Left threatened Jewish interests and the kind of liberal, meritocratic society in which Jews thrived.

The neoconservatives took themselves very seriously, and the relentless tone of their writings sometimes made it seem that Jews as a community were becoming more conservative. But the picture in the 1970s was more muddled. At root, there was not so much a rise in Jewish conservatism as a disillusionment with liberalism—a groping for a new set of beliefs and values. Thus, Jews could still be liberal but show fears of black anti-Semitism. They could support a strong Israel but remain active in the American peace movement. Even the neoconservatives themselves reflected this confusion. Some, like Kristol, became Republicans, while others, even as they voted Republican, insisted they were still New Deal Democrats thrown out of a party that had lost its way.

Peretz manifested some of this confusion. In 1968, disillusioned with the New Politics Convention, he had become an active backer and contributor to Eugene McCarthy's insurgent campaign to unseat Lyndon Johnson. But in 1972 the candidacy of another anti-war candidate, George McGovern, made Peretz feel uncomfortable. McGovern's slogan, running on a strong anti-war platform, was "Come Home, America." Peretz feared that was just what McGovern meant. Peretz wanted the United States to pull out of Vietnam, but he was not an isolationist. The 1967 war had made him exquisitely sensitive to how dependent Israel was on a strong America. As an anti-communist liberal he also believed that the survival of democracy throughout the world depended on a strong America as well. Peretz did some work for McGovern, but when November came he voted for McCarthy again—a symbolic vote since McCarthy was running as an independent and had made the ballot in Massachusetts but had no real chance of winning.

At Harvard, Peretz was locked into what he readily acknowledged was a second-string career. He was a gifted and popular teacher and had been an instructor and assistant professor since 1965, and a teaching fellow for four years before that. But he did not have the disposition to do serious scholarship and it was clear that Harvard did not consider him tenure material. Harvard offered him a position as a lecturer and as master of Cabot House, one of the undergraduate dormitories. But his ego required more and he felt he could make a contribution to the debate over the future of liberalism that was starting to take shape in the early 1970s. When Gilbert Harrison, the owner of *The New Republic*, a liberal magazine that had been home to Walter Lippmann, mentioned to Peretz at one point that he was thinking of selling the magazine,

Peretz told him, "When you do, let's talk." In May 1974, Harrison agreed to sell *The New Republic* to Peretz.

Seven months earlier, the confidence of American Jews in the security of Israel had been badly shaken by the surprise Arab attack of the October 1973 Yom Kippur War. Egypt and Syria had attacked Israel on Yom Kippur, the holiest day of the Jewish year. The surprise attack swept Egyptian troops across the Suez Canal and brought Syrian troops back onto the Golan Heights—overlooking the heart of Israel—that Israel had seized in 1967. For the first two days, Israel was on the defensive.

If the 1967 war had thrilled America's Jews with the apparent invincibility of Israeli soldiers, the 1973 war brought them firmly back to earth. Coupled with the surprise attack, the Arab countries cut off oil supplies to the West, a potentially devastating weapon that would unhinge Western economies. Unlike the six-day miracle of 1967, this war dragged on. The Israeli army was resupplied by the United States and counterattacked, but was halted before it could encircle and perhaps wipe out part of the Egyptian army. Unlike 1967, there would be no clear victor. The United States did not want Israel to wipe out the Arabs. On October 24 a cease-fire was declared. Egypt declared this a victory; it had certainly dented Israeli superiority in the Middle East. The illusion that Israel would be invincible was over.

At his home in Cambridge, Peretz could not sleep. As news of the war broke, Peretz tried to get more information by telephoning a friend of his in Israel. His friend knew even less than Peretz. Prior to 1967, Peretz had spent part of his summers in Israel and had known people who made *aliyah* and moved there. He had never felt the desire to settle in Israel, but he always felt a sense of spiritual uplift when he visited. He gave to Israeli charities and in the early 1970s had joined the Jerusalem Foundation, a group set up by Jerusalem mayor Teddy Kollek to bolster Jerusalem's cultural centers and to bring Arabs and Jews together. In 1973, as he followed news of the Yom Kippur War from his home in Cambridge, Peretz realized how deeply he felt Israel made up the psychological armor of American Jews.

The explosiveness of the Middle East coupled with the disruptions of the oil embargo made the Middle East a natural topic for any intellectual magazine. America was disengaging from Vietnam; attention was drifting away from Indochina. But as he took over *The New Republic* in the spring of 1974, Peretz pushed concern for Israel to the very forefront of the magazine, rallying editorials and articles to its cause.

For *The New Republic*, Israel was a besieged state surrounded by madmen. There was much truth to that. Following the 1967 war, Israel had enjoyed a brief period of heroism, hailed as a brave country that had turned back the massed force of Arab armies. But as the occupation of the West Bank dragged on and the conflict remained intense, more and more countries became critical of Israel at the United Nations and elsewhere. The Palestinian cause attracted more sympathy. With the Arab oil embargo it seemed as if the Arab world had a weapon that would be effective. "Israel has become in world affairs a pariah nation," *The New Republic* declared in 1975, and "the power of Arab oil is just now great enough to swing both the weak and the mighty to join the anti-Israel chorus." Its borders had never been secure, and the magazine pointed out correctly how important small stretches of land could be. "Worrying about particular hills and valleys is no trifle for the Israelis. It is a bare hour's march from the Jordan River to Jerusalem; geography itself seems almost to threaten both the agricultural settlements in the north and the population centers on the coast."

At issue were the peculiar circumstances of Israel's right to exist. People didn't just want to criticize Israel; they wanted to wipe it off the face of the earth. *The New Republic* became Israel's most articulate advocate among general-interest publications. Its positions were tightly argued and smoothly written. Writing on the Palestinian Liberation Organization, the magazine declared: "Even if this fractured and murderous rump suddenly were to cease its holy war rhetoric and publicly re-

voke its historical commitments, there still would be no reason to believe that its essential purposes had changed or that
an agreement would be anything but a new step for its war
against Zionism. Words, gestures, meanings are fluid in the
Arab world. One day's embrace easily gives way to another
day's killing."

The Arabs never seemed to let up on Israel. In 1972, the
PLO had seized and killed eleven Israeli athletes at the summer Olympics in Munich. Arab terrorists attacked in Israeli
cities and villages like Kiryat Shemona, Ma'alot, and Nahriya,
killing civilians, many of them women and children. Airport
attacks took place at Lod Airport in Israel, in Athens, Munich,
Rome, and Istanbul. Despite all this, the United Nations welcomed Yasir Arafat, the head of the PLO, to speak before the
General Assembly. He came with a gun strapped underneath
his shirt. And in November 1975, after failing in an attempt
to expel Israel from the United Nations, opponents of Israel
passed a resolution in the United Nations that labeled Zionism a form of "racism and racial discrimination." "This day
will live in infamy," Israel's ambassador to the United Nations
said the day of the vote. "Hitler would have felt at home in
this hall."

Peretz believed he could not trust the Arab political culture
that dominated the Middle East. He read widely in Middle
Eastern history and believed there were features of Arab political culture that made Arab politics untrustworthy. In talking with Arabs and reading their statements, he was always
alert to fraudulence. When he went to the West Bank in Israel
to meet with Arabs, as he sometimes did, his distrusting antennae were always up.

The shift in Israeli politics in 1977 with the election of
Menachem Begin and his rightist Likud party troubled Peretz.
It planted the seeds of what would become a dilemma for
American Jews. Begin represented the antithesis of what up
to then had been Israel's image as a progressive, socialist coun-
try, headed by its heroic founders like David Ben-Gurion and
Golda Meir. Begin's roots lay in the revisionist Zionist ide-
ology of Vladimir Jabotinsky and his followers, who believed

that Israel deserved the land on both sides of the Jordan River, not just the part given to Israel under the British partition plan. Begin was an avowed terrorist. In the years leading to Israel's independence, he had been the leader of the Irgun, the underground army that kidnapped British soldiers and attacked Arab targets. When the Irgun blew up the King David Hotel in Jerusalem in 1946 with only a few minutes' warning to those inside, the blast killed ninety-one people, including seventeen Jews. Begin's communiqué extended condolences only to the Jewish victims. For almost thirty years Begin had been the leader of Israel's opposition, a shrill minority spokesman, opposing any concessions to the Arabs in the wake of the 1967 war, proclaiming that the occupied West Bank of the Jordan was part of "Greater Israel."

In office, Begin declared the West Bank to be part of Israel and annexed the Golan Heights bordering Syria. He encouraged Jewish settlers to live in the occupied territories to stake Israel's claim. He lectured Western leaders and American Jews on the Holocaust, told them they had no right to tell Israel what to do. He ordered crushing military strikes in response to terrorist acts against Israel, attacks that often shattered civilian targets in Lebanon. He was cruder, more emotional, more condescending than any Israeli leader America, or American Jews, had ever encountered.

Peretz detested Begin. He strove to ensure *The New Republic* never printed a good word about him. Peretz criticized the Begin government frequently. "Begin's actions are a threat both to the moral fiber of Israel and to the support Israel still enjoys in the West . . ." he wrote in an editorial in 1981, after Begin had ordered the bombing of a PLO headquarters in a crowded residential area of Beirut. Another article by Marie Syrkin, a longtime Zionist and friend of Peretz's, charged that Begin himself was a threat to Israel. "Those genuinely concerned for the future of the Jewish state cannot evade the responsibility of protesting Israeli government policies that are intrinsically wrong," Syrkin wrote.

But Peretz's support for Israel was undiminished, and in disputes between the Arabs and Israel or responding to American pressure on Israel to compromise, to negotiate away the West Bank in exchange for peace, Peretz sided, vociferously, with Israel. Begin's election had not changed the ultimate goal of the Arab states: To destroy the Jewish state. Moreover, Begin was not synonymous with Zionism, or with Israel. It was one of the triumphs of Zionism, Peretz felt, that the Jews of Israel could elect a bad leader. They could make mistakes. That, however, would not imperil the survival of the state or his support of it.

For other Jews, the question was more complicated. They were angry, and embarrassed, by Begin's intransigence, by his expansionistic policies of encouraging settlements on the West Bank.

Many liberal Jews felt Peretz went too far with his attacks on Arabs and his defense of Israel. But despite the ambivalence stirred by Begin, polls of Jews suggested Peretz was in tune with American Jewish feelings. By the late 1970s, Israel had emerged as the core issue for American Jews. One political analyst dubbed the phenomenon "pro-Israelism." A survey of young Jewish leaders in 1978–79—men and women in their mid-thirties who held positions in Jewish organizations—found they gave their highest priority to raising money for Israel. A poll of rank-and-file Jews three years later found 78 percent believed Jews should not vote for a candidate who is unfriendly to Israel. Almost the same number believed Israel's policies in its disputes with Arabs were "about right." Asked about their personal feelings toward Israel, 83 percent agreed with the statement, "If Israel were destroyed, I would feel as if I had suffered one of the greatest personal tragedies of my life." The humanitarian liberalism of the 1950s, with its focus on equal rights for blacks, now competed with—and in some ways was replaced by—a commitment to Israel that occupied a great deal of Jewish personal and political thinking.

If Israel was the overwhelming issue for Jews in foreign policy, affirmative action emerged as the overwhelming issue for Jews in domestic policy.

Affirmative action had first been developed at a time of a

growing economy in response to the paucity of blacks in many jobs. Back in the early 1960s, it was relatively easy to get into law school. Just about anyone with a college degree and a high-C average could get into law school somewhere. Bolt Hall, the law school of the University of California at Berkeley, was one of the top-ranked schools in the nation. It accepted anyone with a B average—three-quarters of those who applied. Yet in 1965, in all the country's accredited white law schools, there were only 434 black students. Blacks made up 11 percent of the country's population, but only 2 percent of its lawyers and 1.3 percent of its law school enrollees. In the late 1960s, driven by the gains of the civil rights movement and protests on campus, colleges and universities adopted a range of "affirmative" measures to attract more black students (the phrase "affirmative action" stemmed from an executive order signed by Johnson in 1965, ordering federal contractors to take aggressive measures to hire black employees). Colleges set up special training programs for blacks, increased financial aid, and recruited blacks aggressively.

But at the same time colleges and universities were increasing their efforts to recruit and accept black students, the competition for jobs and places in law and medical school was stiffening. Getting a law school or medical school credential became more and more important. Between 1964 and 1975, the number of students taking the LSAT, the exam to get into law school, increased by more than threefold. Law schools expanded their classes to meet the demand, but they could not meet it all. By 1970, 70,000 students nationwide were applying for 35,000 law school spots. At prestigious law schools like Bolt Hall or the University of Washington, it was not unusual for five people to apply for every spot.

The upshot was that standards rose. A *B* average was no longer good enough. Only the best and the brightest could get in.

That placed in a quandary liberals committed to expanding opportunities for blacks. The metaphor invoked in the 1960s envisioned preparing blacks before the race so they could make it to the starting line. But by the late 1970s, the starting line kept being pushed up. Programs that might have given disadvantaged blacks the skills to get into law school in 1965 were insufficient to get them into the far more competitive law schools of 1970. Moreover, many blacks believed that racism was deeply entrenched in universities. The only way to guarantee that blacks entered universities and colleges, they argued, was to establish goals, timetables, and quotas. In the late 1960s and early 1970s, many universities adopted preferential policies that brought in minority students under quota, or near-quota, programs. They set aside places for "disadvantaged" students and explicitly directed their admissions committees to seek out blacks and other minorities to fill a certain number of seats.

Two cases—one involving Marco DeFunis in 1974, the other involving Alan Bakke three years later—crystallized the debate on affirmative action. In each case the major Jewish organizations—the American Jewish Congress, the American Jewish Committee, and the Anti-Defamation League, together with many prominent Jewish academics—sided against the affirmative action programs, although some Jews, including Greenberg and the NAACP Legal Defense Fund, supported the black position.

Marco DeFunis was a Jewish student who had applied to the University of Washington Law School in 1970 and again in 1971. Both times he had been rejected even though he was a Phi Beta Kappa graduate of the University of Washington with an A— average. On the numerical scale that the law school used to evaluate applicants, DeFunis scored 76.23. That was at least two points higher than thirty-two minority students who were admitted to the law school. But the law school, in order to guarantee that minorities would attend, picked students from two pools of applicants—one for non-minority students like DeFunis, a second for blacks, Chicanos, American Indians, and Filipino-Americans. So DeFunis was rejected and the minority applicants, who had a lower number than DeFunis, were accepted. DeFunis sued the school, saying that he was being discriminated against because he was white; the law school, he charged, should look at all applicants equally. Although the Supreme Court eventually declined to hear the case, since DeFunis had been provisionally admitted to law school while he brought the case and was set to graduate, the issues he raised framed the dilemma of affirmative action for many Jews.

Faced with the prominent opposition of many Jews to aggressive affirmative action programs, many blacks cried betrayal. Jews appeared to be willing to fight for civil rights when it affected rednecks in the South but not when it threatened their own interests. There was admittedly a healthy degree of self-interest at stake. Jews had not raised great objections to affirmative action programs that focused on blue-collar jobs. But large numbers of Jews routinely applied to medical school, law school, and other graduate schools.

But the objections to affirmative action and quotas were as much rooted in the Jewish psyche as in the hard calculus of self-interest. Favoritism of black candidates over white was a direct challenge to the merit system under which Jews had made enormous strides. The university quota systems of the 1930s, 1940s, and 1950s were a recent and painful memory for even the most liberal Jews. Michael Walzer, Peretz's friend and by the 1970s a full professor at Harvard, the young man who had been so moved by the telling of the Exodus story at the black church in Alabama in 1960, had not even bothered to apply to Harvard or Yale in the 1950s because everyone "knew" they would not allow many Jews in. Education carried great symbolic power for Jews. This was the way they had made it. It was the system they had mastered. In a country where credentials were becoming more and more important, every black getting into a law or medical school might conceivably mean a Jew, like DeFunis, being kept out. Jews could never succeed in a society that embraced quotas; they made up less than 3 percent of the population.

Peretz was not as upset as many Jewish academics with affirmative action as a threat to Jews. Early on in the debate, he attended a dinner party where Seymour Martin Lipset, a political scientist, predicted that the great beneficiaries of affirmative action would be Jewish women. In fact, Lipset turned out to be right.

The New Republic opposed affirmative action, but not with the same fervor that characterized its support for Israel. It published articles pro and con. In a special issue on the Bakke case, the magazine argued that applicants to college and graduate and professional school should be selected on their individual merit rather than on any group merit. Peretz believed in the even-handedness of admissions committees. He believed that this was, in many ways, a new age, that the time of bias and blind prejudice against blacks had passed. His worry, which would become even more important later, was where the good black applicants would come from. Without publicity, he funded an office at Harvard to recruit blacks to apply for graduate school. The results were disappointing. Many blacks did not seem to have the skills to cut it at a place like Harvard. The pool of black Ph.D.s was shrinking. If that pool was not there, there would be no black Ph.D.'s. Where, Peretz wondered, were the blacks who could take advantage of educational opportunity?

What was striking in *The New Republic* under Peretz was how little it talked explicitly about blacks and about black issues. There was a great deal about Israel, Watergate, the oil embargo, and the future of the Democratic Party, but relatively little about discrimination, affirmative action, and black concerns. This reflected the changing definition of liberalism. There were, in the 1970s, many ways to be liberal: feminism, gay rights, concern over the environment. Civil rights no longer commanded the nation's attention as it had in the early 1960s. The treatment of blacks had also materially changed since the late 1950s. Whereas once blacks had been attacked and bludgeoned in the South, now they were more visible, in offices, in government, at universities. The urgency that impelled the fight for civil rights had waned.

Percolating beneath all these factors was the fact that the sympathy that many liberals—including Jewish liberals—had once felt for blacks had turned into frustration over the failures of Great Society liberalism and anger at problems that would not go away. A sizable number of blacks, locked in poverty, seemed immune to the American dream. Whereas fifteen years before, many whites had looked at the gap between blacks and whites in America and concluded that the country was at fault, now the burden of blame had shifted. After years of anti-poverty programs, anti-discrimination programs, and remedial programs, why weren't blacks making it?

When rioting broke out in New York in the summer of 1977 during a major blackout, no one saw it as a cry against injustice and repression. New York had been mugged, the liberal columnist Mary McGrory declared. More than a billion dollars in goods were stolen from 2,000 stores. Thirty-seven hundred looters had been arrested.

"People have begun to think that New York's problems are not the kind that can be solved by spending money," Peretz wrote in a *New Republic* editorial following the Harlem riot. ". . . No city has been more generous in terms of the amount of money or the variety of programs it has offered to help the poor. None paid its civil servants better. None was more generous with its education system; New York City even opened its university to all residents. Thousands of lives may have been made better by this generosity, but there is no evidence that the sum total of poverty and violence was reduced, and those are the curses of New York." In a national poll conducted that same year, 65 percent of whites said they believed blacks had worse jobs, income, and housing than whites "because most blacks just don't have the motivation or will power to pull themselves out of poverty."

Peretz didn't believe that blacks lacked the motivation or will power to pull themselves out of poverty. He did believe that traditional liberalism had stagnated. Roosevelt had been flexible and daring. But from liberals he heard the same old truisms on crime, welfare, busing, and affirmative action. The Democrats, especially Carter, seemed paralyzed. Peretz did not see himself as one of the neoconservatives for whom everything was a seamless world. He did not have a "Jewish" position on every issue. He cared about Israel, yes. But that did not mean he had a "Jewish" stance on the environment, on taxes, on defense policy. On foreign policy he felt more and more strongly about a strong America and opposed to ideas like a nuclear freeze. As the Carter administration unraveled, *The New Republic* began searching out a new Democratic Party politics—one more pragmatic, less fuzzy-headed, less wedded to special-interest groups and what Peretz felt was the discredited liberalism of the late 1960s. In the 1980 election, *The New Republic* endorsed independent John Anderson over Carter. For the first time since Franklin Roosevelt, the Democratic Party did not get a majority of the Jewish votes; defections to Anderson kept Carter's Jewish vote below 50 percent. There was talk of a conservative realignment in the country, and even *Dissent*, the socialist bulwark of Jewish-oriented magazines, conceded that the neoconservatives and the politics they represented were likely to become a permanent fixture of Jewish political life, with American Jews now split into three camps: conservative, left-wing, and a broad liberal-to-moderate middle.

There were still Jewish liberals who sought alliances with blacks. Jews still voted for blacks in local elections and supported some of their causes. But the devotion to civil rights that had characterized liberalism, especially Jewish liberalism, in the early 1960s was gone, replaced by a broader range of concerns and tempered by anger and hostility toward black criticism of Israel and the seeming intransigence of black problems.

New York Mayor Edward Koch, the city's second Jewish mayor, describing a visit to a black church in Harlem in January 1978

I was asked to go up to one of the major black churches—the Convent Avenue Baptist Church at 135th Street and Convent Avenue in Harlem—to read a proclamation on Martin Luther King, Jr.'s, birthday. I went up there with Basil Paterson [a deputy mayor, who was

*black], and when we sat down near the altar I noticed
that I was the only white person in the church. . . . They
call on me. . . . I just start to read the proclamation. Suddenly I see this guy standing up and yelling in the balcony. And he's pointing down at me and yelling in this
church, "Don't let him speak. Send the Jew back to the
synagogues!" I mean you can't get any more vile than
that. And I am just standing there and thinking, Well
somebody is going to get up and say something. Maybe
Basil? Not a word in my defense from him. And this guy
in the gallery is screaming away. Finally a couple of
deacons, the church elders, get up and look at this guy
in the balcony and one of them says, "Hush, brother."
Then the minister quieted him.*

I said to myself, "Hush, brother"?

*I never got over that. I thought, What if Basil Paterson
or Andrew Young got up and read a proclamation at
Temple Emmanuel on Warsaw Ghetto Uprising Day and
someone in the congregation yelled, "Send him back to
Harlem. Don't let him speak"? Why, there would be a
storm of protest in the synagogue and in the community.*

*I did not, as they hoped, roll over. Instead . . . I con-
tinued on aggressively and up front, attempting to deliver
services on the basis of need, and specifically, not on the
basis of who was threatening me or who had political
clout.*

In 1982, Anne Peretz, who had trained as a therapist, opened
a clinic in Somerville and started a series of programs in Roxbury and other black neighborhoods of Boston designed to help
poor black families. As an outside witness to the evolution of
black-Jewish relations—she was neither black nor Jewish—
Anne Peretz viewed the clashes since 1966 as clashes of style
and attitude. People always talked about them as clashes of
politics and ideology, she felt, but their roots were different.

She was more sympathetic than her husband to the demands
for Black Power and black culture. Jews already had a culture,

a deep and identifiable one they could draw on for strength and for a sense of identity. Blacks were still searching for their history and identity. There was in many Jews, she felt, including her husband, a certain arrogance about Jewish culture. It was justifiable arrogance. Jewish culture was so rich, so rooted. It was easy to look at blacks wearing Afros and consider that somehow silly. But many Jews, she felt, could not accept that some people organized their thought processes differently than Jews did. The Jews she knew were very verbal and very quick; they could easily overwhelm blacks at meetings. But it was wrong, she felt, to think that just because you saw the world one way that was the only way to see it. The desire of blacks to run their own organizations in the late 1960s had been an effort to get out from under the shadow of whites and fight their own battles in their own ways.

Anne Peretz believed the world was more complex than her husband sometimes saw it. Their disagreements were not major. She agreed that the old knee-jerk liberal reaction to black problems had been wrong. But as she worked with blacks directly, she talked to her husband about the problems black families faced and how the solutions favored by the quick-witted writers at *The New Republic* were sometimes too pat and too simplistic.

The stories his wife told him about the black families she counseled troubled Peretz. In 1983, in the wake of a demonstration organized by civil rights leaders to commemorate the twentieth anniversary of the March on Washington, he raised those concerns in an editorial on the state of the black civil rights movement.

The frustrations of fifteen years came pouring out. Peretz recapitulated the "desultory history" of the civil rights movement after the assassination of King in 1968: "At SNCC [John] Lewis was forced out as insufficiently militant by Stokely Carmichael, who gave way to H. Rap Brown, who was displaced by the Black Panthers, and so on down a diminishing line. . . . The phenomena of mau-mauing, of guilt-tripping white liberals, of separatist fantasies, of dashiki-clad jive—these have pretty much run their course."

But Peretz then cited a litany of statistics that revealed the deep pain of blacks in poverty: "There is an epidemic—the metaphor of pathology is not inappropriate, for what is involved is the health of the black community—of single-parent families, unmarried mothers, deserting fathers. . . . Forty-one percent of black families are headed by women without husbands present, up almost a third in the last decade. The divorce rate among blacks has almost doubled in a decade, and is now double that of whites. The percentage of black children living in one-parent homes rose from 32 percent to 49 percent in the same period. . . . The fertility rate of black teenagers is by far the highest in the developed world. For every thousand black females under nineteen, most of them unmarried, there are 515 children born into all kinds of disadvantages of life: inadequate mothering or worse, the absence of a father, the chintzy and humiliating public dole as the most common source of income, the trap of dependence."

Peretz offered no solutions. "Though it won't be easy, someone must begin to address the problem now, and it probably should be blacks first," he wrote. But the statistics and the stories his wife told him sobered him. What was happening to poor black families? What could be done?

In the 1950s, the common interests between Jews and blacks had been self-evident; the differences lay below the surface and were not much talked about. But now, not only the problems but the interests of blacks and Jews were diverging. Peretz was increasingly troubled by the persistence of black anti-Semitism and hostility to Israel. A poll in 1983 showed blacks the most hostile to Israel of fifteen groups surveyed. They were also among the groups holding the highest percentage of anti-Semitic attitudes. Anti-Semitic attitudes increased among more educated blacks. Peretz found that appalling: This was the only form of bigotry that increased with education.

Peretz's positions on Israel increasingly made him a controversial figure. Some of his severest critics were other Jews. To read *The New Republic* was to believe that there could never be a Palestinian state, that one could never fully trust the Arabs, that the Israeli occupation of the West Bank and

Gaza Strip would have to continue. Peretz kept up his attacks on Begin and his policies, but Israel's continued occupation of the West Bank and Gaza, and its invasion of Lebanon in 1982, eroded the ability of many liberal Jews to defend Israel's policies. They found Peretz's continued attacks on Israel's critics intemperate, self-righteous, an obstacle to peace. There seemed to be no answer to the effect a generation of occupation was having on Israel and on a generation of Israelis who had grown up in Israel as an occupying power, ruling over 1 million Arabs with no political rights. For these Jews, Peretz seemed a right-wing figure.

The anger that Peretz and *The New Republic* stirred in critics was fed by the magazine's arch style and by the personal attacks that dotted *The New Republic*'s pages, particularly Peretz's own writings. Enemies and people with whom Peretz disagreed were "second-rate thinkers," "self-indulgent, solipsistic," "fellow travelers and their ilk." Peretz conceded that some of his characterizations and comments were unfair. But more often than not he rooted his defense in truth. He would listen to criticism that he was too one-sided, that he was obsessed with Israel. His voice rising, he would say that he had been right: He had been right that Saudi Arabia would not be a trustworthy ally of the United States, right that Syria was not interested in peace, right about the terrorism and the duplicitousness of the PLO.

Were Peretz only a fringe figure and *The New Republic* a magazine of declining influence, he, and it, would have been easy to ignore. Neither was true. While many readers winced at Peretz's style and disagreed with some of its positions, the magazine gained in circulation and influence. Peretz's emergence represented a change in the Jewish community as well. The critique of black America and the defense of Israel unleashed in *The New Republic* were part of the change in the Jewish self-image uncorked by 1967. There was a new self-assurance and willingness to speak out. In Peretz's mind, his attacks on black leadership and on critics of Israel represented an intellectual honesty, a need to speak out clearly. At its extreme, these attitudes represented a kind of muscular Judaism that was also reflected in the confrontational politics of New York's Mayor Edward Koch, who denounced "poverty pimps" and accused black leaders of being anti-Semitic, and in the growth of the Israel lobby in Washington, D.C. More Jews were staking out their turf and defending it. They would not be Bontshas.

This new Jewish assertiveness came at a time when blacks, too, were gaining in political power. They were tired, as many told me when I spoke with them, of white liberals picking their leaders. They would not be told what to do or what causes to support.

In such an atmosphere, the 1984 presidential campaign of Jesse Jackson began.

A radio address by Louis Farrakhan, March 1984

The Jews don't like Farrakhan, so they call me Hitler. Well, that's a good name. Hitler was a very great man. He wasn't great for me as a black person, but he was a great German. . . . He rose Germany up from nothing. Well, in a sense you could say there's similarity in that we are rising our people up from nothing.

What is it about Hitler that you love to call every black man who rises up with strength a Hitler?

What have I done? Who have I killed? I warn you, be careful, be careful. You're putting yourself in dangerous, dangerous shoes. You have been the killer of all the prophets. Now, if you seek my life, you only show that you are no better than your fathers.

Jewish suspicion of Jackson reached back to the events following the 1979 resignation of Andrew Young as ambassador to the United Nations.

On August 13, 1979, *Newsweek* had reported that Young had met with the PLO observer at the United Nations. The story said the meeting had been "inadvertent" and limited to fifteen minutes of social conversation. It soon became clear that the meeting had been more substantive than that and that Young had misled the State Department when asked about it. The United States had a policy that it would not meet with the PLO until it recognized Israel's right to exist. On August 15, in a storm of publicity, Young resigned.

The issue quickly mushroomed amidst accusations from black leaders that Jewish opinion and organizations had pressured Young into resigning. In fact, only two officials had called for his resignation, but the resignation crystallized the feeling that Jews had set up a litmus test for Israel that no one could pass. In meetings, articles, and press conferences, black leaders called into question the roots of Jewish support. "When there wasn't much decency Jews were willing to share decency," Jesse Jackson declared. "But when there is power they don't want to share power."

In the wake of the Young controversy, several black leaders traveled to the Middle East. Jackson went in the fall of 1979. Begin refused to meet with him. In several comments, Jackson appeared to diminish the importance of the Holocaust. And when he met with Arafat in Beirut, Jackson joined the PLO leader in an embrace. The picture of Jackson hugging Arafat was all many Jews felt they had to know about Jackson's policy on the Middle East.

The New Republic began its coverage of Jackson with the best parody of the 1984 election campaign.

On the cover, the magazine pictured Jackson, one hand on the Bible, the other upraised, taking the oath for President of the United States. The headline read, "I have a scheme . . ." Inside, a one-page article contemplated Jackson's candidacy. How much fun it would be to watch Jackson, with his penchant for rhyming one-line slogans, debate President Ronald Reagan. The article imagined what the debate might be like:

Moderator: Mr. Jackson, what specifically are some of the economic policy changes you would bring to this office?
Mr. Jackson: We don't want *free grub*, we want in the *power hub!*

From being porters to giving orders, from saying yessir to the
Social Register.

The one-liners cascaded across the page. "We don't want an
alibi, we want our share of the *economic pie!* . . . From a thirst
for knowledge to the Electoral College . . . From being lonely
and blue to 1600 Pennsylvania Avenue . . . From having no
fun to Air Force One." The article was entitled, appropriately,
"From Chicago Resident to U.S. President."

It was a gem-like example of the new style of *The New
Republic*: clever, acerbic, not afraid to deflate liberal icons. A
lengthier, accompanying article on Jackson was well-written
and well-researched, leaving the impression of an opportunist
running for his own ambitions who might still draw large
black support.

Peretz thought the parody wonderful. As the months went
by and *The New Republic* hammered away at Jackson's candidacy, it usually referred to him as "Jesse" and worked a
rhyme in the headline somewhere. In his rhyming and jiving
talk, Jackson reminded Peretz of no one so much as Muhammad Ali, the boxer. One longtime staffer, Henry Fairlie, became more and more troubled by the magazine's treatment
of Jackson. It showed a lack of curiosity about what Jackson
was accomplishing, Fairlie thought. His objections came out
at a heated editorial meeting in the magazine's Washington
offices. The magazine was going to carry another editorial
about Jackson. Fairlie argued against it. Peretz, who was curious about so many things, had ceased being curious about
Jackson, Fairlie said. In a way, he felt, Peretz's closed-mindedness about Jackson reflected a similar closed-mindedness
about the Third World. Peretz was so angry with Jackson about
his stand on Israel that he didn't even want to listen to him
anymore.

Fairlie appealed to Peretz to do a positive piece on the Jackson campaign, which had defied projections and garnered more
delegates than anyone thought possible. Peretz let Fairlie write
a piece in support of Jackson, but none of this changed his
views. As controversies over Jackson's use of the word "hy-

mie" and his endorsement by Black Muslim minister Louis Farrakhan engulfed his candidacy, Peretz was not surprised. He believed that Jackson was a charlatan and a hustler. He had to wonder about the black community: In their moment of exercising political power they were turning to someone who reminded Peretz most of George Wallace. Peretz could no more support Jackson in 1984 than he could have supported Wallace in 1968.

When the Democratic Convention met in San Francisco, *The New Republic* urged the presidential nominee, Walter Mondale, to pick Tom Bradley, the black mayor of Los Angeles, as his running mate. Peretz believed Bradley had the necessary qualifications: He had governed a multi-racial city. More important, in Peretz's mind, the selection of Bradley would end the question once and for all about whether a black could be named Vice President.

Mondale picked Geraldine Ferraro, a congresswoman from New York, and went down to a crushing defeat, winning the electoral votes of only one state, Minnesota, and the District of Columbia. There was probably no way Mondale could have won, Peretz believed, but with Bradley as his running mate, he could hardly have done worse.

Despite predictions before the election that Ronald Reagan might win a majority of the Jewish vote, Jews voted for Mondale by a margin of two to one. But the votes for Mondale did not erase the bitter legacy of the campaign for black-Jewish relations. In the late 1960s, when charges of black anti-Semitism arose, the so-called mainstream leaders of the civil rights movement—King, the heads of the NAACP and the National Urban League—were quick to denounce it. Now, in 1984, the two most popular figures in the black community, Jesse Jackson and Louis Farrakhan—one the leading political figure, the other the most charismatic—were either overtly anti-Semitic or tied to anti-Semitic statements.

The 1984 election ended with Peretz ascendant. Peretz's style and manner infuriated many. But once one separated that from the ideas of *The New Republic*, one had to acknowledge its influence. Mondale's defeat confirmed *The New Re-*

public's insistence that the Democrats had to find a new way, and new ideas, to recapture the White House. The magazine's views were widely read and respected. Not everyone agreed with Peretz, but there was a new mood among Jews, and in the country. *The New Republic* had captured much of the disaffection with 1960s-style liberalism and the search for something to replace it.

Peretz continued to see himself as a pragmatist. He could not be wedded to a set ideology. He was suspicious of what he called "enthusiasms." Enthusiasms could shift direction quickly. He remembered his parents warning him in the 1940s when the Communist Party supported the creation of the state of Israel: "Now they're for us. Soon, they'll be against us." Peretz saw himself interested in what worked.

Peretz challenged preconceptions and said things others would not say. He asked tough questions and stimulated debate. His criticisms wounded liberals because they so often hit so close to home.

Yet for all his belief in pragmatism and political alliances, and for all the work of *The New Republic* to air new views, there was in Peretz's own writings and in much of what *The New Republic* did an *ad hominem* tone that was troubling and destructive. Peretz could attack people and ideas unmercifully. Much of his own writing and the writing in *The New Republic* lacked compassion. It entertained little self-doubt. This was not the recipe for building coalitions. It was a recipe for balkanization, for fending off attacks rather than reaching out for understanding and solutions.

Peretz's tone reflected the tone of the country—for the country in the 1980s was becoming polarized, pulling into itself. Every side knew its issues, marshaled its arguments, and barreled ahead.

And yet Peretz remained a more complex figure than his magazine suggested. He was genuinely troubled by black poverty and the dilemmas of what came to be called the black underclass. He found himself thinking at times about the day in 1963 when he had joined the great March on Washington. Josephine Baker, the black entertainer, had been living as an expatriate in Paris. She arrived at the steps of the Lincoln Memorial in a whirl, and with a flourish climbed atop the platform. She looked out at the 250,000 people massed below and pronounced: "This is a salt-and-pepper crowd."

Throughout the 1960s, throughout the tumult of Black Power and the bitterness over Israel, Peretz had believed America might still become a salt-and-pepper country. Even after the Jackson campaign and the bitterness it created, the memory of Baker uttering that phrase still gave Peretz a flush.

But Peretz, as he acknowledged to me late one afternoon as we sat talking in his living room in Cambridge, had only one close black friend, a former student who had become a lawyer in Washington, D.C. And that made him sad, he said. That was not the way he believed things were going to turn out when he started out in civil rights.

7

Too Young to Have Marched with Martin Luther King: Donna Brazile

Late at night, Donna Brazile would sneak under her covers with a flashlight and play the beam across the pages of *Soul on Ice* and the *Autobiography of Malcolm X*. Her mother didn't allow such trash in the house. Her parents were the Martin Luther King set: churchgoing, believing in nonviolence and the power of love to overcome segregation, even in their hometown of Kenner, Louisiana, just outside New Orleans, where a dozen years after the *Brown* v. *Board of Education* decision the schools were still segregated. When Donna was six years old, her grandmother had sent her scurrying down the street to the local church to look in on the civil rights meetings. They were always called in a hurry—someone would call at two to say there was a meeting at six. The talk would be about plans to sit in somewhere or about the bus boycotts somewhere else. There were ten children in the house; Donna's parents had no time to go. Her father was a construction worker, her mother a domestic. Her grandmother was busy with the children, too. Donna would stand in the back of the church and stretch to see what was going on so she could tell her grandmother. Once she got there just as Martin Luther King left.

But now, in 1969, Brazile wanted to read about these new people, Malcolm X and Eldridge Cleaver. She saved her money and sneaked off to the bookstore to buy these books. People told her she was very militant and looked very angry. They would tell her to smile.

"Smile, Donna, why don't you smile?" they would call out to her.

But she couldn't smile. There was nothing nice about life. She had to be mean and vicious. Militant and angry. She was nine years old.

In 1967, when Brazile was seven years old, Richard Hatcher was elected mayor of Gary, Indiana, and Carl Stokes mayor of Cleveland, both becoming—it almost became a part of their names—the first elected black mayors of major American cities. Kenneth Gibson followed in Newark in 1970. Then Tom Bradley, on his second try in Los Angeles in 1973, and Coleman Young in Detroit and Maynard Jackson in Atlanta. The election of mayors was the tip of change across the country. In 1965, before the passage of the Voting Rights Act, there were just seventy-two elected black officials in the South. By 1975 there were 1,600. In 1967, there were just 480 elected black officials in the whole country. In 1975, there were 3,500; in 1984, 5,500. There were twenty-one congressmen by 1984 in the House of Representatives, up from just six in 1967. Soon blacks were being elected not only in cities with large black majorities or in cities, like Newark, that were symbols of urban blight. They were elected mayors of vibrant cities where blacks were not a majority: Los Angeles, with a black population of only 12 percent, kept reelecting Bradley. In 1983 Harold Washington was elected mayor of Chicago, which was about 40 percent black, and Wilson Goode was elected mayor of Philadelphia, which was about 45 percent black. By 1983,

the mayors of four of America's six largest cities were black
—and three of them had needed white votes to win.

Unlike the ministers and civil rights leaders who had led
the movement in the 1950s and 1960s, these black leaders
spoke to different constituencies. The leaders of SCLC, SNCC,
CORE, the NAACP, and the National Urban League had directed their message to blacks, but they had also directed it
to white liberals, whom they relied upon for money and support. The new black political leaders spoke to and for their
own black constituencies, which held them accountable to a
new set of goals and ambitions.

The political upsurge that began in 1967 reached a crescendo
in the 1984 Presidential campaign of Jesse Jackson. The forces
it unleashed sent a shockwave through Democratic politics
and opened a chasm in black-Jewish relations. Brazile had been
too young to march with Martin Luther King in the 1960s.
This time, she would witness it all.

From Soul on Ice *by Eldridge Cleaver*

To a White Girl

I love you
Because you're white,
Not because you're charming
Or bright.
Your whiteness
Is a silky thread
Snaking through my thoughts
In redhot patterns
Of lust and desire.

I hate you
Because you're white.
Your white meat
Is nightmare food.
White is

The skin of Evil.
You're my Moby Dick,
White Witch,
Symbol of the rope and hanging tree,
Of the burning cross.

Loving you thus
And hating you so,
My heart is torn in two,
Crucified.

To grow up in Louisiana is to be acutely aware of matters of color. Centuries of intermarriage between blacks and whites and the sons and daughters of mulattoes have blurred the sharp distinctions of skin color more than in any other part of the country. Someone black can have shades of skin color ranging from very dark to almost white. Blacks can have hair that is tight and curly or long and straight. Even within the same family, there may be variations; Brazile, for example, was dark-skinned with tightly curled, nappy hair. Some of her brothers and sisters had lighter skin and what Brazile called, with envy, "good hair"—the long, soft hair that white people had.

The schools in Jefferson Parish, which included Kenner, were still segregated when Brazile entered school. But even within the all-black schools there were distinctions made on the basis of skin color. The children with the lighter skin and softer hair got the better treatment. The teachers fussed over them, shunting the darker-skinned kids like Brazile aside as problem children. As news of Black Power and the Black Consciousness movement seeped into Kenner, Brazile challenged her teachers. They were believing what the white man was telling them. She was not going to play their game, be shunted aside because her skin was darker than the other black children's. The teachers told her she had a discipline problem.

Brazile was eight when King was assassinated and that, as much as anything, turned her away from what she considered her grandmother's stuff—the civil rights meetings down at the church, all that talk of love and nonviolence. It was a time of Black Power, and as much as a nine-year-old could be, she was swept up in it.

As she read Malcolm X and Eldridge Cleaver, she thought about her hair. Her mother made her straighten it for school. Brazile decided that when she was sixteen her first act would be to get it cut, short and nappy. Sixteen was the liberation age and straightening your hair for school was a sign of oppression. It meant you weren't proud of the way you looked.

It was around this time, in 1969, that Jefferson Parish started busing children to a neighboring all-white school, T. H. Harris, for integration. Brazile had gotten C's in conduct in her all-black school, but she had always gotten A's in everything else. The students looked up to her as a leader. Once they started being bused to the white school, the black students found themselves outnumbered. Almost at once, they started fighting: for their territory, for where they would stand when they got off the bus, for where they would sit in the lunchroom, for inclusion in the athletic programs.

Brazile incited many of the racial fights that first year of busing at T. H. Harris. At home, with her mother, she would be a sweet girl. But when she went out the door, she would put on her little cap and her gloves and she would be a terror. The buses would come at 7:30 A.M. When they arrived at the school, the principal would make the black students stand behind a yellow line before they could file inside. The white students stood over in a covered area. New Orleans could get damp and rainy in the winter. Why did she and her friends have to stand in the open behind the yellow line while the white folks stood underneath a cover, Brazile wanted to know? After two weeks of this, Brazile got up early. Before the school buses came, she got on her bicycle and rode around to every bus stop in her neighborhood that she could get to before seven-thirty and told the students to bring eggs. Brazile understood white people's place just like she understood black people's place. And the blacks' place was to be in first place.

"We are going to bring eggs," Brazile told the students. "And, behind the yellow line, we are going to throw eggs and have ourselves a demonstration."

Word got out; the white students brought eggs, too. The ensuing riot and egg fight brought out the police to quiet things down.

Brazile started writing poetry around this time. One poem that she saved read:

There's going to be a fight tonight
Black-White, Black-White
Man, there's going to be a fight tonight
Black blood, oh so precious.
White blood, oh so bad.
Fight, fight, Black-White
Man, you're going to see some killing tonight.

The Black Panther Party had come to Kenner, and while its activities were underground, Brazile found herself caught up in the debates over integration and nationalism, moderation and accommodationism, Martin King versus Malcolm X. The names of black history spilled over her: Marcus Garvey, Booker T. Washington.

This was all a far cry from the image of a handful of silent Negro children walking through rows of angry white parents in Little Rock in 1957. The new assertiveness of blacks, especially younger blacks, cut across the grain of many whites, who disliked the violence and threats of violence that went with it.

Gradually, conditions at T. H. Harris calmed down. Brazile and the school's assistant principal reached an agreement that black students would be included in more school activities. Nationally, the country's racial climate was quieting after a period of black militance and black nationalism. In 1976, when Brazile was in eleventh grade, Jimmy Carter was elected President and named Andrew Young ambassador to the United Nations. Brazile felt good about that. It seemed things for blacks were changing for the better. It was a time for feeling good about yourself.

Young was a hero. He was alive—unlike King or Malcolm X or all the other blacks who had been killed—and he was talking the truth. He was healing the rift between the United States and Africa and taking great strides toward making peace a part of foreign policy. He was letting black people know that Africa and Asia and the Middle East were important things to think about, that blacks had to live beyond their day-to-day reality and see the connections between their community and the world. There were some crazy people around, people like Jesse Jackson, who were criticizing Carter for not doing enough. But Brazile felt Jackson was just a turncoat or jealous. Everyone could see that Carter was appointing lots of blacks to top positions.

Brazile went to LSU, where she studied industrial psychology and was secretary in the student government. She became LSU's representative to the United States Student Association, a lobbying group headquartered in Washington, D.C. After she graduated, Brazile got a job with the group's national office. She arrived in Washington, D.C., in the summer of 1981.

Speech by Reverend Jesse Jackson, 1983

In 1980, I looked at Reagan's victory. He won by the margin of our despair.

He won Virginia by 200,000, more than 400,000 unregistered. Rocks just layin' around.

He won Tennessee by 4,710; 160,000 blacks unregistered. Rocks just layin' around.

He won North Carolina by 39,000 votes; 500,000 blacks unregistered. Rocks, layin' around.

He won eight southern states by 182,000 votes when there were 3 million unregistered blacks.

Rocks, little David, just layin' around.
SLAY GOLIATH!

Throughout the 1970s, black leaders elected and supported by their new black constituencies churned up a number of issues that reflected the changing needs of blacks. Their positions often brought them in conflict with liberal whites and especially Jews.

The most important was affirmative action. Affirmative action was the way many blacks saw of breaking out to the next step of economic equality, gaining access to well-paying blue-collar jobs, colleges, and professional jobs. They wanted and expected Jewish support and they did not get it. Many blacks believed Jews opposed to affirmative action were backsliding on civil rights and caving in to selfish interests. Jews, and liberals, had been generous toward blacks when a growing economy promised room at the table for everyone. But as the recessions of the 1970s heightened competition for jobs and education, opposition to quotas and aggressive affirmative action programs toughened. It was a variation of the "not-in-my-neighborhood" attitude. Yes, blacks should gain access to opportunities—but not in the law school my daughter was applying to; not at the expense of my promotion. The opposition to affirmative action by many Jews and the most well-known Jewish organizations was, in fact, finely shaded: Some Jews opposed quotas but supported aggressive recruiting of minorities; others supported recruiting and "goals and time-tables," which they saw as much less inflexible than quotas. But the sources of tension were real. Blacks considered affirmative action essential to their progress. Most Jews, even when they supported affirmative action, did so with reservations and hedges.

It was as if, Stuart Eizenstat, an assistant to President Carter, suggested to me, blacks and Jews had each staked out the other's most vulnerable spot and decided to attack it. Many Jews opposed affirmative action, which struck at the heart of black hope for success; many blacks criticized Israel, which represented an equally deep emotional investment for Jews.

In the bitter months following the 1967 Six-Day War, many Jewish groups denounced black criticism of Israel as the prattling of ignorant people who knew nothing about the Middle

East. Why should blacks care what happened between Israel and the Arabs? It was none of their concern. By the late 1970s, however, Israel had emerged as one of South Africa's largest trading partners and arms suppliers. South Africa was a white supremacist regime. Trade with South Africa was a crucial issue for black Americans and Israel's continued trade incensed them. Moreover, the more blacks learned about the Middle East, the more many of them began to sympathize with the plight of the Palestinians—like blacks not so many years ago, a minority without rights; like blacks an oppressed people. Even setting aside notions of sympathy with Third World people, many blacks resented the way Jews bristled at criticism of Israel and constructed what they considered to be a wall around debate on American foreign policy in the Middle East. At a conference in Washington, D.C., in 1985 on black-Jewish relations, an elderly Jewish woman asked a young black woman why so many blacks supported the PLO despite its terrorist actions. Do you feel a special kinship with nonwhite people, she asked?

"First of all, I object to the condescension of your question," the young black woman responded. "As if we have to have some emotional reason, as if we couldn't support the PLO on the merits."

The resignation of Young in 1979 pushed these issues out into the open. The facts, blacks felt, were clear: Jewish pressure, or fear of Jewish pressure, had prompted Carter to fire Young for his fifteen-minute meeting with the PLO observer at the United Nations. The anger that blacks felt, even in the face of Young's denial that Jews had anything to do with his resignation, stemmed in part from feelings akin to Brazile's that Young was a hero. There were so few black leaders of Young's stature, and here he was being forced to resign for an infraction that seemed minor.

But there was something broader underneath the anger stirred by Young's departure: the simmering resentment that Jews had abandoned blacks, that they kept opposing blacks on issue after issue: decentralization, Black Power, Israel, affirmative action. Now, Jews would reap the whirlwind.

A week after Young resigned, a group of 200 black leaders met in New York. These were not fringe militants but the recognized leaders of all the major black groups, including the NAACP and the SCLC. The group included Bayard Rustin, Jesse Jackson, and the educator Kenneth Clark. At first, the representatives—wary of antagonizing Jewish friends and benefactors—pondered issuing a bland statement on black-Jewish relations. They rejected that approach and established a committee to write up their grievances with clarity and force. The resolutions were accepted with few changes. The group of black leaders denounced the "double standard" under which, they charged, Young had been judged. They endorsed a meeting between Joseph Lowery, the head of SCLC, and the United Nations PLO observer. They condemned Israel's ties with South Africa. Jews, the group declared, had supported black causes in the past when it was "in their best interests to do so." Now, in a new age, "Jews must show more sensitivity and be prepared for more consultation before taking positions contrary to the best interests of the black community."

The resolutions were important; one participant called them a "watershed" in black-Jewish relations. What was even more striking was the near-euphoria that engulfed the meeting as the resolutions were adopted and read in public. "This," said Clark, when the session ended, "is our Declaration of Independence."

Alice Walker, writing in 1983

I remember Egypt's attack on Israel in 1967 and how frightened my Jewish husband and I were that Israel would be—as Egypt threatened—"driven into the sea." When Israel won the Six-Day War we were happy and relieved. I had little consciousness of the Palestinian question at the time. All I considered was the Holocaust, the inhuman fact that Jews were turned away by virtually every country they sought to enter, that they had to live somewhere on the globe (there had been talk by the British in the forties of settling them in Uganda, where Britain had already "settled" thousands of its own citizens), and I had seen the movie Exodus *with its haunting sound track: "This land is mine, God gave this land to me." Over the next several years—thanks largely to a Jewish woman friend who visited Palestinian camps and came home with a Palestinian name—I became more aware. When I tried to talk to my husband about the Palestinians, however (all the Palestinians, not just those in camps or those in the PLO), he simply shut down. He considered my friend a traitor to Jews, and any discussion that questioned Israel's behavior seemed literally to paralyze his thoughts. I understood his fear, and shared it. But when he said, "Israel has to exist," I could only answer, "Yes, and so do those other folks."*

Brazile didn't have anything on Jews when she came to Washington. She had a lot on white people—that just happens when you grow up black, she felt—but nothing on Jews. Indeed, if there were any feelings at all, they were positive. It was known in New Orleans that Jews hired blacks when whites often wouldn't. Brazile's doctor growing up had been Jewish and so had her family's lawyer. When she moved to Washington she had Jewish friends from her work with the Student Association. That they were Jewish wasn't such a big thing. They didn't really talk about it until Brazile asked them about their childhood and learned about growing up in Queens, New York, outside Manhattan.

She had seen the firing of Young as a liberal-conservative fight instead of a black-Jewish conflict. She was in college when he was fired. It was painful. She had a history professor who described how history went in twenty-year cycles, and the country moved from left to right. Carter, she felt, was moving more to the center because he saw the country moving more to the right. Young was expendable because he wanted a foreign policy more progressive and liberal. That was why

Brazile turned against Carter: She felt he was becoming more conservative.

She got jobs working for the Student Association and for the Stevie Wonder march for the Martin Luther King birthday holiday. They were fun, but none of the jobs paid well. By the summer of 1982 she was on her last can of string beans. Then, in June 1982, Walter Fauntroy offered her a job as coordinator of the twentieth anniversary of the March on Washington. It was exciting. When she was three she had wanted to go to the March on Washington and five years later to the Poor People's March on Washington. But she hadn't been old enough. This was a chance finally to be in a civil rights march, like the ones she had always heard about as a child.

She was installed in a basement office and was soon on the phone, negotiating conference calls as the outline of the march took shape. The march started out with five "conveners," five of the acknowledged leaders of the black community, each representing groups that had been instrumental in the 1963 march: Joseph Lowery of SCLC; Coretta King, widow of Martin Luther King; Walter Fauntroy, representative of the District of Columbia; Benjamin Hooks of the NAACP; and John Jacobs of the National Urban League. Then it was time for expansion. Brazile wanted to put more women on the board. Others said the board had to put on a Jew. Then a request came from Jackson that if the board was going to seat a Jew, it should also seat an Arab-American, preferably James Abourezk, former senator from South Dakota and chairman of the Arab-American Anti-Discrimination League. The march was also raising a great deal of money from Arab-Americans. So, in early 1983, adding Abourezk to the organizing committee didn't seem like a bad idea.

The objections started immediately. Jewish groups objected to the inclusion of Abourezk, saying the march should be confined to the original participants—blacks, labor groups, and Jewish groups. Jackson and others said the coalition had to be expanded, to a coalition of conscience that included gays and women's groups and environmentalists. The organizers moved on to the drafting of the "Call to the Nation," and when they got to the section called "Peace," the section read that the march opposed "the militarization of internal conflicts, often abetted and even encouraged by massive U.S. arms exports, in areas of the world such as the Middle East and Central America, while their basic human problems are neglected." The objections swelled again: Why include a reference to the Middle East? The conservative Anti-Defamation League and the more liberal American Jewish Committee, both of whom had participated in the original march, said they wouldn't join this one. Brazile, as coordinator, was handling all the phone calls, and the accusations started flying back and forth. On the conference calls among the conveners and others, Brazile heard stories about Jews—landlord stories, manipulation stories. They just want to control us. They didn't back us on affirmative action.

Brazile kept typing up the various drafts of the "call." Jewish leaders would call her to quiz her.

"Who gave you that language?"

"Who gave you that sentence?"

All this puzzled Brazile. In the years before she left Louisiana, as the civil rights movement was dying, she had found herself asking who the white people were who had come to the meetings in Kenner at the church and was told they had been Jewish people—Jewish doctors and lawyers, who had contributed money and helped develop strategy. As the movement died, the white people stopped coming and Brazile felt sad. It had been something for whites to go to all the trouble of coming into an all-black neighborhood for those meetings. And even at the end, as meetings on civil rights in the 1970s became smaller and smaller, it was still the Jewish people who kept coming. One day they stopped coming, as interest in the movement petered out. Brazile was sad but not bitter. They were good to come, she felt, and they were good because they came.

Now that fight forced her to do some reading. She read about Jews and she read about Israel. She had thought Israel was always a country. She didn't know what had happened in 1948 and about the Arab-Israeli wars that followed. Brazile had always thought she had a great understanding of history, but none of the history she had ever learned talked about the Jewish Holocaust. She knew Hitler was a bad man and that he had killed 6 million people or 10 million people, but Brazile had never known just whom he had killed.

Many Jewish groups felt uneasy about participating in the march. But David Saperstein, the lobbyist for the Union of American Hebrew Congregations, representing Judaism's most liberal wing, the Reform Jews, believed it was crucial that some Jews participate. Saperstein's father had been a rabbi on Long Island and deeply involved in the civil rights movement. He and Saperstein's mother had spent several months down South in the early 1960s. When Stokely Carmichael came north one summer to attend the funeral of a slain civil rights worker, he stayed at the Sapersteins' home, talking late into the night with their teenage son, David.

Saperstein knew as well as anyone how blacks and Jews had split over affirmative action, Israel, the resignation of Young. But he believed it was essential to maintain a Jewish presence in liberal coalitions. Without Jews, he contended, liberal groups could easily be hijacked by left-wing or pro-Arab factions. They would then pass the anti-Israel, anti-Zionism resolutions that had become staples of organizations affiliated with the United Nations and left-wing groups in America. Keeping Jews in liberal coalitions forced these groups to compromise, Saperstein believed. On several occasions, he had used the threat of withdrawal to beat off attempts by liberal foreign policy lobbying groups to pass resolutions condemning Israel. Saperstein's message to liberal coalitions he joined, and to other Jews, was simple: Let's keep our eyes on the issues before us. Let's work on what we share in common.

Saperstein believed Jews had to be involved in this commemoration of the March on Washington because of its powerful symbolism. Jews had played a seminal role in the 1963 march. This march was shaping up as a major statement on the power of the civil rights movement in the 1980s. Saperstein's office in Washington, D.C., lay across the hall from the conference room where black and Jewish lawyers had worked in the early 1960s to draft the phrases that became the Civil Rights Act of 1964. The Union of American Hebrew Congregations, Saperstein felt, should be there at the Lincoln Memorial, just as it had been twenty years before.

Saperstein peppered Brazile with articles about Israel and about anti-Semitism, trying to make her aware of Jewish concerns. They talked frequently, and Saperstein grew to respect her enormously. She was negotiating a minefield, but she remained up front and straight with everyone. He was optimistic.

Still, it was clear the march was not going to come off the way the organizers had hoped. Brazile kept attending meetings, taking notes, trying to mediate the various demands. Finally, in Atlanta, she turned to Coretta King and said to her, "Look, the old coalition, whether you want to admit it or not, is dying. It doesn't exist. It exists in your mind. So you have to form a new coalition, because the old one is no longer there."

Somehow, after that, things got better. A last-minute statement by organizers on Israel kept Saperstein and the Union of American Hebrew Congregations in the march. Speakers were divided up between the Lincoln Memorial and a different platform at the ellipse. At the last moment, a group of Jewish donors came through with money which paid for the toilets for the march. Arab-American groups came through with money to cover printing costs. Brazile felt that blacks were caught between Jews and Arabs in a fight that wasn't theirs at all. She also felt that no one had really wanted the march. Jews hadn't wanted it because it involved too much controversy; black leaders hadn't wanted it because they feared that they might be a laughingstock if the march did not attract at least 250,000 people. Brazile felt she had been left with a baby that no one wanted.

Contrary to everyone's expectations, the march came off. On an August day 250,000 people came, and when Jesse Jackson mounted the platform for the keynote speech, the crowd started chanting:

"Run, Jesse, run!"

"Run, Jesse, run!"

Brazile thought Jackson was a showboat in 1979. Many agreed, but he had turned out to be a shrewder politician than many realized. The forces in black politics that were building had continued to grow, and in 1983, Harold Washington had been elected the first black mayor of Chicago on a tide of black votes. It was in the aftermath of Washington's election—with its defiant slogan, "It's our turn"—that Jackson decided he would run for President.

Washington had won election over a Jewish opponent, Bernard Epton. But liberal Jewish voters—the so-called Lake Shore liberals—provided the votes that gave Washington his margin of victory. Washington won only 18 percent of the total white vote, but 43 percent of Chicago's Jewish vote. For a progressive black candidate running against a conservative president like Ronald Reagan, Jews should have been a natural constituency. Three-quarters of Jewish voters in California had voted for Bradley, the black mayor of Los Angeles, in his failed bid for governor in 1982. Half of Philadelphia's Jewish voters had backed Goode when he defeated Frank Rizzo in the 1983 Philadelphia mayoral primary.

But Jackson's relations with Jews had never been good. He did not share the warm feelings of King and others toward Jews and the role they had played in the civil rights movement. When he spoke about his feelings toward Jews, on the eve of the 1988 presidential campaign, Jackson began by telling how he had once attended a lecture given by the black historian John Hope Franklin at the University of Chicago. Franklin talked about Jews who had owned slaves. He was immediately denounced by several Jewish students, who called Franklin anti-Semitic. From the very start of his dealings with Jews, Jackson saw there were two kinds of Jews: the progressive, tolerant Jews, and the conservative, intolerant Jews.

When he was growing up in Greenville, South Carolina, Jackson made no distinctions between whites and Jews. Blacks could not eat in any restaurant—it didn't matter if it was owned by a Jew, a Baptist, a Methodist, a Greek, an Italian. They couldn't use anyone's restroom downtown. Segregation was a black-white issue, not a religious one. As Jackson saw it, white people had privileges. Black people did not have rights. Jews were white. While there had been anti-Semitic behavior in the United States, Jews had not had to pass through the same strictures as blacks. There had been no laws that enslaved Jews in America, no laws or intimidation that denied Jews the right to vote. Indeed, Jackson believed, blacks had often been a buffer between other whites and Jews. The absence of blacks would have meant open season on Jews. Many Jews didn't fully appreciate how the relationship had been mutually beneficial, Jackson felt.

Blacks and Jews shared a certain kinship, Jackson acknowledged. They had both been used as scapegoats. That explained why some of the great civil rights martyrs, like Schwerner and Goodman, were Jews, as well as some of the great civil rights lawyers. American "fascism" and southern apartheid threatened Jews and blacks. The extreme sensitivity of Jews troubled Jackson. Blacks fought with whites all the time—in Chicago it was with the Irish, elsewhere it might be with the Italians, or with whatever ethnic group happened to be in charge. Once the struggle was over, relations improved. But Jews seemed never to forget when Jackson crossed them or upset them.

He recalled an incident when he had gone to Israel for the first time in 1979, in the wake of Young's resignation. He had visited Yad Vashem, the museum commemorating the Holocaust.

As he walked through the museum and saw pictures showing Jews in striped prison uniforms staring out from behind the barbed wires of the concentration camps, Jackson's thoughts went back to his childhood in Greenville, to the striped uniforms on the black men who worked the chain gang in his neighborhood. He lived near the prison and had seen chains there, barbed wire and stockades. He remembered how the police would lock up blacks for all sorts of crazy, groundless reasons.

When Jackson emerged from the museum into the sunlight, a Jewish man asked Jackson how he felt.

"I feel this is one of the great human tragedies of all time," Jackson said.

"Unique?" asked the man.

Jackson thought of other massacres he had read about, and about the chain gangs in Greenville.

"Tragic," Jackson said.

The man persisted. "Unique?"

"Tragic."

"You insult us," the man declared.

It was inconceivable to Jackson that this debate over word usage could be the basis for an argument, though several months later the Jewish writer and Holocaust survivor Elie Wiesel explained to Jackson the importance to Jews of defining the Holocaust as a "unique" tragedy that must never happen again.

Similarly, Jackson did not understand why Jews were so angry about his meeting with Arafat. He had embraced Arafat and shaken his hand—not put money in his hand, not put a gun in his hand. He had told Arafat: "Your objective should be a mutual recognition policy [with Israel], because ultimately you must learn to live together. You should remove any suggestion about driving Jewish people into the sea."

How could shaking Arafat's hand and challenging him to behave that way be seen as an act of hostility, Jackson wanted to know?

There were personal feelings Jackson harbored toward Jews as well. In 1981, his daughter had applied to Harvard and been badgered by a Jewish alumnus who interviewed her in Chicago. The man kept asking her whether she would disassociate herself from her father's views on the Middle East. That was insulting, Jackson thought. She was accepted at Harvard, but instead decided to go to Howard University in Washington, D.C.

In the months leading up to Jackson's announcement of his candidacy, the Anti-Defamation League prepared and sent to journalists a collection of Jackson's statements on Israel that painted him as an anti-Semite. Many of the statements, Jackson felt, were yanked out of context solely to make him look bad. Then, at his announcement, an offshoot of the Jewish

Defense League called Jews Against Jackson disrupted his remarks and had to be carried away by police. The group then
set up pickets around his home, frightening his family and
neighbors. This was an outrage, Jackson thought. If black groups
had done this to a Jewish candidate, it would have been front-
page news. But the press seemed to accept it as a matter of
course. Jackson was livid.

Brazile saw Jackson's candidacy as an extension of her work
on the March on Washington. When she thought about it,
there were other black candidates, perhaps, who might be
better. But Jackson wanted to run. Jackson was going to run.
He was the only candidate of all the Democrats that Brazile
could see supporting. So she joined the campaign as head of
constituency mobilization, bringing along her contacts with
white progressive groups, including Jews. She was twenty-
three years old.

Despite her contacts, the Jackson campaign was able to get
only two prominent Jews to join the campaign and stand with
Jackson: Jack Mendelsohn, who had become a Unitarian minister, and Barry Commoner, the environmentalist. Neither of
them was a leader in the Jewish community and neither could
assuage the doubts of many Jews about Jackson's attitudes
toward Jews. There were about ten Jews working in various
capacities for the campaign. Others would not come near the
campaign. Brazile understood that Jews were not going to be
part of Jackson's Rainbow Coalition—in sharp contrast to Arab-
American groups, who were helping Jackson raise money and
whose influence in the campaign was growing. The best Brazile could do was check with her friend Saperstein before
speeches to make sure that nothing Jackson said would be
offensive.

It was a chaotic but wonderful campaign. Brazile traveled
to Georgia, to Louisiana, to New York, to New Jersey. The
pace was brutal; staffers went to sleep after Jackson went to
bed and got up before Jackson woke up. That often meant
three hours of sleep a night. If Jackson stayed up until 4:00
A.M., the staff stayed up until 4:00 A.M. If Jackson got up at
six, the staff got up at five. The candidate stayed in hotels but

staffers, pinched by the campaign's shoestring budget, stayed
with volunteers. Out in front of hand-clapping audiences,
Jackson would talk about helping the "boats stuck on the
bottom"—the poor and disenfranchised he had made his core
constituency. After some of the speeches, Brazile would go up
to Jackson and say, jokingly, "I've finally figured it out. We're
the boats stuck on the bottom, your staff." Jackson guffawed.

The Jackson campaign had been slow starting. After the
initial excitement following his announcement in late 1983,
it became moribund. Then Jackson went to Syria and brought
back a hostage and lots of attention. The polls then showed
he might take 16 percent in New Hampshire.

The "hymietown" story broke on February 13, 1984. In a
conversation with Milton Coleman, a black reporter with the
Washington Post, at the cafeteria in Washington's National
Airport a few weeks earlier (January 25) Jackson had said,
"Let's talk black talk"—slang, he assumed, for taking a conversation off the record. Complaining about the attention his
positions on the Middle East were getting, Jackson told the
reporter, "All hymie wants to talk about is Israel; everytime
you go to hymietown, that's all they want to talk about."
Coleman passed the information on to another *Post* writer
who was working on a story about Jackson and the Jews. The
information appeared in the thirty-seventh and thirty-eighth
paragraphs of a fifty-two-paragraph story:

> In private conversations with reporters, Jackson has referred to
> Jews as "hymie" and to New York as "hymietown."
> "I'm not familiar with that," Jackson said Thursday. "That's
> not accurate."

The reference to hymietown might as well have appeared
in the headline. A *Washington Post* editorial denounced it as
"ugly . . . degrading . . . and disgusting." It demanded "an ex-
planation and an apology. . . . The offense here is not against
any one group in American life, but against all. It is not typical,
we think, of the way any large number of Americans usually
talk, and certainly not of the way they want political leaders
to talk."

When Brazile first heard of the story, she was furious. She immediately went to Jackson and asked him, "Did you say that?"

"No," he replied. "No. No. No."

She believed him, and fended off calls of outrage from Jewish leaders and from many of her friends. "No, he didn't say it," she told friends. "He didn't say it and damn it, don't y'all stick that to him. You know that's a fabrication. Milton Coleman told a lie."

For two weeks Jackson denied at every opportunity that he had ever used the words "hymie" or "hymietown."

February 25 was Savior's Day in Chicago, the biggest event for the Nation of Islam and its leader, Louis Farrakhan. Farrakhan was not yet as well known as he would be in a few months. Brazile knew him from her work on the March on Washington, where he had appeared as one of the speakers. She was part of the advance team sent by Jackson to help Farrakhan organize the event. Jackson's campaign wanted the so-called Islam vote or Farrakhan vote, which they believed extended beyond the 10,000 people who were members or followers of the Nation of Islam. Farrakhan and Jackson had been friends for several years, visiting each other's homes. On Thanksgiving, 1983, the two men had agreed that Farrakhan would provide bodyguards for Jackson until he received Secret Service protection—the clean-cut, close-shaven "Fruit of Islam" guards ubiquitous in their dark suits, white shirts, and neat bow ties—and would serve as a Jackson adviser. Farrakhan had accompanied Jackson on his recent trip to Syria. At age fifty-one, Farrakhan registered to vote for the first time and urged other Nation of Islam members to do the same.

Before the Savior's Day rally started, Farrakhan and Jackson got together in a back room and started talking about the hymietown controversy. Brazile watched from the side of the room. Brazile had grown up on a street corner, and as she watched the two men talk it dawned on her: This was street-corner time, Jackson and Farrakhan punctuating their discussion with "Hey, man, yeah, man."

"Hey, man, I didn't say that."

"Yeah, man, they're trying to pin me down."

For the first time, Brazile felt something was really wrong. This was the way boys and teenagers talked on the streets in Kenner—that "hey man, yeah man, we all right man" kind of talk, "we're going to whip that white person's ass." But as you got older, Brazile felt, you didn't want to whip anybody in the ass. In fact you didn't want to fight. It's a way of talking bad and saying nothing.

The jive talk went on for several minutes and finally Brazile looked at Jackson and said, "Man, was I lied to?"

He ignored her completely. That night, in a speech introducing Jackson, Farrakhan declared: "I say to the Jewish people who may not like our brother, when you attack him you attack the millions who are lining up with him. You are attacking all of us. If you harm this brother, I warn you in the name of Allah, this will be the last one you do harm." Jackson listened to the introduction but said nothing.

Brazile flew back to Washington, D.C., the next morning. That night Jackson went to a temple in New Hampshire where he confessed that he had, in fact, used the words "hymie" and "hymietown": "In private talks we sometimes let our guard down and we become thoughtless. It was not in a spirit of meanness, an off-color remark having no bearing on religion or politics . . . however innocent and unintended, it was wrong."

Brazile was disgusted. She felt it was reprehensible for Jackson to lie to his own staff. If you do something wrong, she believed, you confess. Brazile didn't believe Jackson was an anti-Semite. She didn't believe he hated Jews; she didn't believe he hated anybody. From her own observation of Jackson, Brazile believed he had a deep need to be loved by everyone, including Jews. To say such hateful things was out of character. But Brazile had to accept the fact that Jackson was a human being, a man who had faults. Like others in the campaign, she felt she had to accept his contradictions.

As primary followed primary, the controversy over hymietown followed Jackson. "He could light candles every Friday night, and grow sidecurls, and it still wouldn't matter . . . he's a whore," Nathan Perlmutter, head of the Anti-Defamation

League, told reporters. Jackson's campaign staff felt that the press paid no attention to the issues Jackson was raising, such as how the second primary system hurt blacks. In many parts of the South, black candidates often won the preliminary election with a plurality of the vote in a crowded field. But then they had to face a run-off election against a single white candidate and would lose. Jackie Jackson, Jackson's wife, was furious; Jackson had apologized and asked for forgiveness, but it made no difference. Jackson's people felt unfairly pursued. He was raising issues that others would not touch. He supported a more balanced foreign policy in the Middle East. He proposed shifting domestic priorities away from defense. Reporters focused on his relations with the PLO but ignored issues he raised about Mondale's position as a director of Control Data Corp., which has business dealings with South Africa. He could stir crowds like no other. But the controversy over his statements about Jews drowned out everything.

The increasingly belligerent speeches by Farrakhan exacerbated the situation. Upon learning that a black reporter had been the source of the "hymietown" quote, Farrakhan denounced Coleman as "a no-good . . . filthy . . . dog," adding, "At this point no physical harm [but] one day soon we will punish you with death." In a radio speech in March, Farrakhan declared, "The Jews don't like Farrakhan, so they call me Hitler. Well, that's a good name. Hitler was a very great man. He wasn't great for me as a black person. But he was a great German. Now I'm not proud of Hitler's evil against Jewish people, but that's a matter of record. He rose Germany up from nothing. Well, in a sense you could say there's a similarity in that we are raising our people up from nothing." In June, Farrakhan called the creation of the state of Israel an "outlaw act" and Judaism "a dirty religion." At campaign stop after campaign stop, Jackson was asked to repudiate Farrakhan. Jackson refused. "I can repudiate the man but not the messenger," he said.

Around the campaign office, things had turned ugly, Brazile hearing talk of Jewish landlords, and jokes that Jews controlled the press, that Jews controlled this, that Jews controlled that.

In meetings with Jewish feminist friends, she found she kept having to defend herself as not being an anti-Semite.

At the height of all this, Brazile received a call from her mother. She considered her mother, down in New Orleans, a part of grassroots America. Her mother called her to say that she no longer trusted her doctor.

This was the Jewish doctor who had been treating her family for their diabetes ever since Brazile could remember. Growing up, she had always heard good things about him. Now, all of a sudden, he had become this evil man.

"He wants my money, he's taking my money," Brazile's mother told her. "He's getting rich off me. He's giving me the wrong medicine. He has no respect for me."

In fact, her doctor one day had given Brazile's mother the wrong medicine, but that wasn't the root of her feelings. Brazile's mother, part of the "Martin Luther King" set, a believer in integration, thought Farrakhan was right: "Jews control everything; you can't trust them."

Brazile realized this was part of a grapevine that was slowly changing the grassroots perceptions blacks had of Jews. Her mother talked to Brazile's aunt and uncle in New York and they would trade stories of Jewish landlords and owners of the corner store. "Yeah, Jesse's right," they would say, "Farrakhan's right." That would come back to New Orleans. When she went home to Kenner she was shocked, talking to the young kids on the street corner, how there was an enemy out there, and the enemy was the Jews.

Brazile was so confused she wasn't sure what was happening. She had gotten burned on the hymie issue but she also didn't like the way she felt the Jewish community had blown things all out of proportion. It was in neither side's interest to fight like this. Jews had suffered a lot at the hands of people, just as blacks had, and they had given their all for the civil rights movement. This was not the right time, she felt, for blacks and Jews to "kick each other's ass." In the larger arena, white America would love to see a fissure between blacks and Jews. The whole thing stank.

Brazile stayed on Jackson's staff through his appearance at

the Democratic Convention and his speech in which he stood
before the audience—a man who, as one television commen-
tator noted, could not sit at a lunch counter in South Carolina
twenty years earlier and be served—and declared:

> Suffering breeds character, character breeds faith, and faith will
> not disappoint. Our time has come. Our faith, hope and dreams
> will prevail. Our time has come. Weeping has endured for night,
> but now joy cometh in the morning.
>
> Our time has come. No grave can hold our body down. Our
> time has come. No lie can live forever. Our time has come. We
> must leave the racial battleground and come to the economic
> common ground and the moral higher ground. America, our time
> has come.
>
> We come from disgrace to Amazing Grace. Our time has come.
> Give me your tired, give me your poor, your huddled masses who
> yearn to breathe free, and come November there will be a change
> because our time has come.

Brazile resigned and signed on with the Ferraro campaign.
The contradictions in Jackson's character were too great. She
would work for some individual projects again but not for
him. This was the next logical step, she felt. Some of Jackson's
people were mad at her for joining Ferraro, but she was un-
fazed. Many of the people connected with the March on Washington had been mad when she went with Jackson. She had
to do what she thought was best for black people.

The legacy of Farrakhan and the bitterness of the Jackson
campaign continued. Over the next year, Farrakhan traveled
across the country, speaking to large groups in major arenas
in Los Angeles, Washington, New York. It became a touring
road show with a familiar pattern. Farrakhan would announce
his appearance. Jewish leaders would demand that black politicians denounce him. They would balk. Farrakhan would
give his speech, polarize people, and move on.

Over and over again, when I spoke to black leaders and
politicians, they made clear that they disagreed with much of
what Farrakhan had to say. But they objected even more to
Jews telling them what to say and what to do. That time was
over: No one would tell blacks who their leaders were.

Speech by Jesse Jackson to the Democratic National Convention, 1984

If in my low moments, in word, deed, or attitude, through some error of temper, taste or tone, I have caused anyone discomfort, created pain, or revived someone's fears, that was not my truest self. If there were occasions when my grape turned into a raisin and my joy bell lost its resonance, please forgive me. Charge it to my head and not to my heart. . . . As I develop and serve, be patient. God is not finished with me yet.

It was hard, in writing and talking about black-Jewish relations, to escape the shadow of the 1984 campaign. In an effort to move beyond the anger and hurt feelings, I made a point of asking blacks I met with across the country their ideas about what had happened and what had gone wrong. For some, the lesson was that blacks had to be treated as equals. For others, it opened deep wounds. For still others, it reaffirmed bitter feelings they had long felt toward Jews.

Alice Walker had met her Jewish husband, Mel Levanthol, a civil rights lawyer, during the Freedom Rides in the early 1960s. Not knowing many Jews in Georgia, she thought all Jews were like Howard Zinn, the adviser to SNCC whose family she befriended during those civil rights years.

Then, one day, she traveled to Brooklyn where Levanthol was cleaning out his apartment, and she was shocked by how coldly his family treated her. A woman on the street—who, she said, was not Levanthol's grandmother but "could have been"—came up to her and said, "You don't belong here." It was her first exposure to Jews who could be bigots like white southerners.

Her feelings about Israel had changed over the years, from joy and hope following the Six-Day War to disappointment and anger at the Israeli occupation of the West Bank. She still valued her Jewish friends and when she worked on the movie version of *The Color Purple* she felt the people on the set who understood the book the best were Jews, including Steven Spielberg, the director. Her changing feelings on Israel were prompted by a Jewish friend, whose sympathy for the Palestinians moved her. But Walker felt no more need for an alliance between blacks and Jews. She felt no sympathy for Israel. At a certain point, she said, you stop struggling with people and with a country. She had reached that point with Israel. And she believed the black-Jewish alliance, whatever it had once been, had ended.

As our conversation ended, she asked me what I thought about Farrakhan. I had emerged that day from a series of interviews with people vociferous in their defense of Farrakhan. I had seen him speak myself and believed that while he was a Jew-baiter, much of his economic message was appealing to blacks. I told Walker this.

"I think he is a bigot and an anti-Semite," she replied simply as our conversation ended. "And I think you must condemn people like that."

As I reflected on that conversation, I considered whether or not Jewish leaders had searched out the middle ground between blacks and Jews. By focusing on Farrakhan they had perhaps inflated his importance, ignoring blacks with whom they could agree about some things and disagree about others.

Ron Walters had been Jackson's deputy campaign manager. As we talked about the campaign he said he could understand why Jews would not back Jackson. He was a black nationalist. He understood Jewish nationalism. If he were Jewish, he wouldn't back Jackson either. Walters brushed aside talk of an alliance now because, in his eyes, things could not be equal until blacks had equal power. For him, everything was a process: Every year more black mayors would be elected. Every year there would be more black politicians. Then, perhaps, Jews and blacks might be able to sit down together.

Julius Lester had traveled a long and intricate road since leaving New York and WBAI. He had gone to the University of Massachusetts at Amherst to teach and, while on sabbatical, had studied the Holocaust. It was a promise he had made to himself during the WBAI controversy—to learn about the Holocaust and understand why Jews had been so hurt and upset.

During that year he studied the Holocaust, Lester found himself waking up from dreams reciting the "Shm'a," the Jewish prayer that declares, "Hear, O Israel, the Lord Our God, the Lord is One." Lester had known that there was Jewish blood in his family, and he decided to study Judaism.

When I spoke with him, he had just finished a book about his conversion to Judaism. He reflected on the WBAI controversy and said, looking back, that he would not have done anything differently. Lester spoke, on occasion, to synagogues about black-Jewish relations. The message he brought them was sobering: Blacks, he said, did not worry much about the collapse of the black-Jewish alliance. Jews worried about it much more. Jews, Lester felt, needed blacks much more than blacks needed Jews. It was one of the ways they defined themselves as good liberals, and as Jews. He told the story of a Jewish woman he met who was asked, "How do you know you are Jewish?" and responded: "I read *The New York Times* and give to the NAACP." Jews interested in rebuilding coalitions, Lester said, had to get to know blacks better, had to get to know them as people, instead of as liberal icons. He reflected, with a smile, that the place where he encountered the least racism was among Hasidic Jews, who saw him as a Jew and felt his race didn't matter.

Jesse Jackson remained unchanged and unmoved by the controversies that had engulfed his campaign. He believed that Israel's continued trade with South Africa was an affront to blacks and that Jewish supporters of Israel had to come to terms with that. Blacks, he felt, had been very restrained in bringing up the issue of Israel's ties to South Africa, but that restraint would not last forever. Jackson was tired of the way people kept examining and re-examining relations between blacks and Jews. Every other day, it seemed, he was asked: "How y'all and Jews getting along?" One thing Jackson knew: When blacks and Jews fought together, they almost never lost. But now there were points of tension, and they were not superficial. An alliance had to be an alliance of equals, not of one group paternally watching over the other.

By 1987, it was clear that Jackson intended to run again for president in 1988. As he prepared to run, however, Jackson refashioned his political message, moderating it to reach out to farmers in the Midwest and blue-collar workers. He appointed a Jewish campaign manager and consulted with a number of liberal Jewish advisers. But Jews by and large still refused to vote for him. As his campaign proceeded, it became obvious that something unusual was happening. Jackson was creating a progressive coalition that included everyone except Jews. People had long talked about Jackson's "Jewish problem"—the angry feelings he stirred among Jews and the obstacle that threw in the path of his winning the Democratic presidential or vice-presidential nomination. Those feelings crystalized when, on the eve of the New York primary, New York Mayor Edward Koch said Jews would be "crazy" to vote for Jackson. But as Jackson broadened his appeal and attracted a steady number of white liberals, gay activists, disgruntled union workers, and farmers, Jews faced the specter of their own "Jackson problem." What would happen if the acknowledged leader of the black community as well as the leader of the progressive wing of the Democratic Party were someone Jews found anathema? For the first time since World War II it was conceivable that Jews might be forced to cede, or at least share, their long dominant role in the liberal wing of the Democratic Party to Jackson and his supporters.

After the Ferraro campaign in 1984, Brazile had moved on to other projects. She helped organize the benefit Hands Across America to raise money for the hungry and a benefit for *The*

Color Purple. She considered going to law school but as the 1988 presidential campaign began, she went to work for Richard Gephardt, a congressman from Missouri, as one of his top staff people.

Brazile worried about the disintegration of black society. She joked with friends that when she married someone, he would have to be ten years older because all the men her age were dead. It was scary, going back home and asking after friends and finding that they were dead.

In 1985 Brazile went on a trip to Nairobi, Kenya, to attend the International Conference on Women. It was an exhilarating trip, and one of her strongest memories had to do with the colors she saw there.

All her life Brazile had thought she couldn't wear red because it didn't go with her black skin. Then she saw people wearing red in Nairobi. She came back and bought red scarves and red skirts and red bandannas. She decided to put red in her room. It was a small thing, perhaps, but Brazile loved the fact that she could now wear red. It made her feel independent and free.

Brazile decided that one day she wanted to visit Israel, to see things firsthand. Several times she had to abandon plans to go because she was just too busy.

She spoke to liberal Jewish groups about the need to build coalitions. She was troubled by a phone call she had gotten from a Jewish friend in the waning days of the Jackson campaign. The friend called her from law school and said, "I'm thinking of going into civil rights law, but I don't know if blacks want me to."

"If you think that," said Brazile, "then we are all in a lot of trouble."

8

Broken Alliance

I began this book gripped by a fondness and curiosity for a past that history books, TV news footage, and my own childhood memories told me had been a time of goodwill and idealism, hope and promise. If only the country could recapture the magic of the civil rights movement, if only we could lock arms together in the shadow of the Lincoln Memorial and sing "We Shall Overcome," the words of Martin Luther King ringing in our ears, we might heal the rift between blacks and Jews and open the way for a new era of cooperation and change.

What I found was far different. The alliance between blacks and Jews was never as strong as it appeared. It was rooted as much in the hard currency of politics and self-interest as in love and idealism. Even at those times when the alliance seemed strongest—when police unearthed the bodies of Schwerner, Chaney, and Goodman; when blacks and Jews worked side by side for the passage of civil rights laws; when Jews in the North and West wrote checks to the NAACP, SCLC, and SNCC— the symbols of cooperation covered a cauldron of ambivalent feelings and conflicting emotions. At civil rights dinners during the 1960s and 1970s it was customary for blacks and Jews to talk as if they were one people. Both blacks and Jews have been oppressed. Both know the pain of injustice. "Let us go forward together." But that rhetoric masked a world of difference. The Chinese have a saying: *Tong chuang yi meng.* "We are sleeping in the same bed, dreaming different dreams." That could have served as a metaphor for the dynamic of black-Jewish relations.

Blacks and Jews were brought together by intersecting agendas. Jews, emerging from the catastrophe of the Second World War, their recent past shaped by their experience of anti-Semitism in the United States and the legacy of Eastern European socialism, latched onto a political agenda which, they believed, would ensure their success in America: Society should not make distinctions based on race or religion. That was good for blacks—but it was good for Jews, too. Blacks, readying in the 1950s for yet another assault on segregation, emboldened by the Supreme Court's decision in *Brown* v. *Board of Education* abolishing segregated schools, were willing to reach out and work with white allies. They accepted the help of Jews as people who could make a difference. There was genuine love and cooperation in the civil rights movement, but for some blacks and Jews, the main motivation was not an alliance but success. The alliance was a means to an end, not an end in itself.

Each group saw the other through its own lens. During the heyday of the civil rights movement, from 1960 to 1965, many Jews saw blacks as other Jews. The misapprehension was easy. The two shared common imagery and a common language drawn from the Bible and the image of the Exodus. Both shared a common desire to break down barriers of prejudice. Both shared a common enemy: the prejudiced white Gentile. Writing in 1970 in a new introduction to *Beyond the Melting Pot,* Nathan Glazer and Daniel Patrick Moynihan noted this phenomenon and its perils:

> From the outset [of the civil rights movement], Jews, in a great variety of roles, defined the new problem. (Not all of them public roles by any means. During this period, if a famous civil rights leader made a speech, the chances were at least even that it had

been written by a Jewish speechwriter.) And the first thing they did was to define the difficulties facing the Negroes as being in most respects identical to those earlier faced by Jews. In essence, this was the . . . approach of a highly competitive group so threatening to the established position of others that artificial barriers are raised to restrict and limit the success experienced by the new group (for example, quotas in medical school).

Reality, Moynihan and Glazer noted, was almost completely the opposite:

The black immigrants in New York City in the 1950s and 1960s were a displaced peasantry, not at all unlike their Irish and Italian predecessors, most, in truth, like the Irish, who arrived with all the stigmata acquired from living under rulers of a different race. . . . The Negroes were not highly competitive; they were undercompetitive. They had been raised that way in the South, and were not instantly transformed by Bedford-Stuyvesant, which became not a ghetto but a slum. Taking all references to racial or ethnic identity out of university admission applications, and forbidding photographs, would not automatically double or triple the proportion of Negroes admitted to the Columbia Medical School. It might have quite the opposite effect.

Many Jews believed that, like Jews, blacks were an oppressed minority, bursting with talent, who would flood the universities and law firms and medical schools once barriers were struck down—just as the Jews had. They didn't consider that blacks might be different, that they might come to power in different ways—perhaps, like the Irish had, through politics, slowly seizing power in large cities through mayoral elections and civil service. When blacks failed to live up to Jewish expectations—when they did not overachieve on college entrance exams but instead demanded quotas and affirmative action—Jews were surprised and betrayed. This was not what they had bargained for at all.

For their part, many blacks who first encountered Jews in the civil rights movement mistook Jewish support for civil rights for endorsement of all the goals of the black struggle as it expanded and evolved. Many black activists seemed genuinely perplexed at Jewish anger toward the Black Power movement. For them, black nationalism was just a variant on Jewish nationalism, Black Power a variant on Jewish power. In much of what they were doing, black leaders believed, they were emulating what Jews, as an oppressed minority, had done. How could Jews not understand that? And even if they could not understand it, how could they not sympathize with the black struggle? They had once been oppressed themselves. The expectations of many blacks, especially blacks active in the South, were skewed by their exposure to a narrow slice of the Jewish community. The Jews who went south in the 1960s or otherwise became intimately involved with civil rights leaders represented the left-liberal edge of American Judaism. They drew from the socialist and left-wing heritage of America's Jews. Greenberg was one of the most conservative among them. They may have represented the best of American Jews. But they did not represent all American Jews. They certainly did not reflect the group of Jewish intellectuals growing up around *Commentary* who by the late 1960s had become uneasy with the turmoil of the past decade and would develop a powerful critique of Great Society liberalism, questioning the increasing demands of blacks. They did not reflect the fear of lower- and middle-class Jews, who were bearing the brunt of change as neighborhoods in city after city shifted from largely Jewish to largely black, and crime and violence rose.

Same bed, different dreams. Michael Walzer visited Montgomery, Alabama, in 1960, heard a black minister preach the story of the Exodus, and believed he was witnessing the reenactment of the Jewish struggle for success and acceptance in America. Alice Walker believed that all Jews were like Howard Zinn, the sympathetic professor and adviser to SNCC who had worked in the shipyards with a copy of Marx's writings in his back pocket. Rhody McCoy saw the struggle in Ocean Hill–Brownsville as a battle for power; many Jews in New York saw it as the outbreak of anti-Semitism.

The different dreams blacks and Jews brought to the struggles of the 1960s shaped their different verdicts on the civil rights movement. For Jews, the toppling of legal barriers and the rout of southern racism between 1960 and 1965 were a great victory. It marked a fundamental shift in America, where merit would count. Here at last was a society in which all could make it on their own, a color-blind society. The burden had shifted now to blacks to take advantage of these opportunities, as the Jews themselves had a few decades before. Politically, Jews basked in the rosy glow of cooperation, congratulating themselves on having been part of a great coalition that had created progressive change and shown how committed they were to the best of liberal Jewish ideals.

For many blacks—at first the most militant but by 1967 even King and other moderates—the gains of the civil rights movement in voting and access to bathrooms and buses were just a start. There now needed to be economic change and access to power. Racism in the North took more subtle forms. There were no governors or sheriffs standing in schoolhouse or courtyard doors. Instead there were civil service exams and admissions standards that skewed benefits toward those already a part of the system and kept blacks out of jobs and out of colleges and universities. Going to a desegregated restaurant didn't mean much if you didn't have a job. The right to vote lost some of its luster when your son or daughter couldn't get into a good college. Passage of the civil rights laws barring discrimination was a beginning, not an end.

Jews who had hoped integration would usher in an era of free mixing and friendship with Negroes—Negroes who beneath their skin color were "just like us"—could not fathom the celebration of black consciousness, black beauty, black art, black language that accompanied the growth of the Black Power movement. They were shaken by a change in attitude among black leaders. By the late 1960s, many blacks were, justifiably, angry. Anyone who stood in their way was an enemy—and the deepest suspicion was directed against those who impeded their progress while claiming to "help" them. These more militant and vocal blacks resented the paternalism that ran through much of the cooperation between blacks and Jews in the 1950s and early 1960s. They resented Jews doling out advice on the "Negro problem" as if they were the elder brothers in suffering.

Dreams—Martin Peretz's dream of a "salt-and-pepper" society, King's dream of a nation where children would be judged "not by the color of their skin but by the content of their character"—died first. By the 1970s, blacks and Jews found not only their expectations diverging, but their interests coming into conflict.

Affirmative action was the first arena of battle. It was the central issue for blacks, especially the most successful blacks, those who were joining corporations and universities. They saw their success and the success of those who followed as being tied to the continuation of affirmative action programs. Yet every Jewish organization, with various degrees of stricture, opposed quotas and certain types of affirmative action. Jewish neoconservatives became the chief architects of the intellectual opposition to affirmative action. And many rank-and-file Jews were queasy about the prospect and opposed it.

Again and again blacks, especially educated blacks, bumped up against Jews in positions of power as they tried to move up in corporations and universities. In the 1960s, Bayard Rustin had noted that of the five people that a black meets in the course of the day—the storekeeper, the landlord, the schoolteacher, the social worker, and the police officer—four were Jewish and one, the police officer, was Irish. By the 1970s, Jews no longer were so visible in ghetto life. The arena had shifted. In the spring of 1986 I visited the campus of UCLA, where the major issues for black students were the small number of black professors, the declining percentage of black graduate students, and the college's investments in companies doing business with South Africa. The president of the university was not Jewish. But the dean of the graduate school was Jewish. The provost who oversaw hiring was Jewish. So was the assistant dean in charge of dealing with demonstrations and protests over issues like divestment.

In foreign policy, black and Jewish interests clashed over South Africa and Israel. Concern over South Africa came to dominate the foreign policy concerns of black leaders in the late 1970s and 1980s. Israel continued its role as one of South Africa's largest arms suppliers and as a trading partner. While many American Jews came to oppose Israel's position on South Africa, and Israel began gradually to reduce its ties, its continued trade with South Africa enraged and frustrated blacks. In 1986, I traveled with a group of blacks and Jews to Israel. One day we met over lunch with officials from the Israeli Foreign Ministry. Blacks in the group asked why Israel continued to maintain relations and trade with South Africa. Israel condemns apartheid and speaks out against it at every opportunity, the senior Israeli Foreign Ministry official answered. But at a time when so many countries have turned against Israel, South Africa has remained a staunch supporter. And why should Israel cut off relations with South Africa, the official asked? Arab countries trade with South Africa. The United States maintains relations with South Africa. African countries trade with South Africa. Why should Israel be the one to stop?

"I understand your point of view," said a black member of the group, "but I am disappointed. I expected more from Israel."

Blacks in the 1970s—especially black leaders and Jesse Jackson—emerged as the most visible critics of Israel. It was black politicians and leaders—like Young and Jackson—who raised questions about the thrust of American policy in the Middle East and who urged dealings with the PLO. Asked in 1984 whether their sympathies in the Middle East lay more with Israel or with the Arab nations, 47 percent of whites said their sympathies lay more with Israel. Only 29 percent of blacks said their sympathies lay more with Israel. Blacks, as a community, were also the only group of Americans that showed a rise in anti-Semitic feelings. Between 1964 and 1981, polls found that the level of anti-Semitism among whites dropped almost 8 percentage points while the level of anti-Semitism among blacks increased slightly. Blacks were far more willing than whites in 1981 to agree with statements like "Jews have too much power in the United States," "Jews have too much power in the business world," "Jews are more loyal to Israel than to America." The Jew-baiting speeches of Farrakhan reinforced the notion that the greatest threat of anti-Semitism lay in the black community.

There was plenty of blame to go around. From their first encounters with Jews, blacks confused Jewish money with Jewish power. As Jewish income, education, and influence rose, blacks could not understand how Jews could talk as if they were still insecure. By every economic measure, Jews had reached the pinnacle of success. Yet they still spoke as if they were an imperiled minority, discerning a threat even from blacks. Such a view missed the historical roots of Jewish insecurity. The Jews in Spain had been the most influential and wealthiest in Europe just before the Inquisition. Jews in Germany did very well economically before the Holocaust. Wealth was no protection, Jews had learned, if politics changed and the world turned against the Jews. Black critics of Israel failed to understand the emotional power Israel's survival held for American Jews. Leaders like Jackson did not understand American Jewish insecurity and, not understanding it, dismissed it.

For all their talk about wanting to work together as equals, Jewish and black leaders in the 1970s and early 1980s showed little interest in building genuine coalitions. Most of the issues on the black-Jewish agenda in the 1970s—affirmative action, an end to discrimination, combating racial violence—were issues that benefited blacks. To develop a common agenda would have required adding support for Israel, concern over anti-Semitism, concern over Soviet Jewry. That would have been a real coalition.

But if blacks denied the historically based roots of Jewish anxiety, Jews failed to acknowledge the realities of their power. Jews do wield great power in America. In 1982, for example, Jews made up less than 6 percent of the national press corps. But they made up 25 to 30 percent of what author Charles Silberman correctly dubbed the "media elite"—people working for *The New York Times*, the *Washington Post*, the *Wall Street Journal*, *Time*, *Newsweek*, *U.S. News & World Report*,

and the news divisions of NBC, CBS, ABC, and public television. Similarly, Jews by 1975 made up 10 percent of all
college professors—but 20 percent of professors at top-rated
universities. At one time or another in the 1980s, the deans
of the law schools at Harvard, Yale, Stanford, and Columbia
were all Jews, as were the presidents of Princeton, Dartmouth,
and Columbia. Members of the white elite, Jews could not
escape criticism for the underrepresentation of blacks in corporate suites, college faculties, newsrooms, Hollywood. "Anybody can observe the Sabbath," Alice Walker observed, "but
making it holy surely takes the rest of the week."

Yet Jews were, by and large, shocked at suggestions that
they had become part of the American elite. Most Jews still
saw themselves as outsiders. A friend of mine told a revealing
story about a parents' meeting she had attended at an exclusive
New York private school. The parents in her child's class were
gathered in a circle in a classroom. The parents from old,
monied families—the kind that had been sending their children to private schools for generations—sat next to each other
in one part of the circle. The Jewish parents next to them.
The handful of black parents next to them. Looking at the
black parents, one Jewish woman leaned over to the Jewish
woman next to her and asked: "When they look at us, how
do they see us?" The answer was clear. The black parents
looked across the room and saw the Jews as white. The Jewish
parents, still uncomfortable in such a setting, saw themselves
as outsiders.

Jews, like most whites, failed to understand what it was
like to be black in America. They underestimated the depths
of discrimination and racism. That America had become a
"color-blind" society was a naive notion. It was truer than it
had been in the 1950s and 1960s. But the question of color
remained, as it had been throughout the century, America's
preeminent dilemma.

In the bitterness that has followed the breakup of black-
Jewish cooperation, it is tempting to argue that the conflict
was inevitable, that the alliance was a temporary one that was
bound to die. Jews, some black scholars now argue, first be-

came involved in civil rights in the early twentieth century as a way to win "civil rights by remote control" for themselves. They used blacks to interpose someone between themselves and white society, using blacks as long as it suited their interest, and then shifting over to the white majority when conditions eased and supporting black causes and liberal causes was no longer in their economic and social interests.

Jewish intellectuals, especially the neoconservatives, have urged Jews to disassociate themselves from the liberal coalition of the Democratic Party. Economically, they contend, Jewish interests lie more naturally with the Republicans. A safe Israel depends on a strong America and Republicans are far more likely to ensure that than liberal Democrats with their penchant for cutting defense spending.

There is also a class interpretation, which argues that it was class interests that brought blacks and Jews together for a time in the 1940s and 1950s but that this was an aberration. The dissolution of the alliance was inevitable as Jews became more well-to-do and many blacks became mired in poverty.

There are elements of truth in all these arguments. But to write off the period of black-Jewish cooperation and the feelings it stirred as a cynical manipulation or sociological aberration is to miss something vital, I think, about the spirit and the hope that infused the country and the civil rights movement in the early 1960s.

Cooperation between blacks and Jews—the direct cooperation between black leaders and Jewish leaders and the resonance that it struck in both communities—grew and flourished at a time of hope and idealism. These were optimistic times when great changes seemed possible. It is fashionable these days to exalt the Kennedy era and the spirit of hope it unleashed in the country. But to talk to anyone who lived through those years is to hear a sense of loss for a spirit that no longer exists. That spirit was not Kennedy's alone. To reread Martin Luther King's speeches today is to find in them a vision of hope, not just of chastisement or bitterness. It is, decades later, to still feel a shiver of emotion at an inclusive vision that strove to overcome differences. In his speech on the steps of the Alabama state capitol at the end of the voting rights march from Selma to Montgomery in 1965—a speech that probably would have ranked as his greatest had he not given his "I have a dream" speech in 1963—King declared:

> Our aim must never be to defeat or humiliate the white man but to win his friendship and understanding. We must come to see that the end we seek is a society at peace with itself, a society that can live with its conscience. That will be a day not of the white man, not of the black man. That will be the day of man as man.
>
> I know you are asking today, "How long will it take?" I come to say to you this afternoon however difficult the moment, however frustrating the hour, it will not be long, because truth pressed to earth will rise again.
>
> How long? Not long, because no lie can live forever.
>
> How long? Not long, because you still reap what you sow.
>
> How long? Not long. Because the arc of the moral universe is long but it bends towards justice.
>
> How long? Not long, 'cause mine eyes have seen the glory of the coming of the Lord, trampling out the vintage where the grapes of wrath are stored. He has loosed the faithful lightning of his terrible swift sword.
>
> His truth is marching on.

Blacks and Jews did not live in a vacuum. The years 1960 to 1965 unleashed a flurry of activities that linked idealism and patriotism, liberal vision and religious belief. It was a time of dreams, when—naively, in retrospect—all things seemed possible. By 1968, that spirit had faded. The divisions over Vietnam, the student protests on college campuses, opened a chasm in the country and altered the atmosphere of protest. The politics of civility shifted to a politics of confrontation. A deep cynicism spread that doubted that people of goodwill and vision could change things. Rhetoric escalated. People of opposite views said things that would hurt each other. Once rhetoric passed a certain point—once blacks called Jews racists and Jews called blacks anti-Semites, once anti-war protesters accused the government of genocide and supporters of the Vietnam War accused protesters of being unpatriotic—political confrontation developed a life of its own. It spiraled beyond any recall to common ground.

The inflation of the 1970s fueled a change, too. In an expanding economy, the notion of expanding opportunity was acceptable. But inflation and recession eroded people's confidence. The world was not as safe as it appeared. There was fear about the future and jobs. The tendency of blacks and Jews to look after their own interests in the 1970s mirrored a national trend to turn inward and protect what each person had as the economy became uncertain.

The 1970s and 1980s also saw a dearth of pragmatic leaders. For all their soaring rhetoric, King and Kennedy were pragmatists, sensitive to how to build coalitions and how to bring people along. They were often criticized for being too conservative. So were others involved in building the civil rights movement: Bayard Rustin, James Farmer, Paul Parks, Jack Greenberg. They were all, at root, tacticians, most concerned with moving from one point to the next, pushing the cause ahead. They kept to their goal but understood the importance of compromise.

The alliance between blacks and Jews flourished in an atmosphere of inclusiveness and a hopeful vision. It was held together by the heart as well as the head. That was why the Ebsteins marched with Martin Luther King in Chicago—not just out of a calculus of self-interest but because they felt part of a greater American journey. That was the spirit Donna Brazile felt she had missed because she was too young to march with King. As that spirit faded and the political atmosphere of the country changed, the black-Jewish alliance was one of the casualties.

What does the future hold? Will blacks and Jews come together again?

A return to pragmatism would help. After so many years of fighting it would be a tonic to see blacks and Jews work together again. In their battles, they have often resembled two allies battling it out in an arena while an audience—made up of people not particularly supportive of either side—looks on, smiling. There is a network of connections, still, among blacks and Jews working for social service agencies and foundations and among political and civil rights lobbyists. In Chicago and Philadelphia, Jews have provided the victory margins for black mayors. In 1986, when John Lewis defeated Julian Bond for a congressional seat in Atlanta, Jews provided the key swing votes. In Congress, the Black Caucus, under the leadership of Philadelphia congressman William Gray, has worked with Jewish representatives, exchanging support of aid to Israel for support of sanctions on South Africa.

But such a move may require the passing of Jesse Jackson as the preeminent black political leader. Jackson stirs too much suspicion among Jews; the baggage from his past statements about Jews and Israel weighs too heavily. As other black leaders of national reputation emerge—like Gray or Andrew Young or others—they may be able to take the first steps to create a coalition of pragmatism yoking black and Jewish interests together.

To be frank, however, if Jews often express a nostalgia for the alliance, or puzzlement that it went awry, blacks, by and large, do not. They never liked the paternalism that infused cooperation during the civil rights movement. And many younger Jews wonder why they need to worry about blacks anymore. A conversation I had with two lawyers, on opposite coasts, illustrates the depth of the breach.

"I'm totally bored with hearing the history of Jewish involvement in the civil rights movement," Melanie Lomax, a thirty-five-year-old, politically active black lawyer in Los Angeles, told me. "I'm only interested in what's possible now. The Jewish community's support of reverse discrimination has undermined affirmative action. . . . Jews see blacks as an underclass. Theirs is a patronizing, condescending attitude."

Across the country, in New York, Marc Stern, a thirty-year-old Jewish lawyer, also had little time for nostalgia over the old civil rights coalition. "There is a sort of romantic Camelot attitude toward that civil rights era that has a lot of emotional power for the older generation of Jews. It doesn't have that power for a lot of younger people. The terms of the relationship will have to be renegotiated."

"My parents have had this group of liberal Jewish friends for as long as I can remember—people they fought with to integrate theaters, restaurants, etc.," said Lomax. Many younger blacks, she said, "don't respect my parents' generation that was so much in the pocket of the Jewish community. . . . Younger blacks are intent on breaking that stranglehold."

For blacks like Lomax, Jews have become the enemy, the obstacle they must overcome in fighting for political and professional success. Among supporters of Jackson, the question has become not whether the black-Jewish alliance can be restored, but which whites will replace Jews as partners in future progressive coalitions.

In the end, the future of black-Jewish cooperation, like its past, rests less with blacks and Jews than with the future spirit of the country. The black-Jewish alliance came together in a framework created by others: a time of King and Kennedy, when it was at once patriotic and liberal to oppose discrimination and work together for change. It is tempting to look back over the years and become pessimistic, to focus on what was not accomplished and miss what was. Like a rocket that takes off and has its trajectory altered just a bit at the very beginning, the changes wrought by blacks and Jews have become more visible over time. Who would want to live in a country without the changes in civil rights laws and attitudes that blacks and Jews, in the civil rights coalition, created? Blacks and Jews, for all their failings, misapprehensions, and anger, created that rare thing in America: an interracial coalition. The lessons they learned will loom larger as the country becomes more diverse.

Today, the alliance lies in pieces. But one day, perhaps, someone will come along and again lift America's vision upward, talking of the goals that unite people, of optimism and hope.

When that time comes, the call will go out. Blacks and Jews will respond. Maybe not all. But enough to nudge the trajectory of history once again.

Epilogue
The Fire Next Time

Back in 1988, when I finished *Broken Alliance*, it was still possible to be optimistic about the relationship between blacks and Jews.

Jesse Jackson's second presidential campaign began promisingly. As he did in 1984, Jackson surprised nearly everyone with his showing. In 1984 Jackson had won more than 400 delegates and 3.3 million votes. Four years later, he had increased that to over 1,100 delegates and nearly 6.8 million votes, finishing as runner-up to the eventual nominee, Michael Dukakis. Jackson was helped by a crowded field of white candidates who divided the white vote. But in many states Jackson won as much as 20 percent of the white vote. He surrounded himself with white, often Jewish, advisers, and kept his distance from Louis Farrakhan. He spoke carefully of the need for Israel to live securely with its neighbors. After the bitterness of 1984, Jackson and the Jews were exchanging uneasy glances, each side wondering if coexistence was possible.

Organized Jewish groups, however, remained wary of Jackson's approaches. Jackson himself became frustrated that his well-organized efforts, and well-coordinated public relations, failed to allay Jewish suspicions. Neither side could lower their guard. The question of Jackson's relations with Jews hovered around the edges of his campaign. It finally exploded in New York a few weeks before the New York primary when Mayor Edward Koch said that Jews in New York would be "crazy" to vote for Jackson. Koch's statement was crude, but it reflected a political reality. Despite Jackson's 20 percent support among white voters in 1988, he never received more than 10 percent of the Jewish vote in any of the Democratic primaries. He often received less than 5 percent of the Jewish vote. Twenty-five years after the March on Washington a black man was mounting a serious run for the presidency, and Jews were the one white group that did not seem able to support him.

That same year newspapers in Chicago reported that a black aide to Chicago's black mayor, Eugene Sawyer, had given anti-Semitic speeches before Louis Farrakhan's Nation of Islam organization for three years. The aide, Steve Cokely, had told his audiences that Jews were engaged in a conspiracy to control the world and that Jewish doctors were injecting the AIDS virus into black babies. He mocked Jesse Jackson and other black leaders for becoming too close to Jews and to whites. A month before news of the speeches became public, representatives of the Anti-Defamation League had gone to Sawyer privately, armed with tapes of Cokely's speeches. They urged Sawyer to take action. Sawyer did not. After news of Cokely's speeches became public, Sawyer continued to balk at firing Cokely, apparently waiting for him to resign. Lu Palmer, a black activist who had been instrumental in mobilizing support for Harold Washington, said it was "certainly possible that Jews, not just Jews but whites, are in a conspiracy to rule the world. Why would I be surprised at doctors injecting AIDS into black children?" A black minister who was in line to be the next director of the Chicago Commission on Human Relations, said Cokely's remarks had "a ring of truth." After four days of controversy, Sawyer fired Cokely. But the hostility between many blacks and Jews lingered, emerging again when the Art Institute of Chicago hung a picture that depicted Washington dressed in women's lingerie. Several black aldermen demanded that the museum remove the picture. One said that it was what one would expect from a "Jewish artist." The artist was not Jewish.

Chicago had never been the hotbed of black-Jewish tension that New York had been since 1968. The eruption of black-Jewish hostility in Chicago reflected the way tensions between blacks and Jews at the national level were now leeching down into local politics and into personal relationships. When Sawyer ran for election, he lost. One reason was that the Jews who had supported Harold Washington in 1983 in his race to be the first black mayor of Chicago refused to vote for Sawyer, who had become mayor after Washington died while in office. In 1983, Washington had won 18 percent of the white vote but 33 percent of the Jewish vote, even though he was running against a Jewish opponent. Those Jewish votes, along with overwhelming support from blacks, helped give Washington victory. In 1987, Washington had increased his Jewish support, and his margin of victory. In 1989, though, with the controversy over Cokely still fresh in their minds, Jews shied away from Sawyer and backed his white opponent in the Democratic primary. Together with divisions among black voters, their defection was enough to ensure victory for a white candidate, Richard Daley, son of the former Chicago mayor. Having gained the mayor's office in Chicago—an event so momentous it had prompted Jackson to run for president in 1984—blacks now had slipped back and lost it.

Nevertheless, Jews in 1989 were still more willing than any other white group to vote for black candidates for local office. Whites typically shied away from backing a black candidate for mayor. Jews did not. Their support ranged from the 32 percent who voted for Wilson Goode, the first black mayor of Philadelphia, to the 75 percent of Jews who backed Tom Bradley, the longtime black mayor of Los Angeles. The support of Jews as "swing voters" was crucial in cities where blacks made up more than 40 percent but less than a majority of the population. However, the importance of the Jewish vote was magnified by the willingness of Jewish Democratic contributors and fundraisers to support local black candidates across the country. Jews were crucial in electing David Dinkins the first black mayor of New York in 1989. By the late 1980s the power of the black-Jewish coalition behind Bradley in Los Angeles was so strong that it scared most other contenders out of the race. Once debate moved beyond emotional issues like affirmative action and Farrakhan, polls showed that blacks and Jews held virtually identical views on issues like civil rights, aid to cities, abortion, and government programs to create jobs. The emergence of a new generation of black political leaders skilled in the arts of compromise and coalition building, like Congressman John Lewis of Atlanta, Mike Espy of Mississippi, and William Gray of Philadelphia, suggested the possibility of rebuilding the coalitions. The freeing of Nelson Mandela and the beginning of the end of apartheid in South Africa eliminated the touchy subject of Israel's ties to South Africa. Glimmers of hope in the Middle East suggested that disputes over Israel might ease too.

That optimism turned out to be misplaced. Relations between blacks and Jews, and between blacks and whites, deteriorated rapidly. By the mid 1990s blacks had attacked Jews on the streets of Crown Heights in Brooklyn, resulting in the stabbing death of Yankel Rosenbaum, a Jewish theological student from Australia. Anti-Semitic speakers were packing lecture halls at black colleges. A chill, bordering on hostility, had descended upon relations between black and Jewish organizations. More and more Jews were growing angry—and frightened—by the rise of black nationalism and the influence of black radicals like Farrakhan and the Reverend Al Sharpton in New York. While it is tempting to view the latest eruptions of black-Jewish tension as confined to only blacks and Jews, it reflects something deeper: the growing hostility between blacks and whites. It offers a chilling glimpse of a bleak future, a polarization of the races that James Baldwin once warned would lead to "the fire next time."

The latest downward spiral in black-Jewish relations began in 1991 in Crown Heights in Brooklyn when, for the first time, tensions between blacks and Jews broke out into open violence. For years, blacks and Hasidic Jews had lived in uneasy proximity in Crown Heights, which had once been a Jewish neighborhood. Like Roz and Bernie Ebstein's neighborhood in Chicago, it changed complexion in the 1950s and 1960s. Blacks had moved in; crime had increased; city services had deteriorated. Many Jews had left. But a group of Hasidic Jews, known as the Lubavitchers, considered it the center of their religious community and were determined to stay. This was not a neighborhood where blacks and Jews mingled. The Hasidic Jews in Crown Heights were an insular, self-sustaining community that shut out anyone who was not part of their sect, black or white, Jewish or Christian or Moslem. These were not Jews who had once marched with Martin Luther King, Jr. They were conservative and ultraorthodox. They voted Republican, were pro-life, and set up anticrime patrols that targeted black residents. They focused their political energy on Israel, their own internal conflicts, and getting better services from the city of New York. Blacks were at first mystified by the Hasidic Jews, distinctive in their black coats, black hats, and side curls. Later many came to resent them. The Hasidic Jews were wealthier and competed with blacks for scarce housing. Many blacks believed the Hasidic Jews got better police protection and better city services than they did.

On a hot August night, a car bringing home the leader of the Hasidic sect ran a red light and struck a seven-year-old black boy, Gavin Cato. An angry crowd of blacks gathered. What happened next is disputed. An ambulance from a Jewish ambulance service arrived. Police directed the ambulance to take away the Jewish driver of the car who was surrounded by angry blacks and was in danger. A minute later, a city ambulance arrived and took Cato to the hospital, where he died. Crowds of blacks, enraged that the driver of the car was not immediately arrested and that the Jewish driver had been taken away by ambulance before Cato, surged through the streets. Three hours later, a group of black teenagers descended upon Yankel Rosenbaum, a twenty-nine-year-old Hasidic Jewish scholar visiting from Australia. "Kill the Jew!" they shouted, and stabbed Rosenbaum to death. The black teenager arrested for killing Rosenbaum, Lemerick Nelson, Jr., was later acquitted.

Four days of attacks and rioting followed. Blacks attacked Jewish buildings and stores, breaking windows, looting stores, and setting fire to cars. They threw stones at Jewish and white passersby. A Jewish woman called the police:

"They're breaking all the windows on my block!"

"They're breaking all your windows?" the police operator responded.

"Why aren't they [the police] here. Why are they stalling?" shouted the woman.

"Police are on the way, Ma'am."

"No they're not. I don't see them."

"Ma'am, calm down."

"What are you doing to us?"

David Dinkins, the black mayor of New York, hesitated to deploy vast numbers of police to stop the rioting. He and the city's black police chief hoped the rioting could be contained and tempers calmed by restraining the police. Dinkins went to Crown Heights to appeal for calm. He had been elected as a peacemaker, and was a politician used to finessing differences between groups and harnessing them into a political coalition. In Crown Heights, that strategy proved disastrous. The attacks against Jews continued for four days; Dinkins himself was unaware of the chaos enveloping Crown Heights. It was only when he was booed and jeered by angry black residents during a visit to the neighborhood that Dinkins realized the depth of the problem. Dinkins finally flooded Crown Heights with police and brought the rioting to a halt. But the damage had been done. Dinkins was seen as indecisive and out of touch with a riot in his own city. Jews dubbed the rioting the first American pogrom. Many blacks saw it as an explosion over injustice and long-simmering tensions. They said the Hasidic Jews, with their all-Jewish schools, their all-Jewish houses, and their Jewish patrols had created an American apartheid. When the police arrested 163 people to end the rioting, the *Amsterdam News*, New York's largest black newspaper headlined, "MANY BLACKS, NO JEWS ARRESTED."

Once again: Same bed, different dreams.

Because New York was home to most prominent black as

well as Jewish organizations, as well as being the media center of the country, news and pictures of the Crown Heights riot spread rapidly across the nation, inflaming tensions between blacks and Jews far from the streets of Brooklyn.

At the same time, a new trend was developing among black students on college campuses: the rise of Afro-Centrism which charged that traditional history ignored the importance of Africa and blacks to the development of world culture, science, and politics. At the extreme edge of this movement stood several black scholars who charged that Jews had played a special role in controlling and putting down blacks. They used as their text a book called *The Secret History of Blacks and Jews*, published by the Nation of Islam, laden with footnotes and pseudoscholarship that claimed that Jews had financed the slave trade in Europe and America. They said Jews had controlled the civil rights movement and now controlled the world's finances. In their charges and even their language they echoed "The Protocols of the Elders of Zion," an anti-Semitic pamphlet written by the Russian secret police at the turn of the century that claimed to transcribe "secret" lectures by Jewish leaders outlining their plans to subjugate Christians and dominate the world. In 1991, Leonard Jeffries, Jr., a professor at City University of New York, said Jews had bankrolled the slave trade and spoke of "a conspiracy, planned and plotted and programmed out of Hollywood," by "people called Greenberg and Weisberg and Trigliani."

"Russian Jewry had a particular control over the movies," Jeffries said, "and their financial partners, the Mafia, put together a financial system of destruction of black people."

The tensions on campus reached an apogee in 1993 and 1994 when black students groups at colleges around the country invited Khalid Abdul Muhammad, the national spokesman for the Nation of Islam, to speak. A national uproar followed when reports of his speeches became public. Soon Muhammad was a fixture on campuses. After Muhammad appeared at Howard University, a black law student stood up and began leading a chant:

"Who controls the Federal Reserve?"

"The Jews!"

"Who killed Nat Turner?"

"The Jews!"

Back in the 1950s and 1960s, when the Nation of Islam launched its first big recruiting drive under Malcolm X, the group had focused on ghetto street corners and prisons. Now their target was universities and black professionals—the up-and-coming elite of black America. Traditional black organizations like the NAACP and the Congressional Black Caucus began to explore ways to work with Farrakhan. Talking to African-American college students, black professionals, and poor blacks in the inner cities, it became clear why these groups were reluctant to ostracize Farrakhan, despite the wrath of many Jews. Like a rock star, Farrakhan had more fans than followers; few college students or black professionals flocked to the Nation of Islam after his speeches. But Farrakhan touched a chord in blacks. He stirred more passion and drew larger crowds than any other black leader except Jesse Jackson. Benjamin Chavis, the former head of the NAACP, was lucky if he could draw 500 people to a speech. Farrakhan could draw 20,000.

The reason for this was not just because Farrakhan was anti-Semitic, though blacks responded with alarming enthusiasm to his hatred and tirades against Jews. To attend Farrakhan's speeches was to see how the mainstream press had misinterpreted his appeal—a mistake for which all of us in the press bore some responsibility. At a speech of Farrakhan's that I attended in New York, 20,000 people poured into Madison Square Garden, many of them black professionals. Farrakhan began by speaking about Islam. At 10:40 P.M., he physically turned to the largely white press corps seated off to one side of the arena and launched into a twenty-minute attack against Jews. That allowed reporters to get his most inflammatory comments on the nightly television news shows. Farrakhan knows that the mainstream press pays little attention to him when he speaks about Islam or economic development in black neighborhoods. Farrakhan's anti-Semitism reinforced his outlaw image; it underlined his willingness to "stand up" to white people and break any taboo. It was to this image, as much as Farrakhan's anti-Semitism, that blacks responded.

Most of the reporters left the rally in New York after Farrakhan had completed his attacks on Jews; everyone else stayed. For the next two hours Farrakhan delivered a passionate attack on crime and drugs. He told blacks they had to help themselves, build stronger families, rebuild the moral and economic fabric of black life. He attacked not just Jews, but all whites whom he said had conspired to keep blacks down and would never treat them as equals. The crowd cheered.

Farrakhan has tapped into a rage that now fills all classes of black America.

The decade of the 1980s had seen not only the development of the well-publicized black "underclass," cut off from jobs, education, opportunity, and hope. It had also seen a loss of faith by middle-class blacks in the promise that America would one day be an equal society. Travelling across the country, I was struck by the bitterness and anger of successful black executives in Atlanta, blacks who by every definition—with their BMWs in the driveway and their big-screen color televisions in the den—had "made it" in America. These successful blacks spoke angrily about what they saw as the retreat on affirmative action, the "glass ceiling" that impeded their own progress, the looks of fear their teenaged boys received from whites whenever they shopped downtown. Many of them were planning to send their children to all-black colleges. They spoke almost wistfully at times of the days of segregation and the sense of community that segregation created among blacks cut off from, but also safe from, the white world. Earning high salaries and living in leafy suburbs did not mean to these blacks that the struggle for equality was over. They still felt the sting of discrimination themselves and saw the despair and destruction that now enveloped poorer blacks trapped in the inner cities. A poll in 1994 showed blacks becoming increasingly radical politically. Half now backed the creation of a separate, all-black political party. A majority describe their status as a "nation within a nation."

In *Broken Alliance* I had described how black history in the

United States had moved in cycles, from the black nationalism of Marcus Garvey in the 1920s to the more open, integrationist philosophy of Martin Luther King and the civil rights movement in the 1950s and 1960s. The 1980s had made blacks angrier; they were responding not by reaching out but by turning inward.

Farrakhan represented the extreme edge of a growing black disillusionment. In the early 1960s whites, especially northern white liberals, had been so transfixed by King and the civil rights movement in the South that they missed the rise of Malcolm X, which foretold the explosion of black power several years later. So too there is now a danger that America as a whole will look back in five or ten years and realize that the rise of Farrakhan reflected a sea change in American race relations.

For Jews, the 1980s were a decade of more and greater success. In their homes and around the dinner table, Jews still talked about the discrimination they and their parents had faced in the 1930s, 1940s, and 1950s. But by any objective measure, the strides Jews were making in America were enormous. At one point in the 1980s, the dean of every Ivy League Law School was Jewish. In the 1990s the presidents of Harvard, Yale, Princeton, and Dartmouth were Jews. When President Bill Clinton nominated his first two judges to the Supreme Court, both were Jews. No one even remarked on it.

Jews were turning more and more outward—through intermarriage, success at universities, better jobs in business and government. One morning, I appeared on "The Oprah Winfrey Show" with a group of blacks and Jews. The Jews began talking about historic discrimination against Jews in the United States. They described how Jews were still a minority, and still ran into prejudice and hate. Benjamin Hooks, then the head of the NAACP, interrupted. "I look here and I don't see a group of blacks and Jews," he said, "I see black people and white people." This was a view echoed by many blacks. It never ceased to astonish Jews. They did not see themselves as "white." They saw themselves as "Jews," a minority historically oppressed and discriminated against not only in the United States but around the world. But in many ways the black perception was true. Jews were still a "minority" when it came to religious issues like prayer in public schools and hate crimes. But in the new racial and ethnic politics of the 1990s, Jews were more and more allied with whites than with America's other minorities. The demands for diversity in businesses, college campuses, and elsewhere did not include Jews; rather Jews were among the targets of the calls for change. They were seen as part of the white power structure that now had to open up. Many Jews, especially Jewish men, identified now with other white males under pressure from minorities. Jewish interests in many areas were now the interests of the majority, not the minority.

This was especially true among younger Jews. At Yale University, a Jewish senior approached me after a speech and said: "You know, my parents tell me all about this black-Jewish alliance and about Schwerner, Chaney, and Goodman. But the only way I know about blacks is through affirmative action. I know it is going to be harder for me to get into law school because I will be competing against someone black."

For many Jews, anti-Semitism in America now had a black face. The hostility Jews encountered from blacks contrasted with their increasing acceptance among whites. The rise of attacks on Jews among African-American college students and black professionals especially upset Jews. American blacks now appeared to be one of the few groups where hostility towards Jews and anti-Semitism increased with higher education and higher incomes.

Many influential Jewish writers gleefully declared that the alliance between blacks and Jews was over. Most of these Jews were conservatives or neoconservatives whose disillusionment with blacks had been growing ever since the late 1960s, when the rise of Black Power took over the civil rights movement and the Six Day War pushed Israel and questions of Jewish identity to the forefront of American Jewish concerns. These Jews said the alliance between blacks and Jews was over in 1968 when the two groups clashed in New York during the

Ocean Hill–Brownsville school strike. They said it was over in the 1970s when black and Jewish groups clashed over affirmative action. They said it was over in the late 1970s when United Nations Ambassador Andrew Young secretly met with officials of the PLO. And they said it was over in 1984 when Jesse Jackson first ran for president.

More troubling this time around is the exhaustion of many Jewish liberals. The rise of "Farrakhanism" comes at a time of growing white disillusionment with blacks, a generalized racial weariness with the intractability of inner-city problems and frustration with the growing anger of black professionals and college students—the very groups who have "made it" in American society. It is tempting for many Jews to give up and walk away from any hope of restoring black-Jewish cooperation. Certainly Jews, even liberal Jews, have other causes they can fight for.

What would be the consequences of abandoning the black-Jewish alliance—burying it with history and moving on?

It is easy to look back through the hazy nostalgia that has enveloped Jewish participation in the civil rights movement— when Jews contributed three-quarters of the money given to Martin Luther King, Jr., and other civil rights leaders; when Abraham Joshua Heschel and Jewish rabbis marched hand-in-hand with blacks across the South; when Jewish students made up two-thirds of the white volunteers who crossed Mississippi during the "Freedom Summer" of 1964—and mock the way helping blacks became part of the Jewish identity of many Jews. "I remember asking a Jewish lady in New York once how she knew she was Jewish," a one-time black militant told me. "She said, 'I read *The New York Times* and write checks to the NAACP.'"

Most of the Jews who went South and participated in the civil rights struggle were not religious Jews. Most were quite secular. But the movement touched their spirit. It filled an almost religious gap in their lives. For many Jews, identifying with civil rights became part of their identity as a Jew. Thus the tenacity with which Jews clung to the notion of a black-

Jewish alliance long after the two sides had split apart. Thus the pain that permeates many Jews when they speak of the collapse of black-Jewish relations.

For many Jews, especially liberal Jews, a commitment to social justice, to righting society's wrongs, remains a crucial part of their understanding of the Bible and the Jewish prayer book—as important a secular touchstone as supporting Israel or making sure that the Holocaust is remembered. Turning their backs on black America, however temporarily satisfying, could in the long run nag at their consciences. Even more alarming, the growing tensions between blacks and Jews threatens to curdle Jewish views of blacks. Fewer and fewer Jews could point to constructive relationships they had with blacks, or even black friendships. The growing anger of many Jews towards blacks threatened their own reputation for tolerance; it led some neoconservative Jews to make statements that evinced racism.

More concretely, the collapse of cooperation between blacks and Jews bodes ill in three areas in which Jews have historic, present, and future interests: colleges, cities, and the Democratic Party.

The rise of black-Jewish tensions at colleges imperiled the one institution where Jews, more than any other group, has thrived—as students, professors, and administrators. Colleges, as Jews know better than most, are where ideas are shaped and future success determined. In addition to preserving the civility of college campuses, Jews had an interest in ensuring that the hate-filled stereotypes being spread among many black students were counteracted before they could harden into prejudice. Walking away from the black-Jewish alliance meant risking a generation or more of blacks who saw Jews as the enemy.

Cities are another area where breaking off efforts at black-Jewish cooperation could harm Jewish self-interest. Many Jews, like many Americans, have moved to the suburbs. But more than any other white group, the interests of Jews, and much of their power and influence, is tied to the health and future of cities, whether it is the financial and media center of New York where Jews make up a significant proportion of idea shapers and decision makers, or the entertainment capital of Los Angeles. In the past decade almost every major American city has been governed by a black mayor. Politicians come and go; black candidates win and lose. But the reality of black political power in New York, Los Angeles, Chicago, Philadelphia, and other major cities is a fact of the political landscape. As people who live and work in these cities, and who wield power in them, Jews need to come to an accommodation with black citizens and black politicians. The alternative is the crippling tension that has enveloped New York, which has not only poisoned relations between blacks and Jews but physically endangered the Hasidic residents of Crown Heights.

The Democratic Party is the third area imperiled by the collapse of the black-Jewish cooperation. Many neoconservatives saw the growing tensions between blacks and Jews as another wedge to push Jews out of the Democratic Party and into the Republican Party. These neoconservatives, many of whom supported Ronald Reagan in 1980 and 1984 and George Bush in 1988, sought to wean Jews of their historic liberalism. For years they have argued that 1960s-style, big-government liberalism has failed and that the Republicans defend the interests of Israel more staunchly than Democrats. Now they asked: How could Jews remain in a Democratic Party that would always be beholden to black demands? Back in the 1960s sociologists joked that Jews lived like Episcopalians but voted like Puerto Ricans. Jewish conservatives and neoconservatives think it's time Jews voted like Episcopalians, a stereotype of affluent, conservative Republicanism.

That's a fine argument. It is also one that a majority of Jews have rejected ever since it was first mounted in 1968, when Richard Nixon made a concerted pitch for the Jewish vote. About two-thirds of Jews still regularly vote Democratic in presidential elections. And that means they make their home in the Democratic Party—a party in which blacks have a significant voice. Neoconservatives argue that the Republicans are more supportive of Israel, oppose affirmative action, and lash out more quickly at black extremism—all issues presumably important to Jewish voters. But on just about every other important issue—abortion rights, school prayer, the rise of the Christian right—polls show that Jews and Republicans are at loggerheads. The religious right and evangelical Christians are steadily gaining strength in the Republican Party. As the 1996 presidential campaign got underway, evangelical Christians and the religious right were planning to build on the momentum of victories in local school boards, state caucuses, and Republican state committees to shape the selection of a Republican presidential candidate. Did Jews find the prospect of dealing with Pat Robertson and the religious right more comforting that dealing with Jesse Jackson and blacks?

The danger for blacks of the collapse of black-Jewish cooperation was even more stark.

In the 1960s, blacks faced a white population stirred by guilt, idealism, and self-interest into accommodating many black demands. Blacks in the 1990s found whites increasingly resistant to their demands, and other ethnic groups, such as Hispanics and Asians, who are jockeying for a position in the new American society of the twenty-first century. Attacking Jews drove away the most important allies that blacks have in fighting for political and social change. Blacks who sat by quietly as Farrakhan attacked Jews, or who minimized his anti-Semitism, must answer a question: Where did they think future coalitions will come from, especially at a time when Hispanics will soon surpass blacks as the country's largest minority? Already, blacks have lost the great mayoral victories they won in the 1980s. New York, Philadelphia, Chicago, and Los Angeles have all replaced black mayors with white, centrist mayors. These mayors have been elected by coalitions that include white ethnics, Jews, conservative Hispanics, and Asians, and exclude blacks.

For most blacks, certainly for most poor blacks, the debate over black-Jewish relations was a distant speck on the horizon. Their concerns were far more immediate: jobs, poverty, school, crime, drug abuse, the collapse of inner-city black neighborhoods. When they thought of Jews specifically, it was in the context of the Jackson presidential campaigns or the attacks on Farrakhan. They viewed Jews as the enemy. Yet polls still showed that on all these issues of key importance to blacks, Jews were the most supportive and Jewish politicians the most liberal. Cutting off Jewish support meant further isolation for black America. Despite their at times bitter anger toward each other, blacks and Jews still seemed caught in what Martin Luther King called an "inescapable web of mutuality."

For America, the death throes of the black-Jewish alliance had consequences too. Out of sight of most of their countrymen, blacks and Jews since the end of World War II have been on the cutting edge of American race relations, from the cooperation of the 1950s and 1960s to the debates over affirmative action and other disputes in the 1970s and 1980s. Now, the growing hostility between blacks and Jews presages an even darker time, a time of different groups pulling inward, rallying for their own special ethnic interests, balkanizing the country.

Blacks and Jews used to share the same space. They often shared the same physical space in city neighborhoods that changed rapidly in the 1950s and 1960s from Jewish to black. They shared the same political space in the Democratic Party where they worked together for a common goal—an end to prejudice and discrimination—and for a broad liberal agenda. They even shared the same spiritual space. The civil rights movement was shaped by southern preachers, who drew powerfully on the Old Testament and the black fascination with the Jewish Exodus. Both blacks and Jews sang "Let My People Go."

All that has changed. The change has accelerated rapidly since 1988. Jews, like most whites, have moved to the suburbs. Most blacks remain trapped in, or tied to, the cities and their problems. Disagreements over affirmative action, Jesse Jackson, Israel, and Farrakhan have fractured the underpinnings of the liberal Democratic coalition. The rise of Farrakhan's message of hatred and separatism, coupled with the separate but growing influence of black nationalism among blacks, has eroded even the spiritual ties that once existed between blacks and Jews.

The space that blacks and Jews now seem to occupy is a boxing ring. Blacks and Jews seem so preoccupied with slugging it out with each other that they have lost sight of their audience. These spectators, including conservatives and the religious right, do not like blacks or Jews. They cheer the fight on. Pow!—Affirmative action! Bam!—Jews controlled the slave trade! Left jab!—Louis Farrakhan! Right hook!—Crown Heights! The fight enervates blacks and Jews, just as it enervates civil rights and a vision of a more inclusive America. It is still unclear how the battle will end—whether blacks and Jews will be able to put their gloves down and see how they can work together again in their mutual interests. Or whether they will keep slugging away, until one or both collapse, bloodied and exhausted.

Acknowledgments

Many people helped in the research and writing of this book.

My first thanks go to the subjects of the six biographical chapters—Paul Parks, Jack Greenberg, Rhody McCoy, the Ebsteins, Martin Peretz, and Donna Brazile. Each spent many hours with me, often in multiple interviews, sharing their recollections, thoughts, and feelings. I suspect that they will not agree with everything that is said here, but their generosity and willingness to cooperate made this book possible.

There were others who shared their insights and experiences with me who are mentioned in the text. Some who are not mentioned or who especially helped shape my thinking, and change it: St. Clair Drake, David Levering Lewis, Alice Walker, Michael Meltsner, Alan Gartner, Marilyn Gittell, Richard Kluger, Ron Walters, Alvin Poussaint, Julius Lester, Don Rose, J. Anthony Lukas, David Garrow, Taylor Branch, Amiri Baraka, Clayborne Carson, Robert Hill, Derrick Bell, Chaim Seidler-Feller, Robert Coles, Leonard Fein, Dotty Miller Zellner, and Randall Kennedy.

The Alicia Patterson Foundation supported me for a year with a fellowship that allows journalists to research and write on a topic of their choice. Helen Coulson and Cathy Trost were enormously supportive, and Trost was the first sounding board for several of the ideas here. I would also like to thank those who sponsored me for the fellowship: Michael Janeway, Leonard Zakim, Meldon Hollis, Robert Armstrong, H. D. S. Greenway, and Tom Winship (the best editor a reporter could ever hope to work for).

At the *Boston Globe*, Jack Driscoll, Ben Taylor, Michael Janeway,

301

and Al Larkin gave me a year's leave of absence to work on this book, extending it for another three months so I could finish my research. Many of the concerns touched on here first occurred to me while doing stories for the *Globe*. I am fortunate to work at a place that values this kind of reporting and that encourages its reporters to write books.

Michael Carlisle, my agent, supported this project from the beginning and saw it through with jolts of enthusiasm, counsel, editing ideas, and humor. He began as my agent and quickly became my friend.

Reporters are only as good as their sources; writers are only as good as their editors.

Ross Gelbspan read this book starting from the draft of the proposal and through the drafts of various chapters. He and I spent long lunches teasing out ideas and themes. Ross's ideas and his comments helped me when I got stuck and clarified me when I got muddled. You can only say this once, so I will say it here: I could not have written this book without him.

At Scribner's, I owe a special debt to Robert Stewart, who provided several shrewd, and crucial, changes of focus that taught me some important lessons about writing books and made the writing of this one flow easier. Ann Bartunek, my copy editor, and Dale Jagemann helped whip the manuscript into shape. Milly Marmur and Maron Waxman were enthusiastic backers of this project at its start. Betsy Rappoport read an early draft and peppered me with editing suggestions that helped shape the final copy.

Several people read the manuscript in whole or in part and offered criticisms and suggestions.

Over several years of conversations, Meldon Hollis has taught me a great deal about black politics and black perceptions. But that doesn't begin to capture his energy, enthusiasm, and warmth. He was an enthusiastic backer of this project from the start, read the book in manuscript, and offered advice and encouragement throughout. Teresa Hollis cheered me on and occasionally acted as my advance scout in deciding whom to speak with. Together, the two of them welcomed me to Baltimore, suggested interviews across the country, and opened many doors. With these two as backstops, I knew I could not go far wrong, though of course where I have gone wrong, it is my responsibility, not theirs or anyone else's cited here.

Leonard Zakim arranged for me to join a trip of blacks and Jews to Israel, read over the manuscript, and argued and discussed the dilemma of black-Jewish relations over lunches, phone calls, and at parties. His knowledge and willingness to engage in debate pushed my thinking, and his support buoyed me. We often joked about whether someone or something was, in that familiar phrase, "good for the Jews." Lenny is.

William Strickland at the University of Massachusetts at Amherst, and Larry Sternberg at Brandeis, each read the first two chapters and shared important thoughts, correcting some errors. My conversations with both of them helped adjust my balance.

Jonathan Reider, a writer I much admire, read the manuscript on short notice and offered valuable suggestions on the introduction and conclusion. Terri Minsky and David Blum, writers and friends, read the entire manuscript and were especially helpful with the Peretz and Greenberg chapters, sharpening my style and filling gaps.

In addition to those who read the manuscript, I had conversations with several people that shaped my thinking about the writing and structure of the book. My thanks to Lisa Drew, Harriet Rubin, Peter Davison, Fletcher Roberts, David Ownby, Tim Cheek, and Barbara Howard. It was Mike Janeway's idea to insert "newsreel" footage, an idea that germinated for many months before taking root. Kirk Scharfenberg encouraged my thinking about some of the broader issues in American politics that shaped the black-Jewish conflict. Sean Mullin and Charles Liftman at the *Globe* helped me get the book from computer disk to manuscript.

One of the pleasures of working on this book was the chance it gave me to visit friends in other cities and bounce ideas off them. In New York, Terri Minsky and David Blum put me up and listened as I wended my way from proposal to research to writing to publication. They were always there for phone calls and advice—and laughter. In Chicago, Geoff Tabin gave me the run of his apartment, even though his residency kept him at the hospital for most of my stay. As always, he came through in a pinch. In Washington, D.C., Deb Knopman and Don Weightman made sure my shoes were polished before I forayed out for fellowship interviews. I relished our long evenings of conversation. In San Francisco, Richard Seeborg turned over his living room and phone to me and endured multiple visits to the Hunan and Brandy Ho. Someday I hope he will meet Alice Waters. In Los Angeles, Shirley Peppers both put me up and suggested several interviews. Her insights and her friendship over the years have meant a great deal to me, and prompted many of the questions I found myself asking as I proceeded with this project.

Closer to home, Bob Richards, Ralph Child, Eliza Blanchard, David Shapiro, Tim Cheek, David Ownby, Anne Wheelock, Michael Frisby, Fletcher Roberts, and Karol Roberts all bolstered my spirits during what was at times a lonely business. Special thanks to Peter Gosselin, who was a sounding board for many peaks, and many valleys.

Barbara Howard was part of this book from the start and endured more than I probably want to acknowledge in mood swings, preoccupied evenings, and missed days at the beach. But, I would like to think, she also shared in the highs of exaltation, giddiness, and fulfillment. Writing this book was an adventure for both of us. May there be many more.

Chapter Notes

Introduction

p. 2.   "The Negro identifies himself . . .": James Baldwin, "The Harlem Ghetto," *Commentary*, February 1948. Reprinted in *The Price of the Ticket: Collected Nonfiction, 1948–1985* (New York: St. Martin's/Marek, 1985), p. 7.

Chapter One

p. 15.   The disappearance of the three civil rights workers: Details are taken from William Bradford Huie, *Three Lives for Mississippi* (New York: WCC Books, 1965); Jack Mendelsohn, *The Martyrs* (New York: Harper & Row, 1966), pp. 109–32; *The Boston Globe*, 6/25/64, 6/30/64, 8/5/64, 8/9/64; *New York Herald Tribune*, 8/6/64.

p. 17.   Jackson speech to the Democratic Convention in 1984: Excerpted in Clayborne Carson, Daid J. Garrow, Vincent Harding and Darle Clark Hine, eds., *Eyes on the Prize: A Reader and Guide* (New York: Viking Penguin, Inc., 1987), p. 292.

p. 17.   "The reverence in which Andrew Goodman . . .": *Andrew Goodman, 1943–1964* (Memorial volume prepared by the Goodman family).

p. 18.   Newspaper reports at the time: *The Boston Globe*, 8/5/64, 8/9/64; *New York Herald Tribune*, 8/6/64; Huie.

p. 18.   "It never even occurred to any of us . . .": Interview with Carolyn Goodman.

p. 18.   David Dennis speech: reprinted in Juan Williams, *Eyes on the Prize: America's Civil Rights Years, 1954–1965* (New York: Viking Penguin, Inc., 1987), pp. 238–40.

p. 19.   Well over half the white students heading South that summer were Jewish: Murray Friedman, "Jews, Blacks and the Civil Rights Revolution," *New Perspectives* (U.S. Commission on Civil Rights, Fall 1985). The estimates for Jewish participation and fund-raising are a general consensus of civil rights leaders interviewed. In their study, *CORE: A Study in the Civil Rights Movement* (New York: Oxford University Press, 1983), August Meier and Elliott Rudwick write that about 95 percent of CORE's national contributors in 1964 were white "and they were disproportionately Jewish." On a list of top New York contributors "the majority of the names were also Jewish."

p. 19.   A routine by Lenny Bruce: reprinted in William Novak and Moshe Waldoks, eds., *The Big Book of Jewish Humor* (New York: Harper & Row Perennial Library, 1981), p. 60.

p. 20.   "Of all European peoples . . .": Hannah Arendt, *Anti-Semitism: Part One of the Origins of Totalitarianism* (New York: Harcourt Brace Jovanovich, 1968), p. 23.

p. 20.   "Any group bigger than a minyan": Interview with Martin Peretz.

pp. 20–21.   Jews who came to American . . . treaded cautiously: the role of Jews in early reform movements and their transformation into opponents of discrimination is discussed in an essay by Oscar Handlin in Nathan Glazer, Joseph L. Blau, Herman D. Stein, Oscar and Mary F. Handlin, *The Characteristics of American Jews* (New York: Jewish Education Committee Press, 1965).

p. 21.   Sol A. Benjamin hauled into court: Morris U. Schappes, *A Documentary History of the Jews in the United States, 1654–1875* (New York: The Citadel Press, 1950), p. 280.

p. 21.   Report of the American and Foreign Anti-Slavery Society: Robert G. Weisbord and Arthur Stein, *Bittersweet Encounter: The Afro-American and the American Jew* (Westport, Conn.: Negro Universities Press, 1970), p. 26.

p. 22.   Advertisement by Abraham Seixas: Ibid., p. 20.

p. 22.   Sermon by Rabbi Raphall and reaction to it: Schappes, pp. 405–18.

p. 24.   these new immigrants brought with them a new ideology: The rise of socialism among Jews is discussed in the Handlin essay in *Characteristics*; Henry L. Feingold, *A Midrash on American Jewish History* (Albany: State University of New York Press, 1982), especially chapters two and six; Nathan Glazer, *The Social Basis of American Communism* (New York: Harcourt, Brace and World, Inc., 1961), pp. 167–68; Jonathan Frankel, *Prophecy and Politics: Socialism, Nationalism and the Russian Jews* (New York: Cambridge University Press, 1981); Nora Levin, *While Messiah Tarried: Jewish Socialist Movements, 1871–1917* (New York: Schocken Books, 1977).

p. 26.   "You colored workers . . ."; "It was just a case . . .": Hasia R. Diner, *In the Almost Promised Land* (Westport, Conn.: Greenwood Press, 1977), pp. 217–20.

p. 26.   For those Jews who adopted or flirted with Communism: Mark Naison, *Communists in Harlem During the Depression* (Urbana: University of Illinois Press, 1983), especially pp. 321–27. For the story of Leibowitz's involvement in the Scottsboro Boys case, see Dan T. Carter, *Scottsboro, A Tragedy of the American South* (Baton Rouge: Louisiana State University Press, 1979).

p. 26.   upsurge in political activism . . . fed by religious changes: *Characteristics*, pp. 96–97.

p. 28.   discrimination against Jews had become widespread: *Characteristics*, pp. 265–67; Charles Silberman, *A Certain People* (New York: Summit Books, 1985), pp. 28–72. The Columbia chant and Wolfson quote are cited in Silberman.

p. 28.   In 1913, Leo Frank: Friedman.

p. 29.   Yiddish *Forward* . . . began writing extensively about blacks: Diner, pp. 36–81. Diner cites extensive quotes from the *Forward*, including those here.

p. 30.   In 1909, when the "call" was issued: Ibid., pp. 118–33.

p. 31.   Jewish philanthropists: Ibid., pp. 166–76.

p. 31.   "one of the 'minorities' . . .": *Characteristics*, p. 277.

p. 32.   "Jews live with this fact . . .": *Commentary*, November 1945.

p. 33.   "Ante-Bellum Sermon": reprinted in Joseph R. Washington, Jr., ed., *Jews in Black Perspectives* (Rutherford: Fairleigh Dickinson Press, 1984), p. 37.

p. 34.   "It seems unlikely . . .": Baldwin, "The Harlem Ghetto," *Price of the Ticket*, p. 9.

p. 34.   It was on plantations: John Gibbs St. Clair Drake, "African Diaspora and Jewish Diaspora: Convergence and Divergence" in *Jews in Black Perspectives*, pp. 19–41.

p. 34.   In 1822 . . . Denmark Vesey: Vincent Harding, *There Is a River* (New York: Vintage Books, 1983), pp. 68–69; Drake.

p. 36.   In one of his earliest memories: Interview with St. Clair Drake.

p. 36.   "all of us black people . . .": Richard Wright, *Blackboy* (New York: Harper & Row Perennial, 1966), p. 70.

p. 37.   There was even a competing anti-Jewish religious myth: Drake, pp. 37–38; Interview with Drake.

p. 37.   the great migration: August Meier and Elliott Rudwick, *From Plantation to Ghetto* (New York: Hill & Wang, 1976), p. 232.

p. 38.   "The Jewish boys . . .": Baldwin, "The Fire Next Time" (1963), *Price of the Ticket*, p. 347.

p. 38.   article for a Harlem Newspaper: Roi Ottley, *"New World A-Coming"* (Boston: Houghton Mifflin Co., 1943), p. 126.

p. 38.   In 1935, when rioting broke out: Ibid., pp. 124–25.

p. 39.   "Don't Buy Where You Can't Work": Ibid., pp.114–15.

p. 40.   The Civil War and Reconstruction: The condition of blacks during Reconstruction is detailed in C. Vann Woodward, *The Strange Career of Jim Crow* (New York: Oxford University Press, 1974), pp. 11–65. The growth of segregation and disenfranchisement is detailed on pp. 67–147. The growth of lynching and racist scholarship is described in Woodward and in *From Plantation to Ghetto*, pp. 194–211.

p. 42.   In 1917, race riots: *From Plantation to Ghetto*, pp. 236–39.

p. 43.   "The struggle for, with, and against white allies . . .": *Eyes on the Prize: A Reader*, p. 7.

p. 43.   "No people can be free . . .": *River*, p. 172.

p. 43.   Du Bois . . . wrote frequently . . . during the 1930s of the rise of anti-Semitism: Herbert Aptheker, *Annotated Bibliography of the Published Writings of W. E. B. Du Bois* (Millwood, New York: Kraus-Thomson Organization, 1973).

p. 43–44.   "We may be expelled . . .": *Bittersweet Encounter*, p. 53.

p. 44.   "The African Movement . . .": Robert Weisbord and Richard Kazarian, Jr., *Israel in the Black American Perspective* (Westport, Conn.: Greenwood Press, 1985), p. 14.

p. 44.   "A new spirit . . .": Ibid., p. 16.

p. 44.   "Gone is the intensity . . .": Hortense Powdermaker, "The Channeling of Negro Aggression by the Cultural Process" in August Meier and Elliott Rudwick, eds., *The Making of Black America* (New York: Atheneum, 1969), II, p. 104.

p. 45.   "Our victory will not be a victory for Montgomery's Negroes alone": David J. Garrow, *Bearing the Cross* (New York: William Morrow and Co., Inc., 1986), p. 67.

p. 45.   The ministers and sons of ministers: James Farmer, *Lay Bare*

the Heart (New York, New American Library, 1985), p. 33;
Interview with Bayard Rustin.

p. 46.   "The hibernation is over . . .": Ralph Ellison, *Invisible Man* (New York: Vintage Books, 1972), pp. 567–68.

p. 46.   After their son's body was found: Interview with Carolyn Goodman.

Chapter Two

p. 51.   Paul Parks liked to tell this story: Interview with Paul Parks.
p. 53.   "We are looking for . . .": Huie, pp. 249–50.
p. 54.   His people were from central Florida: Interview with Paul Parks.
p. 55.   Although Indiana had not joined the Confederacy: Conditions for blacks in Indiana and Indianapolis are described in Emma Lou Thornbrough, "Segregation in Indiana During the Klan Era of the 1920s" in Meier and Rudwick, *The Making of Black America*, II, pp. 184–203.
p. 56.   Gabe Segal: Interview with Paul Parks.
p. 56.   Parks was a bad kid: Interview with Paul Parks.
p. 57.   There were only ten black students on campus: Interview with Paul Parks.
p. 59.   The years of the New Deal had seen . . . easing in hostility toward blacks: *From Plantation to Ghetto*, pp. 259–61.
p. 60.   It was in the army: Interview with Paul Parks.
p. 62.   Working for a series of engineering firms: Interview with Paul Parks.
p. 63.   "Six years ago . . .": Alice Walker, "The Civil Rights Movement: What Good Was It?" *In Search of Our Mothers' Gardens* (San Diego: Harcourt Brace Jovanovich, 1983), p. 124.
p. 64.   What was so striking: The history of the early days of the civil rights movement is detailed in Howell Raines, *My Soul Is Rested* (New York: Penguin Books, 1983), pp. 37–74, and in Williams, *Eyes on the Prize*, pp. 59–90.
p. 65.   organized a benefit rally: David L. Lewis, *King: A Biography* (Urbana: University of Illinois Press, 1978), p. 76.
p. 66.   Jewish contributions: *CORE*, pp. 225, 336, 411; Interview with David Garrow. Interview with Bayard Rustin.
p. 66.   Jesse Jackson recalled: Interview with Jesse Jackson.
p. 66.   "*Judeo*-Christian tradition": Interview with David Garrow.
p. 66.   "As sure as Moses . . .": *My Soul Is Rested*, p. 56.
p. 66.   Traveling around the country: Interview with Marvin Rich.
p. 66.   Stanley Levison: Garrow, pp. 465, 272ff. The importance of Levison and King's refusal to cut off his ties with him is discussed extensively in David Garrow, *The FBI and Martin Luther King, Jr.* (New York: W. W. Norton, 1981).
p. 67.   Rich . . . Alan Gartner . . . Howard Zinn: Interviews with Rich, Gartner, Zinn.
p. 67.   Robert Moses: Interview with Robert Moses.
p. 67.   Stokely Carmichael: Clayborne Carson, "Blacks and Jews in the Civil Rights Movement," *Jews in Black Perspectives*, pp. 113–31.
p. 67.   "All I want . . ." "maybe some day . . .": Clayborne Carson, *In Struggle: SNCC and the Black Awakening of the 1960s* (Cambridge: Harvard University Press, 1981), p. 13.
p. 68.   Julius Lester: Interview with Julius Lester.
p. 68.   "If we are wrong . . .": *Eyes on the Prize: A Reader*, p. 45.
p. 68.   at a press conference: *Eyes on the Prize*, p. 132.
p. 68.   Paul Parks embraced the chance: Interview with Paul Parks.

p. 71.   "That was a terrible night . . .": *My Soul Is Rested*, pp. 152–53.

p. 72.   "to have white people": *In Struggle*, p. 99.

p. 72.   "Profoundly influenced by the overthrow of white colonialism": reprinted in August Meier and Elliott Rudwick, *Black Protest Thought in the Twentieth Century* (Chicago: Quadrangle, 1970), p. 380.

p. 72.   "white liberal-labor syndrome": James Forman, *The Making of Black Revolutionaries* (New York: Macmillan, 1972), p. 381.

p. 73.   Mississippi Freedom Democratic party: *Eyes on the Prize*, pp. 232–49; Interview with Dotty Miller Zellner.

p. 73.   Parks believed the compromise was necessary: Interview with Paul Parks.

p. 74.   "Something is happening to people . . .": quoted in *In Struggle*, p. 101.

p. 74.   when Stavis issued a call for lawyers: Interview with Morton Stavis.

p. 75.   The Muslim came into SNCC's office: Interview with Dotty Zellner.

p. 75.   "this mealy-mouth, beg-in . . .": Peter Goldman, *The Death and Life of Malcolm X* (Urbana: University of Illinois, 1979), p. 6.

p. 75.   "When a man is hanging . . .": Ibid., p. 14.

p. 76.   In CORE, younger and more militant members blocked efforts by Farmer to name one of his Jewish advisers: *CORE*, pp. 293–94; interview with Alan Gartner.

p. 76.   In April 1965 King . . . met with blacks in the basement of a church: Interview with Paul Parks.

p. 77.   Parks flew out to Chicago: Interview with Paul Parks.

p. 78.   King had flown south: The rally in Greenwood is described in *Eyes on the Prize: A Reader*, pp. 191–94.

p. 78.   Parks believed King was losing control of the movement: Interview with Paul Parks.

p. 79.   "If America don't come around . . .": *In Struggle*, p. 255.

p. 79.   "If America chooses to play . . .": *In Struggle*, p. 254.

p. 80.   "There is no such thing": Interview with Paul Parks.

p. 80.   SNCC issued a leaflet: the story of the SNCC leaflet is recounted in *In Struggle*, pp. 266–72 and in *Israel in the Black American Perspective*, pp. 29–45. The poem from the Black Panther magazine is cited in *Israel in the Black American Perspective*, p. 43.

p. 81.   Harold Cruse: Harold Cruse, *The Crisis of the Negro Intellectual* (New York: Quill, 1984).

p. 82.   "is singled out": Baldwin, "Negroes Are Anti-Semitic Because They're Anti-White" *The New York Times Magazine*, April 9, 1967, reprinted in *Price of the Ticket*, pp. 431–32.

p. 82.   Parks was upset: Interview with Paul Parks.

p. 82.   In October 1963 . . . a poll: John A. Williams, *The King God Didn't Save* (New York: Coward-McCann, 1970), p. 210.

p. 83.   The night King was assassinated: Interview with Paul Parks.

p. 83.   "This is our basic conclusion . . . ": *Report of the National Advisory Commission on Civil Disorders* (New York: Bantam, 1968), p. 1.

p. 84.   Parks would achieve: Interview with Paul Parks.

Chapter Three

p. 85.   Jack Greenberg always insisted: Interview with Jack Greenberg.

p. 86.   In late 1964: Gary Marx, *Protest and Prejudice: A Study of Belief in the Black Community* (New York: Harper & Row, 1967), p. 152.

p. 86.   "For years we used to hear stories": Peter Golenbock, *Bums: An Oral History of the Brooklyn Dodgers* (New York: Pocket Books, 1986), p. 189.

p. 87.   The year Jackie Robinson broke into the majors: Interview with Jack Greenberg.

p. 89.   Morton Stavis . . . made the rounds of Wall Street: Interview with Morton Stavis.

p. 89.   some of his professors: Interview with Walter Gellhorn.

p. 89.   Unlike many of his classmates: Interview with Jack Greenberg.

p. 90.   One day he received a call: Interview with Walter Gellhorn. The conversation between Gellhorn and Marshall is also recounted in Richard Kluger, *Simple Justice* (New York: Vintage Books, 1977), p. 436.

p. 91.   established a legal vigilance committee: *Simple Justice*, p. 101.

p. 91.   to write a blueprint: Ibid., pp. 132–34.

p. 91.   There were few black lawyers: Ibid., p. 125.

p. 91.   extraordinary alumni association: Ibid., p. 272.

p. 92.   Esther Brown: The details of Esther Brown's involvement are drawn from Kluger's account in *Simple Justice*, pp. 388–90, 401, 411.

p. 93.   Kenneth Clark . . . paper funded and written: Friedman.

p. 93.   a poll showed: Silberman, p. 57.

p. 93.   In cities across the country: *Bittersweet Encounter*, pp. 134–35; Interview with Earl Rabb.

p. 94.   Carter . . . welcomed: Interview with Robert Carter.

p. 94.   Frankfurter . . . called one of his clerks: Interview with Dan Greenberg.

p. 95.   "How many bubbles . . .": Jack Greenberg, *Race Relations and American Law* (New York: Columbia University Press, 1959), pp. 141–42.

p. 95.   "Travel without embarrassment . . .": Ibid., 131n.

p. 96.   "A case can hardly be won . . .": Jack Greenberg, *Litigation for Social Change: Methods, Limits and Role in a Democracy*, 30th Annual Benjamin N. Cardozo Lecture Delivered Before the Association of the Bar of the City of New York, October 31, 1973 (New York: Association of the Bar of the City of New York, 1974), p. 36.

p. 97.   "When the Freedom Riders left . . .": *Black Protest Thought*, pp. 396–97.

p. 98.   Fund-raisers from the Federation: Interview with Alan Gartner.

p. 98.   Black and Jewish lawyers began meeting: Interview with David Saperstein.

p. 98.   When Henry Schwartzchild: Interview with Henry Schwartzchild.

p. 99.   "There was no doubt . . .": Paul Cowan, *An Orphan in History* (New York: Bantam Books, 1983), p. 6.

p. 99.   "It is in the context . . .": Woodward, p. 132.

p. 100.   synagogue was dynamited: *Bittersweet Encounter*, p. 137.

p. 101.   "There on the pulpit": Michael Walzer, *Exodus and Revolution* (New York: Basic Books, 1985), pp. 3–5.

p. 101.   "We are confronted . . .": *Eyes on the Prize: A Reader*, p. 120.

p. 102.   called Greenberg into his office: Interview with Jack Greenberg.

p. 102.   Carter was disappointed.: Interview with Robert Carter.

p. 103.   the appointment stirred controversy: Louis Lomax, *The Negro Revolt* (New York: New American Library, 1962), pp. 194–95.

p. 103.   "After all": Ibid., p. 202.
p. 104.   "Yes, they should, and with few exceptions they do": Jack Greenberg, "An NAACP Lawyer Answers Some Questions," *The New York Times Magazine*, August 18, 1963.
p. 105.   set up a separate account: Interview with Jack Greenberg.
p. 105.   "Let him know": *Garrow*, p. 386.
p. 106.   Greenberg fought against using lawyers affiliated with the National Lawyers' Guild: Carson, *In Struggle*, p. 107; James Forman, *The Making of Black Revolutionaries* (New York: Macmillan, 1972); Interviews with Dotty Miller Zellner, Henry Schwartzchild, Jack Greenberg.
p. 106.   When Greenberg thought about: Interview with Jack Greenberg.
p. 108.   "Two ideas puzzled me . . .": Norman Podhoretz, "My Negro problems—And Ours," *Commentary*, November 1963, pp. 93–101.
p. 109.   "As the Negro masses have become . . .": Nathan Glazer, "Negroes and Jews: The New Challenge to Pluralism," reprinted in Nathan Glazer, *Ethnic Dilemmas: 1964–1982* (Cambridge, Mass.: Harvard University Press, 1983), pp. 29–43.
p. 110.   Andrew Goodman's family: Interview with Carolyn Goodman.
p. 110.   Howard Zinn . . . had moved to Atlanta: The story of Zinn's introduction to civil rights is drawn from an interview with Zinn.
p. 112.   Like Zinn, Dotty Miller: Interview with Dotty Miller Zellner.
p. 113.   traveled uptown to Greenberg's apartment: Interview with Marilyn Gittell.
p. 113.   "Some support the all-black school . . ."; "The Urban Coalition": Jack Greenberg, "The Tortoise Can Beat the Hare," *Saturday Review*, February 17, 1968, pp. 57ff.
p. 114.   "[Tommie] Smith had just won": *Time*, October 25, 1968.
p. 115.   In 1971, the fund split badly: Interviews with Margaret Burnham, Michael Meltsner, Jack Greenberg, James Nabritt.
p. 117.   stunned to discover that the Anti-Defamation League had filed a brief: Interview with Jack Greenberg.
p. 118.   There was no love lost: Interview with Jack Greenberg; Interviews with officials of the American Jewish Congress.
p. 118.   Open letter to Harvard students: copy in author's possession.
p. 119.   For several years in the late 1970s: *The Washington Post*, July 26, 1982; Christopher Edley, Jr., "The Boycott at Harvard" (op-ed article), *Washington Post*, August 18, 1972; Interview with Derrick Bell.
p. 120.   "Many of us were excited . . .": Edley, "The Boycott at Harvard."
p. 120.   "This course is concerned . . .": Open Letter to the Harvard Law School Community.
p. 121.   "W. E. B. Du Bois . . .": *The New York Times*, August 11, 1982.
p. 121.   "Bad times make for bad moods . . .": *Denver Post*, August 16, 1982.
p. 121.   Black students used the boycott: Interview with Muhammed Kenyatta; Randall Kennedy, "On Cussing Out White Liberals," *The Nation*, September 4, 1982; Interview with Derrick Bell; Interview with Randall Kennedy.
p. 121.   Greenberg seemed more annoyed than hurt: Interview with Jack Greenberg.
p. 123.   For Chambers: Interview with Julius Chambers.

Chapter Four

p. 127.   King had debated for several days: Garrow, *Bearing the Cross*, pp. 339–40.

p. 127.   "What are you middle-class niggers . . .": Interview with Bayard Rustin.

p. 127.   That night he and Rustin talkcd: Interview with Bayard Rustin.

p. 128.   "The Supremes' 'Where Did Our Love Go?' . . .": *The Autobiography of LeRoi Jones/Amiri Baraka* (New York: Freundlich Books, 1984), pp. 209–10.

p. 131.   "It's better to be free . . .": Interview with Paul Parks. The preceding information on Parks and McCoy is drawn from interviews with Parks and Rhody McCoy.

p. 131.   "There are few things under heaven . . .": quoted in J. Harvie Wilkinson III, *From Brown to Bakke* (New York: Oxford University Press, 1979), p. 272.

p. 131.   black teenagers roamed the streets shouting at police: *The Death and Life of Malcolm X*, p. 205.

p. 132.   His years in New York up until then had been years of frustration: This and most of the details that follow about McCoy's attitudes and beliefs are drawn from interviews with Rhody McCoy.

p. 133.   McCoy found the private Malcolm quiet and passive: Interview with Rhody McCoy.

p. 134.   "Whatever else he was or was not . . ." Ossie Davis, "On Malcolm X," *The Autobiography of Malcolm X* (New York: Ballantine Books, 1973), pp. 457–60.

p. 136.   "There are far too many Jews from Jewish organizations . . .": Cruse, *The Crisis of the Negro Intellectual*, p. 497.

p. 137.   Jews owned about 30 percent of the stores: *Bittersweet Encounter*, p. 73.

p. 137.   Of the five people that a black meets: Interview with Diane Ravitch. The saying is sometimes attributed to Bayard Rustin.

p. 137.   New York was the capital of black America: *Bittersweet Encounter*, p. xxiv; *Jews in Black Perspective*, p. 105–12.

p. 137.   New York was also the capital of Jewish America: Nathan Glazer and Daniel P. Moynihan, *Beyond the Melting Pot*, Second Edition (Cambridge, Mass: The M.I.T. Press, 1970), pp. lvii–lxviii.

p. 138.   approximately two-thirds of New York's teachers . . . were Jewish: Interview with Albert Shanker. Interview with Marilyn Gittell. *Beyond the Melting Pot*, p. 146.

p. 138.   Crime had skyrocketed in the 1960s: Figures are taken from Peter Steinfels, *The Neo-Conservatives* (New York: Simon and Schuster, 1979).

p. 138.   heaviest Jewish opposition: *Beyond the Melting Pot*, p. xxvi.

p. 139.   Oliver was becoming increasingly concerned: Interview with C. Herbert Oliver.

p. 140.   black twelve-year-olds reading two years behind: This and the figures for black teachers and principals are taken from Martin Mayer, *The Teachers Strike* (New York: Harper and Row, 1969).

p. 141.   anger . . . coalesced over the opening of Intermediate School 201: Diane Ravitch, *The Great School Wars* (New York: Basic Books, 1974), pp. 292–311.

p. 141.   Bundy report: Ibid., pp. 329–37.

p. 142.   Ocean Hill–Brownsville was a natural candidate: Maurice Berube and Marilyn Gittell, *Confrontation at Ocean Hill–*

Brownsville (New York: Frederick A. Praeger, 1969), pp. 24; 36–37.

p. 143. "We are witnessing today in New York City ...": quoted in *Bittersweet Encounter*, p. 152.

p. 143. different roles for different audiences: Interview with Rhody McCoy; interview with Mario Fantini.

p. 143. Oliver and the parents liked ... McCoy: The feelings of the various participants on the board are drawn from interviews with C. Herbert Oliver, Mario Fantini, Sandra Feldman, Marilyn Gittell.

p. 144. "Men are capable of putting an end ...": quoted in Mayer.

p. 145. small, unheated triangular office: Interview with Rhody McCoy; Interview with Reverend John Powis.

p. 145. Shanker's creed: Interview with Albert Shanker.

p. 145. Shanker called up Bayard Rustin: Interview with Albert Shanker.

p. 146. "I don't want to give you a choice ...": Interview with Rhody McCoy.

p. 146. create an all-black part of the school system: Interview with Rhody McCoy.

p. 147. The Ferguson appointment created a blaze of controversy: Ravitch, pp. 325–28; Interviews with Rhody McCoy, Sandra Feldman, C. Herbert Oliver.

p. 147. Most [teachers] ... worked two jobs: Interview with Fred Nauman. Nauman, who headed the union chapter in Ocean Hill–Brownsville, also provided salary figures.

p. 147. Nauman considered himself more liberal: Interview with Fred Nauman.

p. 148. Barely a few weeks into the school year, the teachers pulled their representatives: The details of the events leading up to and during the school strike are drawn from Ravitch, pp. 320–78; *Confrontation at Ocean Hill–Brownsville*; Mayer.

p. 148. "I don't want you reading the book ...": Interview with Rhody McCoy.

p. 149. walls plastered with signs: Interview with Fred Nauman.

p. 149. "Wake up, black people ...": copy of leaflet in author's possession.

p. 149. "If whitey taps you on the shoulder ...": Interview with Fred Nauman.

p. 150. McCoy persuaded them to compromise: Interview with Marilyn Gittell.

p. 150. No one ... took much notice that almost all ... were Jewish: Interviews with Rhody McCoy, Marilyn Gittell, C. Herbert Oliver, Mario Fantini.

p. 151. "By a grotesque accident of history ...": Jason Epstein, "The Real McCoy," *The New York Review of Books*, March 1969.

p. 151. a black arbitrator heard the charges: *Confrontation at Ocean Hill–Brownsville*, p. 79.

p. 152. What had moderation gotten black people: Interview with Rhody McCoy.

p. 152. "Are you afraid of black kids?": Interview with Rhody McCoy.

p. 152. 70 percent of the teachers ... were white. Half were Jewish: *Bittersweet Encounter*, p. 173; Jason Epstein, "The Real McCoy," *The New York Review of Books*, March 13, 1969; *Confrontation*, p. 170.

p. 153. Shanker distrusted McCoy: Interview with Albert Shanker.

p. 153. "If African American History and Culture ...": quoted in *Bittersweet Encounter*, pp. 169–70.

p. 154.　several of the union handouts were inaccurate: Fred Ferretti, "New York's Black Anti-Semitism Scare," *Columbia Journalism Review*, Fall 1969.

p. 154.　reprinting the leaflets was a mistake: Interviews with Sandra Feldman and Nauman.

p. 155.　"open admissions" at the City University of New York: For the importance of City College to Jews in New York, see Irving Howe, *World of Our Fathers* (New York: Harcourt Brace Jovanovich, 1976), p. 281.

p. 155.　McCoy . . . had never seen the anti-Semitic leaflets: Interview with Rhody McCoy.

p. 156.　McCoy met with a group of 100 rabbis: Interview with Rhody McCoy.

p. 156.　taken out an advertisement in *The New York Times*: the advertisement is reprinted in *Confrontation at Ocean Hill–Brownsville*, pp. 170–74.

p. 156.　he would pass a Jewish Yeshiva school: Interview with C. Herbert Oliver.

p. 156.　"I can't in a public meeting . . .": Interview with Mario Fantini.

p. 157.　suspended the Ocean Hill–Brownsville community board: Ravitch, pp. 376–77.

p. 157.　"This city is polarized . . .": quoted in *Bittersweet Encounter*, p. 202.

p. 158.　to investigate stories he had heard of Jewish teachers: Interview with Julius Lester.

p. 158.　why . . . couldn't Jews understand that blacks wanted an organization of their own: Interview with Julius Lester.

p. 159.　"I want you to read this on the air": Interview with Julius Lester. Lester also recounts this incident in his autobiography, *Lovesong* (New York: Holt, 1988).

p. 159.　"Hey, Jew boy . . .": quoted in Ferretti.

p. 160.　"That was a very ugly poem": the comments about the poem are quoted in Ferretti. Ferretti obtained a tape of the Campbell show and the shows that followed.

p. 160.　Shanker and the United Federation of Teachers filed a complaint: Ibid.

p. 160.　Lester was handed a leaflet; his answering service recorded threats against his life: Interview with Julius Lester.

p. 161.　Robert Goodman . . . called a press conference: Interview with Carolyn Goodman.

p. 161.　"In Germany, the Jews are the minority . . .": quoted in Ferretti.

p. 161.　He would never be able to forgive Shanker: Interview with Julius Lester.

p. 161.　"There exists a predetermined script": Rhody A. McCoy, Jr., *Analysis of Critical Issues and Incidents in the New York City School Crisis, 1967–1970, and Their Implications for Urban Education in the 1970s* (University of Massachusetts Dissertation; submitted May 1971).

p. 161.　McCoy settle in San Francisco: Interview with Rhody McCoy.

p. 162.　McCoy had confounded the liberals: Interview with Mario Fantini.

p. 164.　Fantini was shouted off the stage: Interview with Mario Fantini.

p. 164.　The vital core was gone: Interview with Mario Fantini.

Chapter Five

p. 165.   believed blacks were moving "too fast": Louis Harris and Bert E. Swanson, *Black–Jewish Relations in New York City* (New York: Praeger Publishers, 1970), p. 65.

p. 165.   Jewish vote was being siphoned off: figures are taken from Richard Scammon and Ben Wattenberg, *The Real Majority* (New York: Coward, McCann and Geoghegan, Inc., 1971), pp. 65, 238–45.

p. 166.   Bernie had been a child in Germany: The details of Bernie Ebstein's experiences growing up and in the civil rights movement are drawn from a series of interviews with Bernie Ebstein and Roz Ebstein.

p. 166.   her mother had taken her to a demonstration: Interview with Roz Ebstein.

p. 167.   getting ready to march: Interview with Bernie and Roz Ebstein.

p. 167.   King had arrived in Chicago: Stephen B. Oates, *Let the Trumpet Sound* (New York: New American Library, 1983), pp. 378–80; 387–92.

pp. 168–69. Bernie and Roz carried a banner: Interview with Bernie and Roz Ebstein.

p. 169.   heard King speak demanding an end to police brutality: *Oates*, pp. 406–8.

p. 169.   Blacks were crammed into two areas: The details of the growth and development of Chicago ghettos are drawn from Arnold Hirsch, *Making the Second Ghetto: Race and Housing in Chicago, 1940–1960* (Cambridge: Cambridge University Press, 1983).

p. 169.   "The plight of the Negro": Abraham Joshua Herschel, *The Insecurity of Freedom* (New York: Farrar, Straus & Giroux), pp. 97–98.

p. 172.   "In our distaste for violence:" reprinted in Milton Himmelfarb, *The Jews of Modernity* (New York: Basic Books, 1973).

p. 173.   noticed a black kid in his class: Inteview with Steven Ebstein.

p. 173.   remained committed to public education: Interview with Bernie and Roz Ebstein.

p. 174.   a riot erupted in Roz's old neighborhood: Oates, pp. 408–11.

p. 174.   "I've never seen anything like it": Oates, p. 413.

p. 174.   Bernie joined a circle: Interview with Bernie Ebstein.

p. 175.   they turned on the whites: Interview with Bernie Ebstein.

p. 175.   polls showed that widespread support . . . had begun to evaporate: cited in Oates, p. 418.

p. 176.   black girls had begun to frighten David: Interview with David Ebstein.

p. 176.   "Fear is the order of the day": *Boston Globe* clipping file.

p. 177.   "I've just sold several houses . . .": Interview with Roz Ebstein.

p. 178.   buying their homes "on contract": This was common practice in Chicago. See James Alan McPherson, "In My Father's House There Are Many Mansions—And I'm Going to Get Me Some of Them Too!," *The Atlantic*, April 1972.

p. 178.   drew up an oversized testimonial: Interview with Bernie and Roz Ebstein.

p. 178.   the anger with which some of their friends talked: Interview with Bernie and Roz Ebstein.

p. 179.   "If those things go down . . .": Interview with Bernie Ebstein.

p. 179.   "take Steven out of this school": Interview with Bernie and Roz Ebstein.

p. 179.   he was angry when Steven was transferred: Interview with David Ebstein.

p. 180.   had canvassed door-to-door for Lyndon Johnson: Interview with Bernie Ebstein.

p. 181.   They were sickened by what they saw: Interview with Bernie and Roz Ebstein.

p. 182.   a reality he was reluctant to face: Interview with Bernie Ebstein.

p. 182.   "The fact is inescapable": *Testament of Hope,* pp. 64–72.

p. 183.   one of the black girls . . . grabbed his pen: Interview with David Ebstein.

p. 183.   saw the kid sitting there on a bench: Interview with Bernie and Roz Ebstein.

p. 183.   a thriving, cacophonous place: Interview with Marshall Rosman.

p. 184.   vans pulling in front of people's homes at night: Interview with Marshall Rosman.

p. 184.   "We need to advertise . . .": "That's racist . . .": Interview with Marshall Rosman.

p. 184.   center moved most of its activities: Interview with Bernie and Roz Ebstein; interview with Marshall Rosman.

p. 185.   membership began declining seriously: Interview with Bernie and Roz Ebstein.

p. 185.   Roth had seen it all before: Interview with Walter Roth.

p. 186.   they would lie in bed: Interview with Bernie and Roz Ebstein.

p. 187.   half the homes on the street had been sold: Interview with Roz Ebstein.

p. 187.   the two had made a pact: Interview with David Ebstein.

p. 188.   "easier to integrate": Interview with Robert Marx.

p. 188.   Blacks were used to whites moving away: Interview with Vernon Jarrett.

p. 188.   a theory of interstitiality: Interview with Robert Marx.

p. 189.   "Who are you": Interview with David Ebstein.

p. 189.   "You believe this stuff": Interview with Roz and Bernie Ebstein.

p. 189.   "He was never to hear the black man's voice . . .": Saul Bellow, *Mr. Sammler's Planet* (New York: Viking Compass, 1973), p. 49.

p. 190.   Bernie advocated moving to Hyde Park: Interview with Roz and Bernie Ebstein.

p. 190.   It was unreal: Interview with Roz Ebstein.

p. 191.   put her in two different worlds: Interview with Roz Ebstein.

p. 191.   That was a victory of sorts: Interview with Bernie Ebstein.

p. 191.   feared that she had turned her David and Steven into bigots: Interview with Roz Ebstein.

p. 192.   he was proud of his parents' involvement: Interview with David Ebstein.

p. 192.   he didn't feel like an underdog: Interview with Steven Ebstein.

p. 192.   agreed with more conservative Jews: Interview with Steven Ebstein.

p. 193.   threw it out: Interview with Roz and Bernie Ebstein.

Chapter Six

p. 197.   "His sufferings were unspeakable": Reprinted in William Novak and Moshe Waldoks, eds., *The Big Book of Jewish Humor,* pp. 293–300.

p. 199.   "As soon as the Arab armies . . .": Arthur Hertzberg, "Israel and American Jewry," *Commentary,* August 1967.

p. 200.   "As of today, there no longer exists . . .": Leonard J. Davis and
            Moshe Decter, *Myths and Facts 1982* (Washington, D.C.: Near
            East Research, Inc., 1982), p. 31.

p. 200.   "When the Arabs take Israel . . .": Charles Silberman, *A Cer-
            tain People* (New York: Summit Books, 1985), p. 182. Silber-
            man gives an excellent recounting of the emotions stirred among
            American Jews by the events leading up to the Six-Day War
            and the war itself.

p. 202.   "In those days many of us felt . . .": Silberman, pp. 183–84.

p. 202.   "Students shall be excused": copy in author's possession.

p. 203.   Zionism . . . played a large role in Peretz's life: The details of
            Peretz's childhood are drawn from a series of interviews with
            Martin Peretz.

p. 205.   answers revealed how modest a place: Marshall Sklare and
            Joseph Greenblum, *Jewish Identity on the Suburban Frontier*,
            2nd edition (Chicago: University of Chicago Press, 1979), pp.
            321–22.

p. 205.   planning guide published for Jewish agencies . . . mentioned
            Israel only in passing: National Community Relations Advi-
            sory Council, "Background for the 1955–56 Plan." Copy in
            author's possession.

p. 206.   Many of the blacks he had known: This and the details that
            follow about Peretz's involvement in the early civil rights
            movement are drawn from interviews with Martin Peretz, Anne
            Peretz, and Michael Walzer.

p. 207.   Farnsworth would regularly give between $10,000 and $50,000:
            Garrow, *Bearing the Cross*, pp. 429, 542, 562.

p. 208.   Peretz was awakened by the sound of people singing: Interview
            with Martin Peretz.

p. 208.   "You know, you're picking on puny victimizers": Interview
            with Martin Peretz.

p. 209.   Peretz soon found himself caught up in the vortex of Black
            Power and increasingly radical politics: Two accounts of the
            National Convention on New Politics are Renata Adler, "Let-
            ter from the Palmer House," *The New Yorker*, September 23,
            1987, and Peter Steinfels, "Alice in Newleftland," *Common-
            weal*, September 29, 1967.

p. 209.   "These cats don't know . . .": quoted in Adler.

p. 210.   "We in SNCC have been the victims of the liberal-labor circle
            lies . . .": Forman, *The Making of Black Revolutionaries*, pp.
            498–503.

p. 210.   New Politics Convention . . . had been neither new nor politic:
            Steinfels, p. 610.

p. 211.   New Politics Convention left Peretz profoundly disillusioned:
            Interview with Martin Peretz.

p. 212.   "You know, one of the things I've been thinking about . . .":
            Interview with Martin Peretz.

p. 213.   Jewish studies . . . boomed in the 1970s: The figures on the
            boom in Jewish studies and on the percentage of Jews attending
            seders come from Silberman, *A Certain People*, pp. 226–34.

p. 213.   what *Commentary* called "revolutionism": The phrase was
            used to unite a cluster of articles that appeared in *Commen-
            tary*, February 1971.

p. 214.   "Whatever the case may have been yesterday . . .": quoted in
            Stephen D. Isaacs, *Jews and American Politics* (Garden City,
            New York: Doubleday & Co., 1974).

p. 214.   "Jewish interests are clearly tied up . . .": Nathan Glazer, "Rev-

olutionism and the Jews: 3—The Role of the Intellectuals,"
Commentary, February 1971.

p. 216.   At his home in Cambridge, Peretz could not sleep: Interview with Martin Peretz.

p. 217.   "Israel has become in world affairs a pariah nation": "Mideast Peace?" *The New Republic*, March 8, 1975.

p. 217.   "Worrying about particular hills and valleys . . .": Ibid.

p. 217.   "Even if this fractured and murderous . . .": "Don't Deliver Israel," *The New Republic*, August 6 and 13, 1977.

p. 219.   "Begin's actions are a threat": "Wrongs and Rights in Lebanon," *The New Republic*, August 1 and 8, 1981.

p. 219.   "Those genuinely concerned . . .": Marie Syrkin, "How Begin Threatens Israel," *The New Republic*, September 16, 1981.

p. 220.   One political analyst dubbed the phenomenon "pro-Israelism": Steven Cohen, *American Modernity and Jewish Identity* (New York: Methuen, Inc., 1983), Chapter 8.

p. 220.   A survey of young Jewish leaders: Jonathan S. Woocher, " 'Jewish Survivalism' as Communal Ideology: An Empirical Assessment," *Journal of Jewish Communal Service*.

p. 220.   A poll of rank-and-file Jews: Cohen, pp. 158–59.

p. 221.   Back in the early 1960s, it was relatively easy to get into law school: Allan P. Sindler, *Bakke, DeFunis and Minority Admissions* (New York and London: Longman, 1978), p. 28. The data for Bolt Hall Law Schoold and the changing standards for law school admission are discussed on pp. 28–37.

p. 222.   Details of the DeFunis case and the positions taken by Jewish organizations are recounted in Sindler, pp. 38–40; Weisbord and Stein, *Israel in the Black American Perspective*, pp. 134–35; J. Harvie Wilkinson III, *From Brown to Bakke* (New York: Oxford University Press, 1979), pp. 256–58; Joel Dreyfuss, *The Bakke Case and the Politics of Inequality* (New York: Harcourt Brace Jovanovic, 1979).

p. 224.   In a special issue on the Bakke case: *The New Republic*, October 15, 1977.

p. 224.   he funded an office at Harvard to recruit blacks to apply for graduate school: Interview with Martin Peretz.

p. 225.   "People have begun to think that New York's problems . . .": "The Mugging of New York," *The New Republic*, July 30, 1977.

p. 225.   Peretz . . . did believe that traditional liberalism had stagnated: Interview with Martin Peretz.

p. 226.   *Dissent* . . . conceded that the neoconservatives . . . were likely to become a permanent fixture: Bernard Rosenberg and Irving Howe, "Are American Jews Turning to the Right?" *Dissent*, Winter 1974, pp. 30–45.

p. 226.   "I was asked to go up to one of the major black churches . . .": Edward I. Koch, *Mayor* (New York: Simon and Schuster, 1984), pp. 83–84.

p. 227.   Anne Peretz viewed the clashes since 1966 as clashes of style and attitude: Interview with Anne Peretz.

p. 228.   "At SNCC [John] Lewis was forced out . . .": "March to Nowhere," *The New Republic*, September 19 and 26, 1983.

p. 229.   A poll in 1983 showed blacks the most hostile to Israel: Interview with William Schneider.

p. 231.   "The Jews don't like Farrakhan . . .": Anti-Defamation League/ Civil Rights Division, *Louis Farrakhan* (Spring 1984 issue of *ADL Facts*).

p. 231.   the 1979 resignation of Andrew Young as ambassador to the

United Nations: the events leading to Young's resignation and the aftermath are detailed in Weisbord and Kazarian, *Israel in the Black American Perspective*, pp. 121–38.

p. 232.   "I have a scheme": *The New Republic*, October 17, 1983.

p. 233.   Peretz thought the parody wonderful: Interview with Martin Peretz.

p. 233.   Henry Fairlie, became more and more troubled by the magazine's treatment of Jackson: Interview with Henry Fairlie.

p. 235.   Peretz continued to see himself as a pragmatist: Interview with Martin Peretz.

p. 236.   Peretz . . . had only one close, black friend: Interview with Martin Peretz.

Chapter Seven

p. 237.   Brazile would sneak under her covers: Interview with Donna Brazile.

p. 238.   election of mayors was the tip of change across the country: Martin Kilson, "Blacks and Politics: A New Maturity," *The Wilson Quarterly*, Spring 1984; Mary Frances Berry and John W. Blasingame, *Long Memory* (New York: Oxford University Press, 1982), pp. 185–94.

p. 239.   "To a White Girl": Eldridge Cleaver, *Soul on Ice* (New York: Dell Publishing Co., 1968), pp. 13–14.

p. 240.   Some of her brothers and sisters had lighter skin: This and the details that follow of Brazile's growing up years and childhood memories are drawn from a series of interviews with Donna Brazile.

p. 243.   "In 1980, I looked . . .": Jackson gave this speech many times in 1983 and 1984. Portions are reprinted in Bob Faw and Nancy Skelton, *Thunder in America* (Austin, Texas: Texas Monthly Press), p. 28.

p. 244.   Stuart Eizenstat suggested to me: Interview with Stuart Eizenstat.

p. 246.   a group of 200 black leaders met in New York: *The New York Times*, August 24 and 25, 1974.

p. 246.   "I remember Egypt's attack on Israel": Alice Walker, "To the Editors of *Ms.* Magazine" in *In Search of Our Mothers' Gardens*, pp. 349–50.

p. 247.   Brazile didn't have anything on Jews: Interview with Donna Brazile.

p. 248.   The objections started immediately: Interview with Donna Brazile; Interview with David Saperstein; *The Washington Post*, August 13, 1983.

p. 250.   Saperstein . . . believed it was crucial that some Jews participate: Interview with David Saperstein.

p. 251.   she turned to Coretta King: Interview with Donna Brazile.

p. 252.   liberal Jewish voters . . . provided the votes that gave Washington his margin of victory: Weisbord and Kazarian, *Israel in the Black American Perspective*, pp. 183–84. The Jewish vote for Bradley and for Goode are also cited here.

p. 252.   He did not share the warm feelings of King and others: Interview with Jesse Jackson.

p. 252.   Jackson made no distinctions between whites and Jews: Interview with Jesse Jackson.

p. 254.   his daughter . . . and been badgered by a Jewish alumnus: *Israel* in the Black American Perspective, p. 180; The New York Times, February 27, 1984.

p. 255. Brazile saw Jackson's candidacy as an extension of her work: Interview with Donna Brazile.

p. 256. "I've finally figured it out . . .": Interview with Donna Brazile.

p. 256. The "hymietown" story broke on February 13, 1984. The details of the incident are recounted in Thunder in America, pp. 49–50 and in Milton Coleman, "A Reporter's Story: 18 Words, Seven Weeks Later," The Washington Post, April 8, 1984.

p. 257. "Did you say that?" Interview with Donna Brazile.

p. 257. Farrakhan and Jackson had been friends for several years: This and following details of Jackson's relationship with Farrakhan cited in Thunder in America, p. 113.

p. 257. Farrakhan and Jackson got together in a back room and started talking: Interview with Donna Brazile.

p. 258. "I say to the Jewish people who may not like our brother . . .": Thunder in America, p. 110.

p. 258. "In private talks we sometimes let our guard down . . .": Thunder in America, p. 52.

p. 258. Brazile was disgusted: Interview with Donna Brazile.

p. 258. "He could light candles . . .": Thunder in America, p. 53.

p. 259. increasingly belligerent speeches by Farrakhan: the speeches are quoted in Thunder in America, pp. 105–18.

p. 259. Around the campaign office, things had turned ugly: Interview with Donald Brazile.

p. 260. Brazile received a call from her mother: Interview with Donna Brazile.

p. 260. When she went home to Kenner she was shocked: Interview with Donna Brazile.

p. 261. "Suffering breeds character . . .": Eyes on the Prize: A Reader, p. 295.

p. 262. "If in my low moments . . .": Thunder in America, p. 193.

p. 262. Alice Walker had met her Jewish husband: Interview with Alice Walker.

p. 263. Walters . . . could understand why Jews would not back Jackson: Interview with Ronald Walters.

p. 264. Lester found himself waking up from dreams: Interview with Julius Lester. Lester describes his conversion to Judaism in his autobiography, Lovesong (New York: Holt, 1988).

p. 264. Jesse Jackson . . . believed that Israel's continued trade with South Africa was an affront: Interview with Jesse Jackson.

p. 265. Brazile had moved on to other projects: Interview with Donna Brazile.

Chapter Eight

p. 268. "From the outset . . .": Beyond the Melting Pot, pp. 1xiv–1xv.

p. 273. why Israel maintained relations and trade with South Africa: Meeting of black and Jewish leaders with David Kimche.

p. 273. level of anti-Semitism among blacks: Interview with William Schneider.

p. 274. made up 25 to 30 percent of the "media elite": Silberman, pp. 152–53.

p. 275. "Anyone can observe the Sabbath": Alice Walker, "To the Editors of Ms. Magazine," In Search of Our Mother's Gardens p. 351.

p. 277. "Our aim must never be . . .": James M. Washington, ed., A

Testament of Hope: The Essential Writings of Martin Luther King, Jr. (San Francisco: Harper & Row, 1986), p. 230.

p. 279. "I'm totally bored . . .": Interview with Melanie Lomax.

p. 279. "There is a sort of romantic Camelot attitude . . .": Interview with Marc Stern.

Index